Owned by The Vampire

Vampire

Created in The Shadows of Heaven

Book 1

Lucy Lyons

© **2017**

Newsletter

This exclusive **VIP Mailing List** from Persia Publishing focuses on delivering high quality content to your inbox that will bring more passion, excitement, and entertainment to your life. Weekly insights, specials offers and free giveaways that you will love!

You are just one click away from getting exclusive access to the **VIP Mailing List**!

Click the "**Get Access Now**" link below to join today!

GET ACCESS NOW

http://www.persiapublishing.com/subscribe-to-romance-lucy/

LIKE US AT

https://www.facebook.com/LucyLyonsRomance/

CAN YOU HELP?

PLEASE leave a quick review for this book if it gives you any value. It provides valuable feedback that allows me to continuously improve my books and motivates me to keep writing.

Thank You!

© Copyright 2016 by Persia Publishing- All rights reserved.

All rights reserved. No part of this publication may be reproduced, distributed, or transmitted in any form or by any means, including photocopying, recording, or other electronic or mechanical methods, without the prior written permission of the publisher, except in the case of brief quotations embodied in critical reviews and certain other noncommercial uses permitted by copyright law. For permission requests, write to the publisher, addressed "Attention: Permissions Coordinator," at the address below.

The information herein is offered for entertainment purposes solely, and is universal as so. The presentation of the information is without contract or any type of guarantee assurance.

Table of Contents

Book 1

Chapter One	8
Chapter Two	21
Chapter Three	30
Chapter Four	44
Chapter Five	60
Chapter Six	71
Chapter Seven	81
Chapter Eight	90
Chapter Nine	101
Chapter Ten	123
Chapter Eleven	130
Chapter Twelve	148
Chapter Thirteen	160
Chapter Fourteen	173
Chapter Fifteen	186
Chapter Sixteen	197
Chapter Seventeen	204

Book 2

CHAPTER 1	221
CHAPTER 2	233
CHAPTER 3	250
CHAPTER 4	273
CHAPTER 5	290
CHAPTER 6	308
CHAPTER 7	326
CHAPTER 8	345

CHAPTER 9	352
CHAPTER 10	366
CHAPTER 11	383
CHAPTER 12	398

Book 3

CHAPTER 1	408
CHAPTER 2	423
CHAPTER 3	441
CHAPTER 4	454
CHAPTER 5	459
CHAPTER 6	474
CHAPTER 7	486
CHAPTER 8	499
CHAPTER 9	520
CHAPTER 10	533
CHAPTER 11	547
CHAPTER 12	573
CHAPTER 13	580
CHAPTER 14	592

Chapter One

Isabel smoothed her hair back from her forehead, taking a deep breath as she glanced around the parking garage. Most of the people who were going out for a Friday night of fun had already managed to make their way to the clubs, and while the garage was two thirds full, it was shockingly silent. All of the drivers were either wandering Royale Street or in one of its clubs. She glanced in the flip-down mirror, smiling to make sure that her lipstick hadn't ended up on her teeth. She turned her head slightly, one way and then the other, checking the contour work she had done; it still looked a little obvious in the stark light of her car, but Isabel knew that in the darker club ambience, it would make her face look slimmer and her cheekbones more prominent.

"Well, the dress looks nice anyway," Isabel said, pressing her lips together and flipping the mirror back up.

She stepped out of her car, tottering slightly on the heels she had convinced herself to wear before locking the door on the old Camry. Isabel had timed her arrival in the downtown area carefully; it was to her benefit that most of the crowd visiting the bars and clubs had already started their revels. Isabel started towards the elevator, balancing her weight carefully on her new heels until her body fell into the right posture to walk in, running through her plan mentally. Most of the guys at her favorite club would be at least one drink in, probably closer to two or three; they would have been shot down by the hottest of women out partying. And the men who were far, far out of her league would have picked up their hookups for the night.

Isabel had never needed the insincere protests from her cadre of going-out girlfriends that "you've got such a pretty face" and "you're not fat, you're beautiful," to know where she stood in the spectrum of available single ladies. Although she had been a waifish child, as soon as puberty had come along, Isabel had struggled with her weight. Although looking back at pictures of herself as a teen, she had to admit that her self-perception of herself as a homely blob had been far from the truth. Her breasts and hips had expanded again and again, while her upward growth had stalled out at 5'6", and while she was curvy, Isabel knew that some of her curves were less than perfectly appealing to a certain subset of men.

It had been a hard-won victory when she had learned to dress for her body type, and found jeans that fit her hips without gaping at her waist. However, for going out, she preferred skirts or dresses. She believed she was a great hookup fodder; pretty enough, cute enough, sultry enough to appeal to men for the purposes of getting laid. Yet not ethereally lovely or perfect enough —thus far —to find the prince charming who would want a relationship that lasted more than a few months on the outside.

Isabel shook her thoughts away as she stepped out of the parking garage and onto the street, looking both ways to take in the general vibe.

Judging by the throng of smokers outside, there seemed to be some kind of event at Rock-a-Billy's, while O'Malley's had its usual crowd of beer-and-whiskey rowdies at the picnic tables in front.

Isabel's gaze landed on the entrance to Underground, her favorite Friday night haunt; the two door men were in position, with Mike at the door itself to check IDs and Clancy seated next to the cash register. There was no line, but movement inside the club told Isabel that there were still plenty of people, and there would probably be more in an hour or so. Underground didn't really pick up until almost midnight.

She made her way across the street, and Mike spotted her first, smiling at her as she approached. "How much is cover?" Clancy shook his head in response to her question.

"You know better than that," Mike said, ripping a paper wristband free of the sheet folded in his hand. "I wouldn't even bother with the wristband, but there are a couple of new bartenders we just took on, and I don't want you to deal with the hassle of explaining to them that you're honorary staff." Isabel grinned, giving Clancy a quick hug while holding out her wrist for Mike to wrap the band around. She had come to Underground almost every weekend for years; she was practically a fixture for Friday, and sometimes, Saturday nights.

"What's the show tonight?" Normally, there was no cover charge at the door unless there was a special event.

"Burlesque," Clancy told her. "They're starting up in about an hour." That would help – in its own way. Of course, the men would flirt with the performers, hopeful to get a half-naked woman to come home with them. But when the lingerie-clad beauties started to filter out of the club with their boyfriends, spouses, or the odd 'Mr. Right for tonight,' the attention would turn back to the regular denizens of the club, with an urgency that would make it easier for Isabel to "close the deal" as the guys said.

She hugged Mike and stepped into the dark entryway of the club, letting her eyes adjust. Pounding rhythms of a Strokes song filled her ears, and Isabel glanced in the direction of the DJ booth to confirm that DD was running that end of things. Which he was, bent over his MacBook to adjust the levels. As soon as she was confident of her ability to navigate the dance floor without either getting doused by some drunk's PBR or stepping on someone else, Isabel made a beeline for the bar.

She saw one of the new bartenders, but waited for Jesse to be free, leaning against the acrylic bar top and looking around. Most of the people in the club were regulars; a few looked like fish out of water; people who had somehow managed to stray from their usual haunts along Royale Street.

"The usual?" Isabel nodded in response to Jesse's question and took her debit card out of her wallet while he poured Jameson into a plastic cup full of ice, and added quick, short dashes of cola to it. He reached out blindly and grabbed an orange wedge from the caddy behind the bar, squeezing the juice into the cocktail and dropping the wedge in, before adding a straw and looking up to take Isabel's card. She might have another two or three over the course of the night – four, if it looked likely that she was going to end up going home without a partner. She would be staying until closing time at 4 in the morning--but the first sip of bitter-caramel-orange sweetness was the best.

"No one makes it better," Isabel told Jesse, giving him a thumbs up before he turned away to start her tab. Isabel reached into her purse and found her pack of cigarettes after a moment's searching, and then her lighter after a little more effort. She had managed to cut back her bad habit to weekends only, and when she was out or hooking up with someone. One day, she was sure, she would end up kicking it entirely.

While she waited for the show to start, Isabel wandered around the club, making her way slowly towards the back, where the patio area was, and then back into the main dance floor, evaluating her options. There were a few guys she thought might be worth subtly trying to encourage; but she would have to wait and see if they managed to catch any of the performers' interest. Isabel chatted with fellow regulars, greeted some of the lingerie-clad women who would grace the stage, and tried to keep herself optimistic for the hours to come. There would be no point in being out if she was going to give up on herself before the night was half over.

As she stood at the bar, Isabel felt someone staring at her. DD was on a run in the DJ booth: Yeah Yeah Yeahs, Depeche Mode, The Cure, in rapid succession, making people feel faintly romantic. Isabel looked around, trying to find the source of the stare, when she spotted a man standing along one of the walls, she couldn't help but wonder if she had met him before. It was hard to make out details in the darkness, and she had already finished her first drink, but he was gorgeous even from afar to be paying such serious attention to her. Especially when there were far more glamorous women in the crowd.

The man was tall, broad across the shoulders, dressed in a tailored suit which fit him so perfectly that Isabel wondered what he was doing in Underground at all. *Why isn't he over at Roxy's, or Martini Blues?* The man had blond hair, combed back from his face to just fall at his collar, and while Isabel couldn't determine the exact color, his eyes were pale from where she stood. She met his gaze and raised an eyebrow, letting him know that she was aware of him staring at her. Instead of looking away, or even signaling her, the man smiled slightly, continuing to meet her gaze. *He must just look like he's looking at me,* Isabel decided. She looked away, flustered, and took a sip of her second drink. Isabel reached for her pack of cigarettes, but her lighter had disappeared. Annoyance replaced her embarrassment as she decided, glumly, that someone had stolen it. "Can I get a packet of matches, Jesse?"

"No need," someone said next to her. Isabel turned in the direction of the low, cool-toned voice. The first thing she saw was a flame, flickering at the top of a vintage lighter —Isabel thought it looked too classy to be a Zippo —extended just in range for her to light a cigarette. She quickly plucked one out of her pack and brought it to her lips, leaning towards the flame.

"Thank you," she said when she pulled back, exhaling the first, quick throatful of smoke. The lid on the lighter snapped shut and the flame extinguished. Isabel glanced at the source of the convenient light and nearly dropped her cigarette in shock. *What the hell is a guy like you doing in a place like this?* The man who had offered her a light was every bit as gorgeous as the one she had caught staring from across the room, but he was quite different in appearance. He had long, slightly curling dark hair that stopped just above his shoulders, and big, deep eyes which Isabel thought were some shade of either hazel or brown. His features were sharply cut, his strong jawline softened by a dusting of dark stubble. Instead of a tailored suit, he wore jeans and a fitted black tee shirt. But just the sight of the man was enough to make Isabel's throat dry, and enough to make her heart pound.

"My pleasure," the man said, smiling slowly. There was something beautiful, and brightly warm about the sight of him. Isabel's heart fluttered in her chest. *Down girl! He's probably here with a date. And if he's not, he'll leave with a date for the night who's so far beyond a "10" that they knock the number scale out of the water! He's probably just nice.* But there was unmistakable warmth in the dark eyes looking down into hers, and something she couldn't quite make out in the curve of his lips; a kind of promise that Isabel hadn't seen before. "You can take it, if you want," the man added, opening his hand and extending the lighter towards her.

"That looks like it probably costs my entire bar tab," Isabel said with a laugh.

"I have a dozen of them," the man told her with a shrug. "I have three on me tonight alone."

"Collector?" Isabel smiled politely. *That explains it, if he's single: he's some kind of nerd.*

"I just enjoy beautiful things," the man said, smiling at her again. "Take it, please." Isabel hesitated a moment longer, but there was nothing in the man's face that made her doubt his sincerity. She reached out and took the lighter. For a moment, she thought that the man's skin felt strange – smoother than she would have expected, almost hot to the touch. But she dismissed it as her fingers closed around the cool metal of the lighter. "I'll see you later, Isabel."

"How do you know my name? And what's yours?" Isabel frowned for a moment, wondering if she had – somehow – gained a reputation beyond the usual for an Underground regular.

"Lucky guess," the man said. "I'm Oz." He leaned in and brushed his lips against her cheek. "I'm friends with one of the performers: Miss Kitty Galore. I need to run, but I will definitely find you later." Isabel highly doubted that, but as the man walked away, she thought that if nothing else, her ego had been propped up by the strangely charming man.

"Ladies and gentlemen! Make sure you have your drinks in hand. The show is about to begin!" Isabel turned her attention towards the stage, pushing the two supernaturally gorgeous men out of her mind in her determination to enjoy the show. She told herself that there was no chance in hell that she would end up with either of them that night; she might as well forget they even existed.

Chapter Two

Isabel stumbled into her bathroom the next morning, groaning as she made a beeline for the shower. She turned the water on and waited for it to heat up, taking care of other physical needs first and wondering what she could have possibly done the night before to feel so utterly exhausted and sore. "Well," she said to herself, sitting on the toilet seat lid and staring blankly at the water shooting down from the showerhead. "One thing I definitely know is that I got laid." She shifted her hips and cringed, pain seething through her.

The possibility that she might have been drugged floated up into her mind, but Isabel dismissed it; it felt more like she had been spectacularly drunk, though she thought she had only had maybe four Jameson-and-Cokes over the course of the evening. "Okay," Isabel said, rising to her feet and reaching a hand into the shower to test the water temperature. "First things first: what do I actually remember?"

She stepped into the hot water and closed her eyes, letting it pound her throbbing skull for a while until she was drenched from head to toe. Isabel started from the beginning of the evening – her arrival at Underground – and tried to work from there. She remembered one or two of the burlesque acts: there had been a debut performer, doing her strip tease to one of Isabel's favorite songs, and a few others that were noteworthy, in a span of maybe ten acts total. "And then what happened?" Isabel turned her back to the showerhead and reached for her soap, racking her brain. The gorgeous man – the second one she had seen, with the dark hair – had approached her at some point. He had offered to buy her a drink, and she had accepted, though she had watched Jesse make it and had taken it directly from the bartender's hands. She couldn't have let the man bring it to her, reasoning as always that one couldn't be too careful.

They had spent the rest of the time – that Underground was open – talking on the back patio, though Isabel couldn't remember what they had specifically talked about. She had a mental image of the man attentively listening to her, nodding occasionally, and heard – in her mind – bits and pieces of things that she must have said: something about what she did for a living, writing ad copy for the agency. Something about the worst client she had ever had to deal with, and about petty office politics.

She could remember the dark-haired man, Oz, she recalled, finally pointing out to her that she seemed more drunk than she should be to drive home. He had offered to drive her to a diner up the street when the Underground's manager announced last call. Isabel frowned again, thinking to herself that Oz had somehow managed to pay her tab as well. She had another mental image of the two of them seated in Bien-Venue, the preferred after-hours eating spot in the downtown area – owned by the same people who owned Underground. She remembered talking while they ate the high-end diner fare.

Isabel began scrubbing herself, turning her head this way and that, hoping that the heat of the shower water would loosen the tight feeling there. She couldn't quite remember what she had eaten at Bien-Venue, only that she had gradually sobered up – not fully, but enough to think to herself that she might be capable of driving herself home.

She had walked with Oz to his car, and somehow – Isabel saw flashes in her mind's eye – she had ended up in the back seat with him. As she slid her soapy hands along one of her legs, Isabel felt a rough patch, like a scab, just below where her hip and thigh met, only inches away from her vagina. "What the hell is that?" Isabel looked down at her leg, turning out at the hip to examine the patch. It looked like something between a small, deep scratch and a bite mark. She scowled at the mark, trying to remember how it had come to be there; certainly, it hadn't been there before that night.

There was no way that there had been enough room in the back of Oz's car for him to have done that, and on top of that, Isabel thought, *it doesn't look like anything a person could have done. Was there some kind of critter in his car?*

Had she done something after getting out of Oz's car when they had finished?

Isabel shuddered, trying to imagine how such an odd mark could have ended up in such an intimate area and failing utterly. "Okay, it'll come back to you later. Think about it later," she told herself. "No sense in getting yourself all worked up."

She finished her shower and grabbed her towel, feeling a small measure more human than when she had stepped into the bathroom, even if there were still bits and pieces of the night before that Isabel thought she would never quite recall. There had been a few nights like that in her life before; she had learned not to worry herself about it too much. But the soreness, the tender feeling between her legs, told her that whatever had happened, she must have been enthusiastic.

Isabel wrapped the towel tightly around her breasts and walked across her apartment to the kitchen. Her head was still throbbing, but she thought it had subsided a little. "Maybe next week, I'll stick with my usual," Isabel mused, pressing the power button on her coffee maker to start it up. She remembered suddenly that she'd also had one or two shots of something – maybe a Fireball, something with cinnamon. The shots hadn't been drugged; but they had utterly destroyed her inhibitions. "No wonder I feel like death warmed over," Isabel murmured to herself. She put a coffee pod in the brewer and grabbed a mug out of the cupboard. The whole evening was so strange; Isabel shook her head in disbelief.

There were other things; that much Isabel knew. Whatever she had done with Oz in the back of his car, it hadn't caused the strange mark on her inner thigh, or the tenderness she felt along her labia and along her inner walls. Isabel snickered softly to herself as the coffee began pouring into the mug. "Whoever else I ended up with, they must have been *big*." She shook her head again.

Isabel —added cream and sugar to her coffee then walked to her couch and sat down, sipping carefully. As the caffeine began to do its work, a few more flashes of the night before came back to her. There had been another man; she couldn't remember who, just the fact of hearing someone call to her, quietly, as she had left Oz's car.

I told him I was fine to drive home, that I didn't feel like going back to his place. Isabel drank down some more coffee and set the mug aside. *And then on the way to my own car ... who was it?* She couldn't remember, only that she had seen the guy earlier in the night at Underground.

There was a second guy, she thought; she had gone to his place. "No wonder I'm sore and feel eaten up," Isabel said, amused at her own decadence and mildly appalled at the same time.

The guy had climbed into the passenger seat of her car; Isabel could remember his voice, cool, low, and calm, directing her to his address – which she couldn't remember the house. She could remember the feeling of him inside of her, and something about his skin being strange under her hands, but that was it. Isabel shuddered, smiling slightly to herself at the memory of how the second man – whoever he was – had felt. *That explains a lot.* It didn't explain the odd marks on her leg, but Isabel pushed that thought aside; there were too many good memories from the night before to wonder about odd scabs on her body. They didn't look like anything that could be an early STD indicator, plus when she had scrubbed at them with the soap, they didn't hurt. Resolving to get them checked out if they didn't clear up within a few days, Isabel turned on the TV and considered how to spend the rest of her weekend.

After she had finished her first cup of coffee, she made breakfast: eggs and toast, with some apple juice to put an end to the dregs of her hangover. Her phone buzzed, and Isabel – grateful that she had plugged it in before passing out – checked it to find that Alicia, one of her friends, wanted to get dinner. She figured that would fill up a few hours, at least. Isabel sighed, looking at but not quite watching the TV, knowing that all too soon it would be Sunday morning, and then it would be Sunday night, and she would have to go back to work. "At least I have a good story to tell about my Friday night out," she mused to herself. She imagined the look on Alicia's face when she told her that she'd had sex with not one, but two guys in the same night.

Setting her plate in the empty sink, Isabel walked back into her bedroom. She started going through her clothes to figure out what to wear that evening, and thought to herself that it was a damned good thing that she hadn't let either man come home with her. "Not that they weren't gentlemen, in their own way," she said, countering her own thought. "But probably just as well not to let them know where I live." Isabel smiled wryly to herself; there was no way that either man would want to have anything else to do with her, as much as she would have liked a repeat performance with either. The fact that she couldn't remember who the second man had been bugged her a little; but there wasn't anything to do about it. She would just have to accept that it had been one of those magical evenings where things went even better than expected, and leave it at that.

Chapter Three

Isabel stepped into the bathroom closest to her desk at the office, feeling a strange skin-crawling sensation all over. *Mondays suck but this is ridiculous,* she thought, hurrying over to one of the stalls.

As she stepped out of the stall, Isabel glanced at herself in the mirror, and froze where she stood, not even hearing the noise as the door to the cubicle slammed shut. She stared at her own reflection, frowning, trying to figure out what was so shocking about it, why it had stopped her dead in her tracks.

After a few seconds of staring, Isabel shook her head in disbelief. She had seen herself in the mirror so many times in the course of her life that unless she was checking her hair or makeup, she barely even looked. But the woman she saw in the mirror in front of her was both the same one she always saw and somehow, indefinably, different at the same time. She continued staring, trying to understand what it was she was seeing.

She reached around to the back of her head, and almost thoughtlessly, Isabel's fingers found the elastic band she had used that morning for twisting and tucking her dark hair into a bun. Isabel felt a sharp tug at some of her hairs, stuck in the elastic, and then the bun unwound, and her hair fell around her face. She gasped at the sight of it; just that morning, or so she had thought, she'd had dark brown hair, stick-straight and healthy, if not particularly glamorous. But the woman in the mirror bore a hood, a cascade made of flowing, crackling, dark wavy hair, that seemed to have a life of its own; shot through with glimmering highlights in warmer coppery and cinnamon colors. It was as if she had spent the morning being pampered at a salon – a high-priced salon – and not at her desk, reviewing a client brief trying to sort out the conflicting instructions.

She hadn't put on makeup that morning, because she had barely managed to get out of bed by the third snooze cycle on her alarm. But the woman in the mirror had artist-worthy makeup, a gleam in her gray eyes that was hot and cold all at once, full lips that promised everything a man could want. "Is my face ... thinner?" Isabel hesitantly stepped closer to the mirror, peering into the image. Her cheekbones looked as if she had gotten them filled in, her chin had somehow become sharper, and the expanse under her cheekbones was firmer. "What the hell is going on?" Isabel lightly slapped at her face, unable to quite fully believe it as the woman in the mirror did the same. Even the clothes she was wearing – a comfortable ensemble made up of a cardigan and shell, and a pencil skirt seemed to look more glamorous on her, somehow.

Isabel shook her head and turned away from the mirror. She remembered that in her distraction she hadn't washed her hands, and turned back, keeping her eyes averted from the hypnotizing woman in the glass as she bent to clean up. "Don't think about it," she told herself quietly, thankful for the fact that she was alone in the restroom. "If you suddenly look like a model, just ... just don't think about it. It's not important."

She dried her hands and left the bathroom, moving quickly towards her desk. Try as she might, Isabel couldn't put the arresting image of herself out of her mind, even as she worked on the copy she had been assigned. Her stomach felt strange; both tight and loose, and she hadn't been able to make herself finish her breakfast. Her options for lunch didn't sound at all appealing to her, though she thought that if she waited too long she would end up making a bad decision in the midafternoon. Isabel sat back in her chair, frowning to herself, remembering the sight of her own reflection. It had to have been a fluke, some kind of weird hallucination, didn't it?

Isabel glanced at her purse, set aside on her desk out of the way of her computer and keyboard. Her fingers itched as she tried to type a few more sentences, but the temptation was irresistible. She grabbed her purse quickly, convinced – or at least hoping – that the compact mirror inside would reveal the woman she had woken up as that morning. She fumbled amongst the detritus in her bag until her fingers closed around the smooth compact. Taking a quick, deep breath, Isabel looked around; everyone in the office was busy at their own tasks, completely absorbed in their computers, paying no attention to her. *At least that much is normal,* she thought.

She opened the compact and steeled herself, not certain whether she wanted the sight she had seen in the restroom to be the truth or a hallucination. *If it was a hallucination, you have bigger things to worry about than just suddenly being weirdly gorgeous,* she thought. *But then again, if it wasn't a hallucination, you're going to have to figure out how to explain to everyone – including yourself – how you suddenly turned into a glamazon.* She closed her eyes and held the mirror part of the compact up to her face, a few inches away from her.

Isabel opened her eyes, and for just an instant, she felt disappointment that the image she saw was exactly what she had seen before leaving for work that morning. But the next instant, her eyes focused, and she saw that if she had been hallucinating before, she still was; she was utterly stunning. *Okay, so this doesn't answer that question.... not exactly, anyway.* Isabel closed the compact and put it aside. She could still be hallucinating; it could still be fake.

"How do you figure out if something is a hallucination?" Isabel glanced around her again, making sure that nobody had overheard her quiet musing. She could take a picture of herself, but somehow it didn't seem like that would be adequate proof; she could hallucinate an image on a screen just as easily as she could the image of herself in a mirror. *The only way to prove that something isn't a hallucination is to confirm that other people see it, too.* She would have to see if someone else thought she looked amazing, but she would have to do it in such a way that she could confirm at least a few specifics of what her eyes were telling her.

Isabel stood up from her desk and stretched against the tightness she could feel in her shoulders and back, looking around the office floor. Who could she ask? How could she do it? Isabel considered.... *Alex? That's who I can ask.* Alex, the Project Manager for the copy department, he had never liked her. At least, that was the impression that Isabel had gotten from the man, who was about fifteen years older than she was, and almost as plain as she had been. Alex had dropped hints that she was homely in the past, remarking that it was a good thing that she wasn't client-facing, and that she was exactly what people thought they would see when they considered a copywriter. "If he notices, then it must be real," Isabel murmured to herself.

She spotted Alex walking near the conference rooms, headed towards his office. Isabel thought about a pretense to waylay him, as she tried to figure something that would justify being in his presence long enough for him to pay attention to her looks. It couldn't just be a quick question – it had to be something that prompted a longer conversation. *The Peterson brief,* she realized quickly.

Isabel grabbed the paperwork from the client file and started across the office, moving to intercept Alex. "Hey! Hey, Al!" Isabel quickened her steps, and Alex barely glanced up from the notepad in front of him.

"What's up, Izzy?" Isabel rolled her eyes; she had always hated that nickname, but no one in the office seemed to care.

"I need to talk to you about Peterson," she said. "Do you have a couple of free minutes?"

Alex looked up fully from his notepad, and stopped short, staring at her for a moment. "Yes, of course," he said, his voice more pleasant than it had been all morning.

"Can we step into your office?" Alex nodded slowly, looking almost as if he were entranced, or maybe drugged.

"Absolutely," he said. "Come on in." He gestured for Isabel to precede him into the office, and she did, glancing back in Alex's direction as he followed her. *As if today wasn't weird enough already,* she thought.

"So," Isabel said, when Alex closed the office door behind them. "I'm having some trouble figuring out what they mean in a few places here."

"You are?" Alex shook his head. "But you're always so good at that." Isabel raised an eyebrow at the compliment and plunged forward, sitting down as Alex somehow managed to get into the chair behind his desk without looking at it. He was staring at her almost without blinking. "What seems to be the problem? And how can I solve it for you?" He smiled, and the sight sent a tingle of both apprehension and pride down Isabel's spine. She had seen a smile like that before, but never on Alex's face. It was the smile like the ones on the faces of men at Underground – or at one of the few other bars she went to— – when they were about to make a move on her.

"It's just that they're contradicting themselves," Isabel said, shrugging. "Totally opposite instructions in different places." She handed the file across the desk, and Alex opened it, glancing at it for just an instant before turning his attention back to her.

"You know," he said, leaning forward slightly and resting his chin on his hands, "I don't know what you've done to yourself, but I can't stop staring at you."

"Thank you ... I think," Isabel said, smiling awkwardly. *Well whatever he's seeing, it certainly can't be that far off from what was in the mirror,* she thought.

"I would give you anything you wanted if you were to come home with me," Alex blurted. Isabel sat back in the chair, staring at Alex in shock. He had never come onto her before. She had never seen him be anything but appropriate with the women in the office, at least in terms of flirting; his remarks about appearance had been somewhat irritating, but always just on the right side of HR standards. "Or ...I mean, we could take a smoke break right now. My car's on the top floor of the parking garage, and the AC is great in it."

"That's inappropriate," Isabel said sharply.

"Of course!" Alex blinked and the slightly leering look in his eyes cleared, only to be replaced once more with the musing softness she had seen before. "I would hate to make you feel uncomfortable, Izzy."

"Don't call me that!" she told him, flustered and irritable in equal measures.

"Never again," Alex promised. Isabel sat for a moment, staring at him gazing at her, and wondered what was happening to her. *Is this just the way guys act around you if you're gorgeous?* Isabel decided to test the idea, weak as it was.

"I think I'd appreciate it even more if you'd call Peterson and tell them to send over new, clearer instructions," she said; her voice sounded strange to her own ears as she spoke: soft and commanding all at once, sultry and amusing. "Maybe then we could talk about your car." Alex reached for the handset to his phone. "Wait!" Isabel leaned forward in the chair. "Wait until I get back to my desk," she suggested.

"Of course, of course," Alex said, nodding agreeably. "Whatever you want."

"What I want is to go home early," Isabel said wryly, thinking out loud more than anything else.

"Then you should do that," Alex told her. Isabel stared at him.

"But then I won't get paid," she pointed out.

"Why not?" Alex looked genuinely confused.

"Because I won't be working. I need to be here to get paid, don't I?"

"Don't you?" Alex looked so genuinely confused, so earnest, that Isabel started to feel afraid again.

"Are you saying I could go home right now and you'd just ... let me get paid for the day?"

"If that was what you wanted, then of course, I would," Alex replied.

"Then ... I guess that's what I'll do," Isabel said. "Don't – don't tell anyone you're doing this."

"No, that would be stupid," Alex agreed. "I'll just make sure you're punched out at the right time."

"Okay," Isabel said, staring at him in shock. "Let me know what Peterson says." She rose to her feet, and Alex looked her up and down; for a moment, his gaze almost made Isabel's stomach turn over, it was so full of straightforward lust. "I'll just go now. I'll be back tomorrow morning."

"Can't wait," Alex said cheerfully. "Maybe you could wear a shorter skirt?"

"I'll think about it," Isabel said, shaken. She turned on her heel and left the office.

Chapter Four

"This is absurd," Isabel said to herself, pacing across her living room floor. "Things like this don't happen." She shook her head, reflecting on her drive home. She had been so distracted, so completely bowled over by the shocks of the day, that she had blown right through a red light. Predictably, a police officer had been right behind her when it happened. That, at least, had been more or less how Isabel expected her day-to-day life to go. Right up until the officer had walked up to her window, she had felt comforted by the regularity of the situation in spite of the knowledge that a red-light ticket was going to cost far more than she could afford.

As soon as the officer had leaned in to look at her, in the midst of asking about her license, registration and insurance, Isabel had known that it wasn't going to be the normal process. She thought that Alex's reaction to her newfound desirability was an isolated incident, but the same look of almost drugged enchantment had come over the middle-aged man's face as soon as she met his gaze. "How are you this afternoon, ma'am? You look absolutely fucking amazing."

It had to be more than just becoming attractive, Isabel thought as she continued to pace. She decided to test the luck she'd had with her boss on the police officer, just on a whim, thinking she had nothing to lose. "Thank you," she'd said warmly. "I feel amazing, too."

"I bet you do," the man had said, his voice dropping low. "Any chance I can feel amazing?"

"Not today," she told him. "But maybe you would be willing to do me a favor?"

"Anything you want," the man – whose name tag read Reilly – --had replied. "Anything at all."

"Don't give me a ticket, please," Isabel had suggested. "It would make me so very sad."

"No ticket," Reilly had agreed. Isabel's shock at the strange turn of events had deepened.

"Maybe you'd be willing to drive alongside me, make sure no one else pulls me over for anything?"

"Of course," Reilly had said. "I'd love to."

When she'd arrived at her apartment building, Isabel had been at a loss for what to do with the enraptured officer. She'd finally decided to tell him to get back to his job, and he'd beamed at her as if she'd given him the best treat of his life and gotten back into his car.

"What the *hell* is going on?" Isabel glanced at herself in the big mirror she had put up on the wall opposite her living room window. She was as beautiful as ever. "It can't just be the fact that I'm hot. It can't be." She had known gorgeous women, and while Isabel had heard more than once about their random triumphs, she had never heard of any of them getting off work early with pay, or getting out of a completely valid ticket, much less getting a police escort, just from asking.

Then too, Isabel thought, peering at herself more closely, she wasn't just beautiful; she wasn't even just gorgeous or stunning. As the day had worn on, every time she looked at herself in the mirror, she saw something newly captivating about her face. And she had noticed that her clothes felt just a bit looser than they had when she put them on. Not so much that she worried about them falling off, but enough to notice. There was something *supernatural* about how she looked, how she felt. That was the only word that seemed to fit what was happening; even if it was absurd to think of it that way.

Seized by a sudden thought, Isabel quickly undressed, throwing her clothes aside without paying attention to where they landed in her living room. She sat down on her couch and spread her legs, turning one out at the hip to look at the spot where she had noticed the odd mark only two days before. It was still there, but it had changed; it had healed, somehow, but two little spots lingered, pale pink like scars. "Bite marks don't completely heal in two days?" Isabel brushed her fingers over the spots, and something rose up in her mind: she remembered watching *True Blood* a month before, and the marks the vampires had left behind. "No – no, that's ridiculous," she said, shaking her head dismissively at her own whimsy and looking around for her clothes to put them back on.

Isabel gathered up her office outfit and looked at it distastefully. It had been comfortable enough for sitting at a desk, but she was so shaken by the events of the day that all she wanted was to get into her pajamas. She strode into her bedroom and threw the ensemble into the hamper, pulling a pair of soft cotton shorts and a loose tank top out of a drawer. She didn't expect for anyone to visit her, so there was no need for a bra or a pair of panties.

Almost as soon as Isabel stepped out of her bedroom, dressed for a comfortable afternoon of existential horror and television, she heard a knock at her door. "Of course," she said with a sigh, glancing down at herself. Whoever it was – Jehovah's Witness, someone selling cable packages, or the building manager – they would just have to accept that people in their homes lounged around in pajamas. Isabel padded to the door on her bare feet, irritable at her pensive afternoon being interrupted. She unlocked the deadbolt and twisted the knob lock, not even bothering to look through the peephole before opening the door.

The man on the other side of it was definitely not a Witness, nor was he the building manager; and Isabel was fairly certain he wasn't interested in selling her a new cable package either. For a moment, she stared at the gorgeous man, wondering why he looked so familiar. *I could not have possibly met someone this good looking and forgotten how it happened,* she thought. She took in his dark, shoulder-length hair, his hazel eyes, his broad shoulders and lean, muscled build, and racked her brain for a few heartbeats.

Then, all at once, it came back to her. Friday night, Underground. The man who had paid her tab, who had taken her to a late dinner – or maybe it was an exceptionally early breakfast – and then taken her in the back seat of her car. "Let me in, Isabel," he said firmly, and before she could even think about the command, Isabel stepped back from the door, opening it wider.

"What the hell?" she shook her head, looking down at her hands and then at the man.

"I'm not going to hurt you," Oz said, stepping into her apartment. "You're confused, aren't you?"

"Confused and a little bit scared at the fact that I apparently don't have the self-preservation instinct to close the door on a one-night stand who's stalking me," she said sharply.

"Sit down," Oz told her. Once again, before she could even think about the command, she found herself obeying it. She closed the door and walked over to the couch, seating herself primly.

"Okay," she said. "I think you need to explain what this is, and what's going on." Oz smiled slightly, his eyes gleaming.

"That's exactly why I'm here," he told her. "You're in trouble, Isabel. More trouble than you know."

"You know about what's happening with me," she said, realizing it in an instant. "The whole stuff that happened at work and with the cop." Oz nodded.

"You will listen to me, you will hear me out, and you won't interrupt with any questions until I'm done explaining. Is that understood?" Isabel nodded, in spite of the questions she could feel on the tip of her tongue, almost burning her lips. "You're becoming a succubus."

For an instant, Isabel opened her mouth to retort that what he was saying was ridiculous, but then closed her mouth just as quickly. She frowned…… she had questions, she wanted to say something. *You won't interrupt me.* Anger kindled in Isabel's mind, replacing the instinctive apprehension at the stranger's arrival. *Where does he get off making demands like this?*

"Yes, yes, I know," Oz said, smiling slightly, almost seeming to enjoy her discomfort, or at least amused by it. "Impossible." Isabel nodded, wondering what kind of control that man had on her that she couldn't bring herself to ask the questions churning in her mind. "You humans," he said, shaking his head. "So obsessed with the paranormal but so unwilling to believe it when it happens to you." Isabel raised an eyebrow and Oz looked up at the ceiling. "Since you obviously aren't capable of listening without comment, you can speak," he said.

"First of all: a succubus, really?" Isabel crossed her arms over her chest. "Second of all, how is it that you get to boss me around and I can't help but obey you?" She swallowed against the tight, dry feeling in her throat. "Third: what the hell is going on and how did this happen to me?"

"Yes, really, a succubus," Oz said, sarcastically mimicking her tone. "Because of the circumstances that triggered your change into a succubus, I and one other person have control over you. It's a safeguard, to make sure that your kind don't overrun the planet."

"But a succubus is a kind of demon," Isabel pointed out, grateful that Oz hadn't thought to command her to silence once more.

"Succubi are created, not born," Oz told her. "You are becoming a succubus because you had sex with an angel and a vampire in the same night." Isabel blushed; only a short time before her one-night stand's arrival, she had felt proud at the fact that she had managed to hook up with two guys in one night. Or if not proud, then impressed at herself for the implied attraction both men had felt for her. But something about the way that Oz spoke made her feel petty.

"Wait," Isabel said, her mind latching onto the significance of his explanation instead of the tone.

"A vampire and an angel?" She shook her head. "Neither of those things exist, any more than succubi are real."

"I thought you would say that," Oz said. He reached down and pulled up the hem of his shirt. Isabel frowned as he tugged it over his head and let it fall to the floor before turning his back to her. A shimmery light glowed along his muscular shoulder blades, and before Isabel's eyes, a pair of glorious-looking, gold-tipped, white feathery wings, began to appear, spreading out from the center of Oz's back. Even when Oz turned around, Isabel could only stare at him, bemused and utterly shocked. She had to believe her eyes, right?

"Okay," she said after a long moment. "So you're the angel, obviously." Oz grinned.

"Obviously," he told her. "Vampires have wings that they can summon or hide as well, but theirs are always dark."

"Why do I suddenly get the feeling that my entire life is about to become incredibly complicated?" Oz's grin changed into a wry smile.

"It isn't *about to* become incredibly complicated," he told her. "It already *is*."

"What do you mean?" Isabel's heart beat faster in her chest; she wasn't sure she believed what Oz had said. After all, it was the stuff of fantasy movies and HBO series, but unless he had some kind of mind control ability, she didn't think he could fake the wings she had seen.

Oz folded his wings; they shimmered and disappeared, and he put his shirt back on. "In order to be a succubus, you have to have had sex with an angel, me," he smiled slightly before continuing, "and a vampire." Isabel pressed her lips together and looked down at her hands, remembering the mark on her inner thigh.

"Okay, so I'm turning into some kind of demon-thing," she said. "That's pretty complicated, for sure, but I get the feeling you mean something more than that." Oz nodded.

"First of all: you aren't a demon, and aren't turning into one. You're an immortal being – like I am and like the vampire you also had sex with is."

"Wait. Immortal?" Isabel stared at him.

"You're just starting to transform now," Oz explained. "Within about a week, the process will be complete, and you'll be a full succubus."

"What does that even mean?" Isabel's mind was still struggling to accept what she was hearing.

"You'll find that you can readily control men's minds," Oz said. "As the week goes on, you will become more and more supernaturally beautiful until you are beyond the ideal for the society you live in. More advanced succubi can change whenever they enter a new culture, becoming the height of beauty wherever they are, but that takes a great deal of time and skill to master."

"That sounds good, at least," Isabel said thoughtfully.

"You won't need to sleep. In fact, once you complete the transition, you'll find you don't even want to sleep, and if you do sleep, it will generally be during the day. At night, you will be restless." Oz half-smiled. "You can still eat food, but your body won't derive sufficient nutrients from it. When you complete the transition and fully become a succubus, you will absolutely *have* to have sex every night."

"Have to?" Isabel stared at the angel. She thought it was as good a term as any, in shock. "I've gone weeks without sex before, though." Oz shook his head.

"If you go without nightly sex – without a condom – once you're fully transformed, you'll begin to weaken within days," he said. "You'll find that you have an utterly insatiable appetite for sex, almost an addictive need." Isabel opened her mouth, realized she had no idea what to say to that, and then closed it.

"How am I going to manage to get sex every night?" she asked finally. Oz grinned.

"Did you forget about the control of men's minds?"

"That would-be rape!" Isabel glared at him. "I'm not going to control some guy into screwing me so I can stay alive."

"They will only be too willing," Oz told her drily.

"But won't – are all succubi just walking STDs or something?"

"You're naturally immune," Oz said. "The other thing you could do, which I recommend is to find a 'host' or person you can rely on for your needs." Isabel's face burned as the significance of what Oz said filled her mind.

"So basically, I'm feeding off of whoever I have sex with," she said. "And you think I should find someone who will agree to have sex with me every night?"

"It will be the best sex of their lives," Oz said, shrugging. "Not many would turn that down."

"This is ..." Isabel shook her head. "This is insane, and wrong. How could ...how is this fair? Just because I slept with two guys in one night who happened to apparently be an angel and a vampire?"

"How are you feeling, Isabel?" She stared at Oz in confusion. The question made no sense, but she realized, in spite of the fear, shock, and dismay she felt, she could feel a little tendril of heat working its way through her body, down her spine. "Hungry?"

Chapter Five

Isabel stood and took a few steps back from Oz. "No," she said, shaking her head. Her stomach was gnawing, but there was a throbbing deeper down, between her legs. In a matter of moments, she felt the slickness along her labia. "You've got to be kidding me," she told Oz.

"Tell me the truth," Oz told her firmly. "Are you aroused right now?" Isabel looked down at her feet, unwilling to answer. But unable to help herself.

"Yes," she said, feeling ashamed.

"It's natural," Oz said, his voice more soothing. "You'll find yourself becoming turned on several times a day, more and more often until you're fully transformed. Then, once you're a complete succubus, you'll learn to control your appetite, although it will never go away." He was stepping closer to her, and Isabel felt a mixture of apprehension and desire as she caught the scent of him: warm, sweet, delicious. Was that what he had smelled like during their one-night stand? She didn't think so, but her mouth watered for more. Images flitted through her head, utterly pornographic: falling to her knees, she took Oz's hard cock into her mouth and worshipped it with her lips and tongue with abandonment until he came; or pushing him onto the couch and ripping her clothes off to ride him, hard and fast, eager for his climax; or Oz bending her over the back of a chair, taking her from behind all at once.

"This is insane," Isabel murmured.

"You need to be fucked, don't you?" Isabel looked up at Oz's face, feeling humiliated and needy, as if her whole body were on fire. She nodded, resigned. "Tell me what you want, Isabel."

"I want to suck you off until you come in my mouth." The words left her almost without thought – she had never in her life been so direct with anyone she had slept with.

Oz smiled slightly and his hands moved to the waistband of his jeans. Isabel stared in a mixture of shock and pure, unadulterated desire as Oz unbuttoned and unzipped, then hooked his thumbs into the fabric at his hips. He pushed his pants down, and his boxers with them. His cock immediately sprung free, fully erect. For the span of a few heartbeats, Isabel stood transfixed, wondering if she had actually seen Oz's body before. When they'd had their one-night stand; there was something so deeply arousing about the sight of him, about the lean muscle of his body and the thick, flushed erection in its nest of dark curls, that Isabel thought it was impossible for her to have seen him before.

The next instant, she was on her knees in front of him, licking her lips to moisten them as she leaned in towards the tip of Oz's erection. She darted her tongue out to catch the glistening drop of fluid, and it spread across her taste buds, sharp and salty yet slightly bitter and sweet all at once. Isabel took as much of Oz's cock into her mouth as she could, sucking and licking, swirling her tongue around the sensitive head as she swallowed down the taste of him. The hunger she could feel in the pit of her stomach, in the tightness between her hips, began to sharpen and ease. She pressed forward, wrapping her lips around the thick length of Oz's erection as she took him deeper and deeper into her mouth.

In the back of her mind, Isabel thought that at any moment, she would set off her gag reflex; normally it was fairly sensitive. But as she swallowed, she felt the tip of Oz's cock brushing against the back of her throat – no sudden rejection, no reflexive retch. The hunger was too strong for her to wonder at it too much, especially when she was getting exactly what she wanted. Isabel moved her lips up and down along Oz's shaft, swirling her tongue around the hot, hard cock until she came to the tip, and then pushing back down. Oz's fingers slid through her hair, and then tangled as he brought them to rest on the sides of her head. Isabel could feel the tension mounting deep down between her hips, the heat gathering along her labia. She knew she had to be soaking wet. It was impossible for her to believe it, but as she moaned at the feeling of Oz's erection in her mouth, the taste of him, the sheer satisfaction felt like the first bites of a meal when she was starving. She couldn't argue.

Oz moaned, his fingers tightening in her hair, and Isabel worked him with her mouth, reaching up with one hand to cradle the thin-skinned, warm testicles underneath. She gave them a careful, gentle squeeze and Oz almost shouted, his hands tugging at her head. The pain in her scalp felt oddly good, and Isabel moved faster, coiling her tongue around the shaft of Oz's penis, wrapping her lips more tightly around him. At that point, he was almost too much for her to take; as he began to twitch inside her mouth, his pre-cum flowing more freely, Isabel struggled to keep her momentum up, fought to get what she so desperately wanted from him.

Oz came with a shout, his hands tugging at her hair, his hips thrusting forward, deep into her mouth even as the first gush of his pleasure flooded across her tongue. Isabel swallowed eagerly, eyes closed. In the back of her mind, she was shocked at how good it tasted, how delicious the salty-sharp flavor was. More and more of it rushed into her mouth and Isabel savored every drop, sucking and licking and swallowing until Oz's hips began to slow and she felt the rigid member between her lips begin to soften.

She sat back, panting and gasping for breath, then looked up at Oz. He had his eyes closed, and his chest rose and fell with his heavy breathing. He looked down at her, and Isabel grinned, still feeling the heat coursing through her body. "That has to have been at least half natural talent," Oz told her.

Isabel shrugged.

"You don't remember the night before?" Oz sat down on the couch heavily, still panting.

"You didn't go down on me the night before," he replied. Isabel chuckled and got unsteadily onto her feet. She could feel the pulse of lust still dancing through her veins, along her bones; taking Oz in her mouth had helped, but it wasn't enough. *Good god, this is going to get tricky if what he says is right,* she thought, even as she began stripping her clothes off, almost unconsciously.

Oz watched her, and Isabel saw the mixture of interest, amusement, and renewed desire in his eyes. "If you're an angel, why are you having sex?" Isabel began letting her hands move over her body slowly, making as much as she possibly could of her curves, for once utterly unself-conscious about the belly she'd had since puberty, or her heavy thighs.

"Your concept of angels isn't the real thing," Oz told her. Isabel saw one of his hands reach down and he began to touch himself, slowly and lightly but steadily. "There's a lot that humans don't know about us. We're not innocent or naïve, and we definitely have sex." Isabel giggled.

She climbed onto the couch, focused solely on the man sitting there, stroking himself to hardness once more. Isabel slipped one hand between her legs, and she felt how hot and wet she was: utterly soaking, her fingers coated in an instant. She found her clitoris by touch and began to rub it, in light, swirling touches, closing her eyes as a tingling jolt of pleasure mingled with need shot through her. "Stop that," Oz said sharply. Immediately, Isabel's eyes opened, and her fingers withdrew. She stared at Oz, confused and disappointed.

"Why?" Oz reached out with his free hand and cupped her vulva, rubbing the heel of his palm against her until Isabel moaned.

"Because," Oz said, his fingers slipping and sliding between her labia, slowly pushing into her, making her shiver and gasp, "you should always let the person you're about to feed on have a taste first." He plunged two fingers inside of her all the way and Isabel cried out; it felt so tight – tighter than it had been the last time they'd had sex, almost as tight as it had been the first time she slept with someone.

Oz withdrew his fingers and Isabel frowned. Every nerve in her body was screaming for pleasure; she *needed* it, not just wanted it. Before she could say anything, Oz let go of his already-hard cock and reached for her. This time, instead of fingering her, he grabbed her by the waist with both hands and lifted her up, until she was just above his lap. "Tell me what you want, Isabel," Oz said.

"I want to ride you, hard and fast," Isabel told him. "I want to feel you come inside me." Oz gently lowered her until her labia barely brushed against his erection, her legs straddling him.

"Then do it," he said mildly.

Isabel shifted on top of him, reaching down to guide the tip of Oz's cock against her slippery, drenched folds until she found the exact spot where she wanted him. She sank down onto him, pushing her hips to take him all at once. Oz's hands moved to her hips, and then back, cupping her buttocks, holding her tightly as Isabel took him in. "Fuck," she moaned. It felt like a minor miracle that he'd fit inside of her at all. She felt so full, so tight around him. Oz's cock throbbed inside of her and Isabel began to move, twisting her hips, rubbing her pleasure center against him as she rode him, taking him deeper and deeper. She gripped the back of the couch to steady herself, moving faster, moaning again and again at the heat of him inside of her, at the sensation of being full where she'd felt so empty only moments before. It was unlike any sex she'd ever had in her life; intense in a way she had never experienced before, her body flexing around the hard cock invading it as if it were simultaneously trying to defend itself and pull him in.

"Did I forget to mention?" Oz began thrusting up into her, rubbing along her inner walls, the tip of his cock brushing against her g-spot with almost every movement. "It's – it's going to be the best sex of – of your life, every time." He claimed her mouth, kissing her hungrily as Isabel moved. She flexed around him, and felt the movement of the muscles, felt the squeeze, and then the reaction from his body as he began to twitch, deep inside of her.

Before she knew it, Isabel felt the mounting tension and heat between her hips reach its highest point, and then all of a sudden it broke; wave after wave after wave of sensation washing through her. Even with the mind-blowing pleasure of her orgasm, she was keenly aware of Oz reaching his own climax, the sticky-slick gush of heat rushing into her body as he moaned against her lips and pushed her buttocks down until he was as deep in her as possible, his fingers pressing into her skin almost hard enough to bruise. Isabel broke away from his lips, shrieking in pleasure, electric sensation crackling through every nerve of her body as she succumbed to the end of their tryst.

Chapter Six

Isabel stared up at the ceiling of her bedroom, feeling the lingering slickness, the tender sensation along her labia. She had retreated to her bed when she had recovered from the encounter with Oz, confused, satisfied, and worried in equal measures. Oz had remained behind, and Isabel was grateful for that; she needed time to think. She needed to wrap her mind around what was happening to her, and what Oz had told her would continue to happen moving forward. "This is so screwed up," she told the ceiling.

She had always had a healthy sexual appetite, but the way she had gone down on Oz, the way she had ridden him, the absolute hunger she had experienced was something totally out of her understanding. Isabel shook her head, baffled by how good the sex had been as well as how much she had not just wanted but *needed* it. "At least I'm good for a day, I guess," she said absently.

"You technically don't need to feed again for another two days, if you don't want to," Oz said from her bedroom door. He came into the room, and Isabel fought off the sense of irritation she felt; she needed way more answers.

"I thought you said I'd need it nightly?"

Oz shook his head.

"Once you're fully transformed, you will," he said. He smiled slightly. "Given your current appetite, I wouldn't be surprised if you were so voracious you needed it a few times a night." Isabel groaned, turning over onto her side, away from him.

"This is humiliating," she said, not bothering to look at the man.

"It's definitely something to adjust to," Oz said. His voice was surprisingly mild. "But there are benefits."

"Oh yes, getting out of tickets and getting my boss to let me leave early for the day with pay are huge benefits," she said. Oz chuckled.

"You're thinking too small," he told her. "You can control the mind of any man – well, gay men are iffy. But think about what that means."

Isabel considered it.

"If you're thinking I can just go around getting guys to give me money ..." the idea felt dirty to her.

"You could," Oz said. "You could also become a model; no male designer would tell you no. You could go into sex work – that way you'd get paid and be guaranteed to get the feedings you need." Isabel cringed. *He's not wrong, but going into sex work just because ...* she shook her head, sighing.

"It would feel wrong," she told him.

"There's a more important concern," Oz said. Isabel turned over to face him, confused.

"What more important concern?"

"You're vulnerable," Oz told her. "Remember how you ended up like this?" Isabel rolled her eyes and sat up, feeling the slick slither of her fluids mingled with Oz's against her labia, along her inner thighs.

"According to you, by having sex with you and also a vampire," she said tartly.

"Right," Oz said. "And unfortunately, that fact puts you in more than a slightly awkward position. That's why I'm here – not just to tell you what you are and to give you a good feeding." He gave her a faint, almost sardonic smile.

"Okay," Isabel said. She licked her lips and combed her fingers through her hair. "So, explain this to me."

"Vampires and angels, we don't get along," Oz said. "Not really, anyway. It's not exactly a good versus evil thing, though you can think of it that way. It's more a question of factions. Vampires are creatures of night; they *can* go out during the day, at least after their first hundred years, but they have to be careful."

"This isn't exactly explaining the awkwardness," Isabel told him.

"Listen to me," Oz said. Isabel subsided, taking a deep breath.

"Explain that, too; the way you can make me do whatever you want, whether I want to or not," she demanded.

"It's because I helped create you," Oz said. "Your body obeys my commands." Isabel raised an eyebrow at that but decided to let it pass; there were more important things to find out. "Vampires and angels, we both have a vested interest in keeping succubi contained. However, we have different opinions about how to accomplish that."

"How so?" Oz sat down on the edge of her bed.

"Angels ... we mostly try to help succubi by setting them up with a host. Someone who can satisfy their needs. Or we steer them into providing sex therapy, or other things like that."

"Okay, and the vampires don't do that?"

Oz shook his head.

"The vampires are big in sex work: prostitution, porn, BDSM clubs and so on," he said. "They're also invested in some unsavory practices that they use succubi in: blackmail, slave trading, things like that."

"So, apparently, it's a good thing you found me," Isabel said, feeling a trickle of fear down her spine.

"The bigger issue is that the vampires are amassing an army," Oz explained. "There are all kinds of paranormal and supernatural creatures on this planet, and the vampires are trying to get as many of them as possible on their side."

"And the angels aren't?"

Oz half-shrugged.

"We're a bit more passive in our recruitment," he said. "We don't feed on humans, vampires do."

"And feeding on humans is relevant because?"

"Because the ultimate goal that the vampires have is war," Oz said. "They want to essentially bring the non-supernatural community under the collective rule of themselves and a few other creatures that exist."

"And succubi are part of that?"

Oz nodded.

"They play an instrumental role," he said. "After all, the ability to control men's minds comes in pretty handy for waging war against them, doesn't it?" Isabel shuddered. She hadn't fully enjoyed even the little taste of mind control she'd had earlier in the day. The thought of that ability being used as a weapon gave her chills. "There's basically been a cold war between angels and vampires for centuries. Angels want the supernatural world to stay quiet and hidden. Vampires want to come out and have the right to feed on whomever they want to, whenever they want to."

"And because of that, I'm in danger," Isabel said, making it not quite a question.

"They'll want to recruit you," Oz said. "If not willingly, then by force. From what we've been able to determine, they starve succubi to make them compliant, and then only give them the opportunity to feed if they agree to do what they're told."

"So, my mind control doesn't work on vampires, I take it," Isabel said grimly.

"It's not as strong, because they have similar abilities," Oz said. "Angels are also partially immune. And if they starve you, your ability to control minds will weaken."

"Clearly, I need to avoid vampires," Isabel said.

"To that point, I want you to stay in my house," Oz told her. "I'll support you financially – there's no need for you to keep your current job, or even find a new one."

"You must be pretty well off to just suggest taking me in like that," Isabel said, looking at him skeptically.

"I have about ten billion dollars," Oz said smiling. "It's not difficult to accumulate wealth when you're immortal."

"That makes sense," Isabel said. She fidgeted, looking at the man she had first considered a one-night stand. He was an angel. *And now I can't tell anyone the story about that night,* Isabel thought, almost bitterly. *I'll be off the grid until ... well ...* "How long would I have to stay with you?"

"Until this matter is resolved," Oz said firmly. "Until you're not in danger anymore."

Chapter Seven

The house that Oz brought Isabel to looked – at first – like a standard mini-mansion, with a landscaped yard, and a modestly sizeable home on it behind wrought iron fencing. But as Oz pulled up onto the circular driveway, Isabel realized that it was something like an illusion; the house was grander, larger, more ornate than she had thought from the street. "How did you pull that off?"

"A little this, a little that," Oz said, matter-of-factly. "There's some illusion magic along the perimeter of the grounds to keep people who haven't been brought here directly from even knowing it's here."

"Magic is real?" Oz smiled.

"Magic is real, vampires are real, angels are real," he said. "There's a whole wide supernatural world out there, Isabel."

"And now I'm a member of it," she said wryly.

"Yes, you are," Oz told her. He parked the car and shut the engine off, and Isabel thought that if she had to be on veritable house arrest for the foreseeable future, she at least had a big, expansive house to be confined to.

She climbed out of the car and followed Oz towards the front door. It was painted red, a deep, bold shade that seemed almost to glow, and the frame was coated in something that Isabel couldn't quite identify, that gave it a slightly shiny finish. The front yard, hemmed in by the wrought-iron fence, was perfectly manicured, with lushly growing garden beds.

Oz unlocked and opened the door as Isabel followed him into the house, blinking in amazement. She had been torn between belief and disbelief when Oz had told her that he was a billionaire; but the marble floors, vaulted ceilings, and the subtle gleam of gold leaf along the molding above set her firmly in the "belief" camp. "Come on, Isabel, let me show you your room," he said.

The whole situation was bizarre; Isabel looked around as she followed Oz through the house, thinking to herself that if anyone ever told her that it had happened to them, she would think they were not just lying, but insane. *I'm a succubus,* she thought. *I'm going to have to make sure I have sex with someone every night or I'll 'starve'.... no matter how much food I eat. Vampires exist.... Angels exist, but they're not like angels from the bible.* Her mind spun in circles, trying to make sense of the situation.

"Here," Oz said. He opened a door to a room that was almost half the size of Isabel's entire home. Looking in, she could see doorways leading into a bathroom and presumably a closet, along with a big, wide bed that dominated the room, a dresser and a vanity with a low bench in front of it. She spotted a flat screen TV, and some kind of terminal – it was turned off at the moment – that had the Wi-Fi symbol on it.

"Not a bad prison, all things considered," Isabel said, stepping through the door. Oz had given her enough time to grab a small suitcase of clothes, and when she had started to pack makeup in her luggage, he'd snorted and pointed out that as a succubus, there would be no —need for makeup ever again.

"It's not a prison," Oz said, his voice firm. "I don't think you understand the urgency in this, Isabel."

"I would be able to understand the urgency in this if I could believe half of what happened," Isabel said. "I'm still trying to figure out how to make sense of becoming a succubus, and you being a literal, real angel, and the fact that I apparently had sex with a vampire. Oh, and that's just the beginning of the bombs you dropped on me today."

"If nothing else," Oz said, starting to lighten a bit, "you know that while you're here, you'll be able to keep yourself from starving."

"I guess," Isabel said. "I'm assuming this isn't just going to be a few days."

"Until further notice," Oz told her. Isabel sat down on the edge of the bed and looked around her room.

"You do realize that I have friends and people in my life, right?" she said as she met Oz's gaze. "People who will miss me if I just disappear."

"I would recommend that if you're going to meet with any of your friends and family, you keep it to the women," Oz told her. "I can't guarantee if you meet with any males who know you – even if they're family – that they won't be sexually interested in you." Isabel stared at Oz.

"If I meet with my Dad …?"

"He will react the same way your boss did, in all likelihood." Isabel shuddered, involuntarily imagining it. *It's not fair! What did I do to deserve this?* She took a slow, deep breath.

"So only women," she said.

"Until you're better able to control your output, yes," Oz said, nodding. "Once you're fully adapted to being a succubus, you might be able to go around male friends and family without having to beat them off of you with a baseball bat."

"But if I have control over their minds, I can just tell them to stop it." Oz smiled.

"Just trust me on this one," he said. "Men will continue to have a difficult time controlling their impulse to hit on you. All men."

"Can you do me a favor?" Isabel looked at Oz.

"Depends on the favor," he said.

"I'd really like some space," Isabel told him. "I need to kind of ... figure things out."

"Of course," Oz said. He smiled slightly. "If you get lonely, or hungry ..." his smile deepened, and Isabel looked away, feeling embarrassed at the knowing look in his eyes.

He left the room, and Isabel let herself fall back onto the bed, staring up at the ceiling. *Nothing at all in my entire life is normal anymore,* she thought bitterly. Her body was changing; she had caught a glimpse of herself in a mirror on the way to the bedroom she would be staying in at Oz's house, and could have sworn that she was slimmer, more svelte. Even though she didn't have the burning, stomach-churning need for sex that she had felt earlier, she could still sense the pulse of her new appetite deep down in her brain.

Oz had said that because he was part of what had turned her into a succubus, he was able to command her. But the vampire and Isabel's brain balked at the idea that had also taken part in her strange conversion: would he have the same ability? *With any luck, I'll never know.* Isabel shuddered, thinking of what Oz had told her about how the vampires treated the succubi; they wanted to recruit.

"I wanted to change my life but this is ridiculous," Isabel said, shaking her head against the mattress. She had wanted to get a different job, or find someone she could maybe consider dating in the long term – not to turn into a supernatural creature that fed off of sexual energy, never slept, and had to be careful around the men in her life she wasn't interested in sexually.

"It's not *fair*," she murmured, turning over onto her side and curling up into a G shape, her knees almost to her stomach, her flatter stomach. The fact that she was losing weight without doing anything different in her life, so much so that her clothes were starting to not fit in a matter of only two days since she'd had her one-night stand with Oz, truly unsettled her.

She didn't feel physically tired, but as Isabel kept her eyes closed, trying to think, to wrap her mind around everything that had happened to her in such a short time she found herself drifting off. Absently, she thought she might as well appreciate the ability to sleep while she still had it, just before her thinking slowed with her breaths, and she slipped into a deeper doze.

Chapter Eight

"I feel ridiculous," Isabel told Oz as they strode through the mall, in the direction of Nordstrom. He'd insisted that she wear sunglasses and a hat, that she pull her hair back under the cap he had given her and wear the most shapeless dress that she had brought to his mansion. It was nearly dusk, and she felt more conspicuous in the "disguise".

"The sunglasses keep you from eye contact with people," Oz explained. "The hat shields your hair. The clothes cover up your body. It was either this or try and order everything online without knowing what your new size is." Isabel pressed her lips together and took a deep breath, following him still.

Two days since she had agreed to stay at his house, under his protection, Isabel had realized that none of her clothes – not even her underwear – fit. She had slimmed down at the waist, thighs, hips, and paradoxically had gone up at least one cup size in her breasts, almost overnight. If it weren't for Oz's patient explanations, she would have already rushed herself to the doctor.

Her irritation at the confused and frankly wondering looks she caught other mall patrons giving her was compounded by the fact that she could feel her hunger rising. Isabel had tried to eat two huge meals already: a big breakfast of eggs, pancakes, bacon, oatmeal, and yogurt, and then a lunch of pasta, steak, salad, and wine. But no matter how much she ate, it seemed, the hunger kept gnawing at her. Isabel glanced at Oz, a few steps ahead of her. She would have to "feed" again soon, and the fact filled her with resentment.

Of all the things that Isabel had tried to adjust to since she had started the transformation, the fact that she *had* to have sex regularly, that it was like eating instead of something she could enjoy whenever she could get it, was the most unfair. Isabel stared at Oz's back, knowing that she was going to end up in his bed that night – and that she would enjoy it, that she would be a fully willing participant – and almost, but not quite, hating him for that fact. It wasn't his fault, strictly speaking; Isabel knew that. But she knew she should be more grateful to him; that he was willing to take care of her, to finance her life and even provide her with the regular sex she needed to stay healthy.

They stepped into Nordstrom and Oz made a beeline for the service counter, reaching back without looking for Isabel's hand. She put her hand in his, and felt a little tingle from her fingers to her shoulder, all the way through her spine. She had begun to suspect that things were different with Oz – not just because he was an angel instead of a regular human, but something more. But as quickly as things had changed, it was too much to try and evaluate.

"We need all female assistance," Oz told the customer service manager at the desk. "We're going to be spending quite a bit of money in multiple departments, but it's imperative that all our customer service people are women." The manager raised an eyebrow at that, looking at Isabel, and she gave him a wry smile from behind her sunglasses. The man frowned, peering more closely at her, and Isabel could see the brief flicker of confused lust on his face. *Okay, so maybe the stupid, ugly disguise was a good idea.*

"Of course," the manager said. "If you can tell me which departments you'll be shopping in today, I'll make sure to have someone on hand in each one to assist you."

"Intimates, women's shoes, and jewelry," Oz told the man. Isabel squeezed his hand reflexively at the last category, even as the manager nodded his assent and stepped over to the phone on his desk to make the arrangement.

"Jewelry?" she tilted her sunglasses down on her nose just enough to meet Oz's gaze.

"My money, I can spend it how I want," Oz told her.

"If you think that this is going to obligate me—"

"You already have to do what I say," Oz interrupted her, a smile tugging at the corners of his lips. "Why would I need to obligate you?"

Isabel took a slow breath and exhaled sharply through her nose.

"Fine," she said. "But don't ... don't think that this makes me ... indebted to you. That's all."

"If I wanted to indebt you to me, I'd write up a contract," Oz said. The manager came back to them.

"Would you like to start in Intimates? One of my best representatives is there, ready to assist in any way she can."

"As long as you have a chain of female attendants for us to go to, I am happy to start wherever you like," Oz told the man. He looked at Isabel. "Intimates, my dear?" Isabel almost started at the familiar name, but quickly realized that unless they played the part of a couple, they'd attract more than their fair share of unwanted attention.

"Sure, babe," Isabel said sweetly.

The woman waiting for them in the Intimates and Sleepwear department was middle-aged, but Isabel could see that she had been lovely – probably even hot – in her younger years. Her skin was duller with age, and her hair had the look of salon processing to cover grays, but she had bright eyes in a well-made up face. She looked curvy enough to have learned the hard way the value of proper lingerie fitting. "Oh, my dear, new wardrobe?"

"From the bottom up, as it were," Oz said.

"Let's get started with some measurements, and go from there," the woman suggested, dividing her attention between Isabel and Oz. "Do you have a budget in mind? I want to make sure to steer you towards the best possible value."

"Money is no object," Oz told the woman. Isabel thought the look that leaped into the attendant's eyes was similar to the expression of someone on the edge of orgasm; the observation was the only point of real amusement she felt at the situation.

Isabel began to relax as she and Oz went from one department to another. She noticed how Oz exuded charm to the attendants they spoke to, but in the most unobtrusive way possible. He was endlessly patient. He was pleasant and smiling, and the women they worked with all responded to it immediately. *Of course, they're probably predisposed to like him on the grounds that he's incredibly hot and rich,* Isabel thought cynically. But it seemed like more than that, and Isabel thought – in the back of her mind – that there must be some kind of angelic magic, or persuasion, to it.

Almost before she knew it, Isabel realized that Oz had managed to rack up nearly a thousand dollars in purchases. He'd had to buy bras and panties separately, instead of in their standard sets, since – as she learned from the attendant – she had gone up two cup sizes to a size F, and down one band size, while her hip measurements had gone down enough inches to bring her to a size 6 panty. They had nearly had an incident while Isabel was trying on clothes in the women's wear department: a man had strayed through, following in the wake of his wife. Isabel had taken off the hat and the sunglasses, and as she emerged from the changing room to get Oz's approval of a dress, the married man stopped dead in his tracks to stare at her without any pretense or attempt to cover it up.

Oz had intercepted the man before he could do more than stare, getting in his line of sight and joking with him for a moment while Isabel scrambled to put her sunglasses and hat back on. That had underscored the fact that she had to be more careful about showing herself in public, at least until she had figured out how to control her "output," as Oz called it, more than any of his warnings had managed to do.

The hunger gnawed at her stomach, and throbbed deep down in her hips, by the time they left Nordstrom; both of them loaded down with bags. Oz had taken his share without complaint or even comment, and Isabel thought of the men she saw in the mall every other time she had been there, glumly carrying their girlfriends' or wives' purchases, holding shopping bags out at arm's length to prove their masculinity in some way. Oz didn't seem to have any of those hang-ups at all, and Isabel wondered at that. "Do you have the energy to stop somewhere else before we leave?" Oz asked.

"You didn't spend enough money at Nordstrom?" Isabel thought of the staggering totals from each department, the incredible charges that Oz had run up without batting a single eyelash, and couldn't believe that he would suggest spending more money.

"You deserve a treat," Oz said. He pointed out a storefront several spots down from where they stood: Lush. Isabel's eyes widened; she knew the store well, even spent a good bit of her own money there.

"Why?" Isabel looked at him. Oz smiled.

"Maybe I want you to be comfortable, happy, and pleased if you're stuck staying with me for the foreseeable future," he said. "Come on. If you don't see anything you like, I won't buy anything."

They started towards the shop, and Isabel tried to fight down her misgivings at the prospect of Oz spending more money on her. As they walked, she felt something – a frisson – deep down in the bottom of her spine. *That's weird,* she thought; it wasn't a feeling she had ever experienced before, and she thought that it must be some function of her new existence as a supernatural creature.

"Oz, you shouldn't have thought you could keep her hidden from us," a voice said. Isabel's heart beat faster in her chest as a group of people surrounded them. All pale, their skin faintly shimmery in the unnatural light of the mall. They wore black suits, regulation-style; to Isabel they almost looked like officials, or some kind of law enforcement. *Secret service? FBI? CIA?*

"You're coming with us dear," a feminine voice said, near her ear. "Best not to fight it." One of the suited figures did something to Oz; the angel struggled, but in a matter of moments, he was subdued. Isabel had no idea how to react as hands clamped on her wrists, icy-cold, like stone wrapped in velvet. "It'll go easier on you if you just let it happen."

<u>Chapter Nine</u>

Isabel wasn't sure what the suited figures in the mall had done to her; but she found herself – an unknown time later – in a dark room, waking up bit by bit. *Oh great, they've left me in this pitch-black room, so whatever is coming for me, I'll never see it.* Except … Isabel squinted, feeling the movement in the muscles around her eyes. Her vision began to adjust, much more than she would have thought possible, and Isabel made out the vague shapes of furniture in the room she had been left in.

She sat up, and realized that she was dressed in some kind of robe, loose around her newly svelte-curvy body. She couldn't feel the sunglasses or the hat. Isabel took a slow breath, trying to still the racing of her heart. *Who the hell* were *those people?* Isabel closed her eyes again and tried to remember whatever had happened. All she could dredge up from the depths of her mind was that they had stone-cold hands, they were pale, and they somehow managed to subdue an angel.

Five hundred says they were vampires, Isabel thought. A week before, she wouldn't have been so confident of it. Even as she had started her transformation under Oz's watchful eyes, she had doubted the reality of vampires even after accepting the existence of angels. *"Oz, you shouldn't have thought you could keep her hidden from us."* That was what one of them — a woman, Isabel was certain — had said. Who else would have an interest in her? Or maybe Oz had lied about the situation with angels, with vampires. *Could angels lie?*

Isabel heard movement, and her heart started beating faster in her chest. *They're going to have to turn the lights on, whoever they are,* she thought. *If someone's coming to check on me, they'll need the light.* At the very least, they would have to open the door. Isabel was certain she was alone in whatever room she had been placed in. She took a slow, deep breath, trying to think what she should do. *You know absolutely nothing at all about vampires,* she thought. *You don't even know if any of the myths about them are true.*

The door opened and light flooded the room. Isabel winced, crossing her arms over her chest, curling her knees up, unprepared.

"Look at me." The voice cut through her distraction and Isabel opened her eyes immediately, in spite of the discomfort of adjustment. The light in the room wasn't as bright as she had thought it initially was – it was yellow-toned, almost soothing once her pupils adjusted to the onslaught. The room, she saw in a quick glance, was about the size of her apartment bedroom, with the bed she was on, a chair, and a door opposite her, along with the door that someone had just entered. "Boy, are you in trouble," the person said, and Isabel heard the door close with a soft murmur.

"Who the hell are you?" She looked at the man who had entered her room – her cell, she thought, might be more accurate. She recognized him: the blond hair, the pale eyes and the tailored suit. "No … no, you can't be the one …"

"The one who helped make you?" The man raised a sand-colored eyebrow, his lips twitching in the start of a smile. "One and the same."

"But you …you would have to be …"

"A vampire, of course," the man said. He sat down in the chair a few feet from the bed she had woken up on. "I wouldn't have been able to come into this room on my own otherwise."

"What about Oz?" Isabel felt her heart beating faster and faster in her chest.

"He's in trouble, too," the blond said cheerfully. Isabel racked her brain, trying to remember not just his name, but the circumstances under which she had ended up having sex with him. The same night she had hooked up with Oz. "Hungry?"

Isabel stared at the vampire. She had been hungry, in the new way that she had begun to feel hunger. She'd forgotten completely. "You're …"

"I'm offering to let you feed," the vampire said. Isabel pressed her lips together; after what Oz had told her about the vampires and how they starved the succubi that fell into their hands, forcing them to do their bidding, amongst other unsavory acts. The idea of having anything to do with a vampire was unappetizing. "Oh," the vampire said, smiling a little more fully. "You've heard bad things about vampires." Isabel nodded.

"I helped to make you," the vampire said. "I have as much claim on you as Oz does."

"I don't even know your name," Isabel told him, knowing her tone was sulky and not entirely caring. The vampire chuckled, his bright – almost unearthly-looking – eyes gleaming.

"Call me Gavin," the vampire said. He held her gaze for a long moment.

"That wasn't an order, was it?" Isabel tilted her head to the side slightly.

"No," Gavin said. "Just a suggestion. You wouldn't be able to pronounce my actual name; it's too old and weird."

"I'm assuming Oz's real name isn't Oz either," Isabel said. She could feel the hunger gnawing at her again. It was as if Gavin's question had brought it back.

"Of course not," Gavin said with a shrug. He rose to his feet. Isabel started when he was somehow right in front of her, inches away from the bed, in an instant. "You didn't answer my question. How long has it been since you fed?"

Isabel shrugged.

"I don't know how long I've been out," she said. She looked down at her hands. "But if it was just a few hours, then … it's been a couple of days." Gavin's eyes widened.

"Oz…" his voice dropped to a growl.

"It's not his fault," Isabel said defensively, without knowing why she felt the need to come to the angel's defense in the first place.

"It is," Gavin said, unbuttoning the blazer of his suit and taking it off. "He should be taking better care of you, if he's trying to keep you away from my kind."

"He made it clear he's available to me whenever I want," Isabel insisted.

"He should have commanded you to feed," Gavin said sharply. He reached out for her, and Isabel gasped at the feeling of his cold hands against her skin. How could she possibly have forgotten sex with a man who felt like that? Whose whole body, as far as she could tell, was like a marble statue wrapped in silk? "You will never – – ever – neglect yourself again, do you understand me, Isabel?" He brushed his lips against her forehead. "Answer me."

"I understand," Isabel said, the words leaving her lips almost before she could consciously think them. Part of her was irritated at the knowledge that yet another person on the planet could command her complete obedience; another part of her thrilled at the knowledge that she was finally about to get what she needed.

"What do you want, Isabel?" Gavin's cold fingers brushed against her cheeks, and Isabel felt her whole body heating up. The hunger that she had been suppressing – since before the ill-fated trip to the mall – rose up, overcoming all sense of hesitation at the fact that the man in the room with her was a vampire. Just like when Oz had first come to her, Isabel found herself picturing what it would be like to be with Gavin in vivid, graphic mental images. She imagined him pushing her down onto her stomach, pulling the hem of the robes she wore over her hips, and taking her. She imagined falling to her knees when he had finished inside of her and taking him into her mouth, tasting herself on his cock as she made him hard once again, and then being thrown onto her back on the bed, her ankles on Gavin's shoulders, as he took her another time.

"I want you to fuck me from behind," Isabel replied. "Hard and fast – as hard as you want to." Gavin smiled.

"And then?" Isabel felt herself blushing in spite of the desperate need she could feel burning away at her pride.

"And then I want to get you hard again with my mouth and have you take me again," she said.

"How many times?" Gavin's breath – strangely cold – brushed against her lips. "How much do you need to feed, little Isabel?"

"I'm starving," Isabel admitted. Gavin's cold hands slid up along her waist, and Isabel realized that she had nothing on underneath the robe. Her nipples immediately hardened into firm little nubs as Gavin's thumbs brushed against them.

"Poor little succubus," Gavin murmured, his voice half-mocking, half-concerned. "You don't know starving yet, but you are *never* to neglect your need to feed again."

Isabel reached down between her body and Gavin's, and she let her fingertips brush against the front of his tailored pants. He was hard. Isabel marveled at the heat she could feel radiating through the cloth. She moaned softly as Gavin claimed her mouth with his, and began to stroke him through the fabric of his clothes. Isabel could barely stop to think of how strange it was, how different Gavin was from Oz, and how different both men were to the regular human men she had been with.

Gavin's fingers hooked into the fabric of the robe, and Isabel broke away from his hungry lips as she heard the telltale sharp noise, and felt the tugging, as he ripped the cloth into shreds and off of her. Isabel pulled back as Gavin drank her in with his eyes, his hands moving to cup her breasts. She gasped as he twisted and rolled her nipples between his cold fingers, sending jolts of pleasure through her body. "I want to hear you beg for it, little succubus," Gavin murmured. He continued his attentions to her nipples and Isabel moaned out as she felt the slick heat flowing along the folds of her labia.

"Beg?" Isabel almost started when she looked at Gavin's face, only to see his fangs emerge between his sharp-tipped teeth. Fear warred with need in her body; the fact that Gavin was clearly something much more predatory than Oz was not quite enough to make her forget the heat flowing through her veins, the hunger twisting somewhere deep down between her hips, as if her vagina led to her stomach.

"Beg me to take you," Gavin said.

"Please. Please, Gavin, take me, I need it," Isabel said. She closed her mouth against the words that had left it almost against her will, feeling humiliated at how easily he managed to gain her obedience.

"Strip me," Gavin commanded her, and Isabel's hands instantly moved to the buttons of his dress shirt. She could feel the coldness of his skin underneath, and wondered once again at the heat she had felt at the front of his pants. It occurred to her that she knew nothing at all about vampires beyond what Oz had told her. But Gavin's command had hold of her; Isabel tugged his shirt off and tossed it aside, feasting her eyes on the muscular expanse of his chest. He was paler than Oz, paler than any man she had been with, his skin cool to the touch. Isabel's hands moved down to the fly of Gavin's pants and she unbuttoned and unzipped them before pulling them down over his hips to reveal a pair of silken boxers underneath. The bulge that showed – as obvious as the sun, straining at the filmy fabric – made her mouth water. Isabel licked her lips and hooked her fingers into the waistband of Gavin's boxers. She eased them down, and Gavin's hard cock sprung free, proudly erect.

She stared at it for a moment, feeling something like shock. Gavin's skin was so pale that she could clearly see the veins, thick with the blood filling the member; his wheat-colored pubic hair was neatly trimmed, forming a nest of curls at the base of the erection, not quite concealing his balls underneath.

Instinct took over, and Isabel wrapped her hand around Gavin's cock, stroking him slowly, achingly slow, but steadily, her thumb rubbing against the uncut tip. Gavin groaned, his hands tightening on her, and Isabel marveled at the difference between the vampire's erection – which felt feverish in her hand – and the rest of him, which was cooler even than the room's temperature.

Gavin's hips bucked, and he shoved Isabel's hand away from him, pulling her face up to kiss her hungrily. His hands on her body seemed possessed of a kind of power, a strength that almost frightened Isabel even as the proximity of his naked body, the feeling of his erection brushing against her skin, turned her on more than ever. She wanted him to the point that it felt as though her bones were shaking inside of her. *How can I want someone I barely even know? Someone I can't even remember sleeping with before?*

Before she could answer that question, however, Gavin's hands tightened on her, and Isabel cried out, startled, as Gavin lifted her off the bed, pressing her body against his for a tantalizing moment before he spun her around and pushed her onto the bed face-first. His hands pulled her hips back, and Isabel caught herself on her forearms, trembling with the desire that surged through her as she felt the heat of Gavin's cock brushing against her slick folds. "Beg me again, Isabel," Gavin said from behind her.

"Please," Isabel murmured, struggling to push her hips back, to take him inside of her. "Please, Gavin, please take me. Take me as hard as you want me!" She felt the thick, hot tip of Gavin's cock rubbing up and down along her labia, not quite penetrating, teasing her, and Isabel trembled, feeling the churning hunger deep down in her body. "Please, please, *please*," Isabel pleaded, twisting her hips trying to push back onto him. It was still difficult for her to believe how quickly her desire rose up inside of her, how she could possibly want someone so intensely in a matter of moments.

Gavin thrust into her hard and fast and Isabel let her head fall forward between her forearms, her forehead against the blankets, moaning out long and low as he filled her up. She rose up onto the balls of her feet, flexing her muscles around the thick, hot intrusion that was Gavin's cock, bowing her back to take him deeper. Gavin groaned from behind her and slid halfway out of her body before slamming back inside of her, his hips slapping against the curve of her buttocks. Isabel cried out as Gavin found his rhythm almost in an instant, thrusting hard and fast inside of her aching, needy body.

It was totally different than being with Oz, but Isabel felt her nerves tingling at the sensation; the cold of Gavin's hands, the heat of his cock inside of her, was thrilling. She twisted her hips, flexing her muscles around him, some bodily instinct taking over to overrule her conscious thought. She felt

Gavin's cold fingers digging into the skin of her hips, felt him speed up – so much so that she almost couldn't keep up with him. Thrusting harder and faster inside of her until Isabel was briefly torn between the intense pleasure of the sensation and legitimate concern that her still mostly-human body couldn't take the friction.

She struggled to hold out, to hold back the tension that she could feel building up in her body, but it was impossible; Isabel gripped the sheets in her hands, buried her face against them, and as the first jarring, body-wide waves of pleasure washed through her, she cried out again and again into the fabric. Her muscles rippled around Gavin's cock as she came, and Isabel – the back of her mind still instinctively monitoring the man's pleasure – felt his cock twitching inside of her, hotter than ever. She heard the long, low groan from behind her, and a gush of sticky-slick heat flooded into her. Isabel gasped, shivering as the flood flowed into her body; she wasn't sure how but Gavin's fluids were so hot they were almost scalding. Even as her orgasm intensified, she felt the sharp graze of the vampire's teeth against her shoulder as he pulled her up and back.

"God – fuck, Isabel ..." Gavin's whole body went tense against hers, and all at once he let go of her. Isabel collapsed against the bed, barely holding herself up by her arms, panting and gasping for breath as she reeled from the intense climax.

He pulled out and Isabel felt briefly bereft, her body almost hollow in the wake of her orgasm. She twisted around and turned over onto her back, looking up at the vampire. "You'll have to give me a minute before you do the rest," Gavin told her. "That was more intense than I was counting on." Isabel grinned, feeling a little surge of pride and power at the fact that she had satisfied a vampire so thoroughly that he needed to recover.

The next moment, though, the hunger was on her again, and Isabel sat up, slithering off of the bed and sinking to her knees in front of Gavin. She looked up at his face, and smiled to herself, briefly nuzzling against his hip before she wrapped her fingers around the base of his not-quite-flaccid dick and brought the tip to her lips. Gavin let out an animal sound as Isabel sucked the member into her mouth and began to swirl her tongue around him. His fingers tangled in her hair, and Isabel gave herself up to the instincts that took over more and more easily; she licked and sucked, her tongue winding around the flesh. Gavin – like Oz – was quite large, even before he became fully erect, for her to handle, but the need to taste him, to take him as much as she possibly could, was greater than her sense of limitation.

Gavin's fingertips rubbed against her scalp, and Isabel felt his cock come to life between her lips, felt it begin to twitch slightly against her tongue as the blood flowed into it, making him swiftly hard once more. Isabel worked him with lips and tongue, even grazed her teeth against his sensitive skin, closing her eyes and giving herself up to the moment. She could taste herself on him, but she also tasted the sharp, slightly sweet taste of his pre-cum as it started to flow. It wasn't like Oz's fluids; it wasn't like any fluid she had ever tasted.

Instead it was almost like honey, both in taste and texture, and Isabel couldn't get enough.

Gavin pushed her away and at the same moment lifted her up, half-throwing her onto the bed. "Still hungry?" Isabel nodded, and Gavin covered her body with his, the heat and cold of him tantalizing her. He kissed her eagerly, his tongue plunging past her lips, twisting and coiling around hers. Isabel gasped at the feeling of Gavin's cold fingers rubbing along her labia, and then made a sound between a cry and a moan as two fingers slid inside of her. She was shocked at how tight she felt; she'd just taken his much thicker cock. "Oh, Oz didn't tell you?" Gavin nipped at her bottom lip with his sharp teeth. "Your body adapts to the size of anything that penetrates it, becoming ..." he began to work his fingers inside of her, "becoming as tight as it needs to be to provide pleasure." Isabel gasped, shivering as Gavin's long, cold fingers slid along her inner walls.

Isabel writhed, twisting her hips and pushing down onto Gavin's fingers as his thumb found her clitoris. "Have you noticed, too, that this seems *so much* more sensitive?" He barely brushed against the bead of nerves and Isabel cried out, reaching for his shoulders blindly. Gavin curled his fingers inside of her, rubbing steadily against her g-spot. Isabel panted and gasped, moving mindlessly as pleasure crackled through her nerves.

Gavin's fingers retreated all at once, and Isabel opened her eyes – unaware of having closed them – and groaned, scowling at him in disappointment. "Greedy little thing, aren't you? Not even fully transformed and you want all the fucking you can get …" Gavin ducked his head away from her face, to her neck. Isabel felt the sharp teeth nip just below her pulse point, felt Gavin's warm tongue lapping at the little bit of blood that welled up. "They could put you in a room with five men and you would feed for hours …" his tongue rasped against her skin, and Isabel whimpered. "And by the time you were through with them, they'd all do whatever it took to get you to fuck them again."

Gavin pulled himself up, his hands gliding down along her legs. "Oh, are you ever in trouble, Isabel," he said with a little grin. He grabbed her ankles and lifted them up onto his shoulders as he moved into place, his burning-hot erection sliding along her inner labia, not quite penetrating her. He held her gaze as he thrust forward, filling her up in one quick movement. Isabel moaned, pushing her hips down to take him deeper. Gavin began moving right away, the tip of his cock rubbing steadily against her g-spot. Isabel gave herself up to the pleasure, to the instincts that were starting to form more of her mind than conscious thought. She twisted and writhed, flexing her muscles around Gavin's erection in fluttering movements, pulling him in as deep as he could go.

Gavin held her exactly where he wanted her, his hands ice cold against her feverish skin, and Isabel had no choice but to let him take her exactly the way he wanted; as she came closer and closer to her third orgasm, her voice cracking from the cries and moans leaving her throat. She felt his teeth sink into her skin, just above her ankle. Heat flowed out of her to meet Gavin's cool lips, and Isabel sank into the simmering pleasure, moaning as her climax shattered through her.

Chapter Ten

"What did you mean I'm in trouble?" Isabel woke once again, without knowing how long she had been out to find Gavin in the bed next to her.

"The people who snatched you have big plans," Gavin said. "Maybe Oz told you a little bit about them?" Isabel shrugged.

"Assuming they were vampires like you?" Gavin nodded.

"They were," he said. "Vampires, but not like me."

"What do you mean by that?"

Gavin smiled slightly.

"The politics of my people can't be summed up in one session," he said. "We're not as simple as the angels are."

"Okay," Isabel said, dismissing the other questions she had. "So why am I in trouble?"

"Because you are the perfect little succubus," Gavin said, reaching out to claim one of her still-naked breasts in his hand. "Even before you started transforming, you were probably pretty sex-hungry, right?" Isabel blushed and looked away, trying to squirm free of Gavin's touch. "You had sex with me no more than fifteen minutes after you left Oz," Gavin pointed out matter-of-factly.

"That's ..." she scowled at Gavin. "I only barely remember that." Gavin chuckled.

"I have some responsibility for your forgetfulness," he admitted. "In my defense, it's standard operating procedure."

"Explain," Isabel said. Gavin raised an eyebrow.

"Because you were so good," he said, letting go of her breast and sitting up on the bed next to her. "I was assigned to follow Oz, to see if he fucked a woman, and then to seduce her myself."

"To create a succubus," Isabel concluded. Gavin nodded.

"So, you're in league with the people who abducted me," Isabel said. Gavin made a face.

"Yes and no," he said.

"You're not going to tell me anything useful, are you?"

"I'm going to tell you that if anyone else, other than me, comes into this room, you need to use whatever you can of your abilities. Just don't give into the temptation to feed on them."

"But you told me before not to neglect to feed." Gavin smiled.

"You won't be," he said. "Vampires and angels are not as susceptible to your charms – at least, the mind-bending aspect of them – but enough time in your company and they'll fall."

"Okay," Isabel said. "So how am I supposed to use that?"

"By insisting that you'll only feed from me," Gavin said. "They're hoping that since I can control you, and since you will need to feed nightly, that they can use me to bend you."

"Bend me?" Gavin nodded.

"With the succubi they find out in the world, they have to starve them," Gavin explained. "Keep them locked up alone until they're willing to do anything to be allowed to feed, and until they've lost the ability to control minds."

"But not me."

"That was why they started sending us to dog angels' steps," Gavin said. "If they knew when a new succubus would be created, they could snatch her up, imprison her, and use her makers against her." Isabel shivered.

"Oz said ... he said that the vampires want to be in the open?" Gavin nodded again.

"Some of them do," he told her. "I'm not one of them, personally – what good is developing years of hunting skills if I can just grab someone off the street and feed on them?" He shook his head irritably. "We're better off being mythical; something that the higher ups don't seem to understand."

"So, you're *not* on their side?" Gavin smiled.

"I'm on my side," he told her. "For the moment, that means getting you out of here, and getting Oz away from them."

"It does?" Isabel stared at Gavin as he climbed out of the bed and began dressing.

"You will tell no one," Gavin said, meeting her gaze. "You will refuse to feed from anyone other than me that the vampires send to you. Do you understand, Isabel?" Isabel nodded. "Say it."

"I understand," she said quickly. She tried to look away, annoyed. "You know, this whole 'unquestioning obedience' thing is irritating." Gavin laughed.

"I'm selling the idea of you as my own personal succubus, to train you up properly until you can be used," Gavin said, moving closer to her. He kissed her lightly on the lips and tweaked one of her nipples with rough, playful fingers making Isabel gasp and shiver. "I'll be back tomorrow night to feed you, greedy little thing." He kissed her again, one hand straying down to the curve of her ass. Isabel felt him smiling against her lips.

He let go of her and turned away, leaving the room so quickly that even if Isabel had had the presence of mind to try and follow him, she couldn't have. The lights stayed on for a moment longer, and then – abruptly – she was in darkness again. Isabel sighed and laid back on the bed, staring up blindly in the direction of the ceiling, trying to understand what had happened to her, and what she could possibly do to get herself out of the situation she was in.

Chapter Eleven

Isabel could feel the hunger beginning to tug at her mind again; she wasn't sure how long she had been in the dark, but it felt as if it were hours, at least. The feeding with Gavin had been enough to satisfy her for a while, but she knew without a doubt that her craving, her need, was growing.

She took a deep breath and exhaled slowly. She had no idea what to think; about Gavin, or about Oz. Oz had been the one to explain to her what she was, and what she needed, but Gavin seemed to know just as much, only about the other side. *Both Oz and Gavin are in agreement that the vampires want nothing but trouble for me,* she thought, scrubbing at her face.

The longer she lay in the dark, the better she could make out the dimensions of the room. *Gavin told me not to feed from anyone else. Oz ...* The thought of Oz being a captive like her, maybe even somewhere in the same building, made her upset without knowing why. Oz had taken her in; he had tried to protect her. *What did they do with all those clothes?* It was a silly – probably an inappropriate – concern, but Isabel wondered about it, nonetheless. It was something to ask if and when Gavin ever came back to see her.

Isabel heard movement in the corridor and blinked a few times, trying to figure out how she might be able to adjust to the light when it inevitably came on. She wasn't sure how she was so certain that whoever was outside of her room was going to stop and enter; but she was sure of it. It was almost as if she could sense the mind on the other side of the door, the intent.

The door opened and Isabel sat up in bed, blinking rapidly as the lights in the room came up. "Good evening, Isabel," a feminine voice said. Isabel tried to fight down her sense of disappointment at the fact that it wasn't Gavin. As her eyes adjusted to the light, she saw it was the woman from the mall. The woman looked different; she wasn't in a suit – instead, she had put on a loose, flowing green dress. Her hair was down, which showed Isabel that it was long indeed: down to the woman's waist, and a red so deep that it almost looked as though it had been stained in blood. "I see you enjoyed your visit with Gavin."

"Who are you?" Isabel pulled the blanket around her, feeling self-conscious in her nakedness.

"Still clinging to some of your more human impulses, I see," the woman said, sitting in the same chair that Gavin had taken when he entered earlier. "Those will go away soon enough."

"You didn't answer my question?" Isabel held the woman's gaze, remembering Gavin's commands to her.

"I'm here to sort of … explain a few things to you," the woman said. Isabel hadn't completely noticed before, but she spoke with a slight, strange accent; one she had never heard before.

"I know I'm a succubus," Isabel said, ticking her points off on her fingers. "I know I have to 'feed' on people or no matter how much I eat, I'll starve to death."

The woman nodded.

"I also know that you're a vampire, and that Oz is an angel, and I know that you kidnapped me from the mall." Isabel licked her lips and crossed her arms over her chest. "So, I assume you're going to continue from there?"

"Do you know *why* we took you out of Oz's keeping, Isabel?" Isabel resisted the urge to roll her eyes.

"I know why Oz said you would try and take me out of his keeping," Isabel replied. "But I'm open to hearing an alternative explanation."

"Succubi are special," the woman told her. "You make people feel the most divine pleasure, and you feed off of it. You're a combination of the best traits of vampires and angels."

"Not hearing an explanation," Isabel said, grateful that there was no way – to the best of her knowledge – that the woman could force her to listen quietly, or make her obey any particular command.

"Your needs and talents make you a natural ally for vampires," the woman said matter-of-factly. "Ultimately, what's good for us is good for you."

"Okay, so you kidnapped me in order to show me how good I could have it?" Isabel gestured around the room. "Maybe I'll understand better how wonderful it is to be kept in a dark room that I can't leave all by myself for hours at a time when I fully transition." She had – in the interests of making sure – checked the door at some point during her time in the darkness after Gavin had left. There was no way to open the door from her side of it.

"We wanted you to be properly receptive," the woman explained. "The lights will stay on after I leave, and of course you can order food if you like it; there's a voice address system. You can bathe, dress yourself, whatever you like. You just can't leave this room unless you're invited out of it." Isabel pressed her lips together.

"Oh yes, I can see how wonderful it will be to be a prisoner," she said tartly. "What an improvement on my previous existence."

"We have to make sure that you understand your new existence," the woman said. "Oz made a mistake in trying to keep you from us. In order to function properly as a succubus, you will need tutelage from vampires, not just from angels." Isabel rolled her eyes.

"What am I supposed to be learning from vampires?"

"How to feed without feeling shame," the woman replied. "How to take what you want and ignore your silly human inclinations." Isabel stared at her in shock. "We have a mutual interest, Isabel, and soon enough, you'll see it."

"Maybe you could tell me what that mutual interest is?"

The woman smiled slightly.

"Vampires want the ability to exist in the world without being covered by myth," the woman replied. "We want to be able to feed when and on whomever we want." She inclined her head towards Isabel. "Doesn't that sound like a cause you can get behind?"

Isabel shrugged.

"Considering the fact that I apparently can control men's minds and get what I want from them, I don't see the issue."

The woman chuckled.

"Isabel, don't you think that if regular humans find out what you are; an immortal creature who feeds on desire and pleasure, then your life will probably not be quite so easy?"

"You haven't given me a chance to find out," Isabel replied.

"I'll make sure someone comes in later to show you the records," the woman told her. "Succubi have *not* been treated well by normal human society…. or incubi, for that matter. The only supernatural creatures who *have* been treated well are the angels. Is it any wonder why they're fine with maintaining the status quo?"

Before Isabel could digest the question, the door opened again; Gavin came into the room, looking every bit at ease as he had hours earlier. "Ah, Portia. I see you're giving my new creation her catechism."

"Oz had his chance to pervert her thinking," — Portia said, shrugging. "Why shouldn't I get my innings in?"

"She's mine to train," Gavin told the other vampire. "The council agreed."

"Why the council trusts you is beyond me," Portia said, rising to her feet. "You've never shown an ounce of loyalty to anyone but yourself."

"You're just worried that I'll succeed with her," Gavin said with a knowing grin. "Then you don't get to get off on torturing the poor thing." Isabel watched the two, thinking to herself that the vampires looked like nothing so much as dogs circling a bone.

Without warning, they advanced on each other, and Isabel slid back on the bed instinctively as she heard sounds of fabric ripping. From behind the woman's back, a pair of dark red-brown wings emerged; at almost the same moment, Isabel saw the fabric give way at the back of Gavin's blazer, and through the tears, a pair of dark gray wings appeared and then unfurled, spreading out to their full expanse.

"Do you want to scare our new recruit, Portia? Because I believe you're defeating your own purpose here, as they say these days," Gavin said, sounding almost bored.

"Do not fuck with me, Gavin," Portia said. She turned to Isabel. "There will be plenty of time later for you to get to know us better." The woman smiled, revealing sharp teeth, fangs extended. "But Gavin clearly wants another mutual feeding, and far be it for me to prevent him." Her wings folded back against her shoulders and Portia turned away, walking towards the door.

Gavin waited until the woman had left, and then Isabel watched as he pulled his own wings back in, and watched them disappear. "Sneaky little bitch," he murmured towards the door. He looked at Isabel. "So, what did you think of our dear Portia?"

"I think she's annoying," Isabel replied. "She reminds me of a friend I ditched back in college." Gavin laughed and sat down on the edge of the bed.

"Manipulative, bitchy, too wealthy for her own good?" Isabel shrugged.

"Something like that," she said, remembering Cara; her former friend had dangled paid trips to the spa, or weekend outings to resorts her parents owned, as an exchange for friendship. Yet, whenever Isabel had gone with her, she'd received more or less constant insults.

"So I don't have to warn you not to trust her, I assume," Gavin said. He held out an arm. "Come here."

Isabel found herself moving towards him almost before she could think of it, and her annoyance at the ready obedience of her body to Gavin's commands returned. Gavin pulled her onto his lap, and Isabel felt a pulse of lust run through her body at the awareness of his masculinity, and the knowledge of what there was under his clothes. "I'm not going to feed you just yet," Gavin said. "I want you to be a little hungry, you see, I do want to train you some."

"Train me?" Isabel looked up into his face, irritable. "Like a dog?"

"Dogs are easier to train than succubi," Gavin said wryly. "They actually *want* to obey."

"If you're just here to lord over how I can't resist you or disobey you, I could kind of do without it," Isabel told him. Gavin chuckled, slipping one hand down between her legs. He cupped her already-slick vulva, touching her lightly.

"Even if I hadn't made you," he murmured, "you would still have this reaction to me."

"I would?" Isabel raised an eyebrow, disbelieving.

"Your body is going to have a continuous low-level arousal for the rest of your existence, whenever you see a man," Gavin told her. "Especially one you've fed from."

"You fed from me, too," Isabel said, remembering that fact. She reached down and touched the marks on her lower leg; they were already starting to heal – much faster than the first ones she had received from Gavin, less than a week before.

"Of course," Gavin said. "Succubus blood is like honey for us." He grinned. "Not exactly a meal, but a sweet treat."

"Oh." Isabel closed her eyes, taking a deep breath and exhaling slowly. "You know, I would really appreciate it if, when people offer to explain things to me, they actually, you know, explain."

"It takes too long," Gavin said. He withdrew his hand and brought his fingers to his lips to lick the traces of her fluids off of them. "We've existed as long as humans have, as long as angels have – that's millennia of politics, of history – you can't expect to learn everything about the supernatural world in a week."

"It would be helpful if I could at least know the full reasons why vampires and angels are fighting over me," Isabel countered.

"You'll learn them all," Gavin said. "In the meantime, we need to get you out of here. Oz, too."

"How are we going to do that?" Isabel gestured around the room. "I have kind of a suspicion that I'm supposed to be forced to stay here."

"Oh, of course," Gavin said. "But you see, my little greedy succubus, I've been working very hard to get an opening for something."

"Why do you want to get Oz out?" Gavin looked away for a moment.

"Oz needs to be out of here because if we don't get him out, they'll kill him," Gavin said.

"How do you kill an angel?" Gavin took a deep breath, and Isabel wondered if anything that the mythology said about vampires – that they were undead, never ate, and had to avoid churches and the sun – was true.

"Angels have a natural impulse – an instinct – to make people feel good," Gavin said. "Some of the more advanced ones can heal injuries, but even the most basic, the weakest of them, can soothe pain and create feelings of peace, relief, pleasure."

"Okay," Isabel said. "That's where that part of the whole succubus thing comes from." Gavin nodded.

"But it drains them," he explained. "They have to recharge – music, kindness, warmth, those kinds of things." Gavin looked at Isabel intently. "The vampires are basically sending a steady stream of injured, depressed, or otherwise people – and entities – in pain into Oz's cell." Isabel considered that and shuddered.

"They're making him heal them, and not giving him what he needs to recharge," she said. Gavin nodded again.

"They want to warp him, to eventually use him against you," Gavin said. He smiled slightly. "Fortunately for you, and for Oz, that fits perfectly into my plans." Isabel frowned, confused.

"How?"

"Just suffice it to say that I am going to bring you to Oz," Gavin told her. "You will not show anything other than hunger when we leave this room, and you are not to tell anyone – no matter how they try and manipulate you – about what I said." He brushed his lips against her temple, and down to her ear. "Do you understand?"

"Yes," Isabel said.

"You're in real danger here, Isabel. Don't let Portia's juvenile behavior blind you to the fact that there are stronger, smarter minds behind her. Minds that see in you a treasure trove."

"Why?" Isabel shook her head, unable to quite believe it.

"Because you are valuable," Gavin told her. "You are one of the more powerful succubi we've managed to create in recent years. Good luck on my part, I suppose." Gavin smiled against her skin. "Oz has excellent taste."

"You talk like you like him," Isabel said.

"I respect him," Gavin replied. "I'd hate to see him drained to death. And I don't want you being wasted on converting the masses."

"You don't?" Gavin chuckled lowly, and Isabel shivered as she felt his sharp teeth graze her neck.

"I have my own plans for you, little Isabel," Gavin said. "And I need Oz to make those plans happen. Do exactly what I tell you, and you'll never want for feedings. That's all you need to know."

Chapter Twelve

Isabel emerged from the shower attached to her room, feeling on edge almost as much as she felt energized and relaxed by the opportunity to get good and clean. *It's kind of amazing how much a shower can change your mood,* she thought, stepping into the main room of her prison cell without even bothering to put on any clothes.

The transformation was still continuing; Isabel had seen her reflection in the mirror, and knew that she was almost at the peak of her beauty as a succubus; her hair seemed to shine with an almost crystalline gleam, and her eyes were bigger and brighter than ever. Her skin was utterly flawless, and the curves of her body were so ripe that if she had seen a picture of herself the way she had become back before the strange turn of events that led to her new existence, she would have insisted that nothing short of intensive, life-threateningly extreme plastic surgery could have accomplished it.

She turned around in front of a full-length mirror in her room, shaking her head at herself once more. The woman at Nordstrom had measured her bra size at a 34 F – and certainly, that size of bra had felt the most comfortable, but the woman Isabel saw in the mirror managed to have almost comically full breasts that drooped only just enough to be real. There was not a single stretch mark, not even the suggestion of a cellulite dimple on her body. One development that somewhat disturbed her was the fact that she didn't seem to have any hair below her neck, almost anywhere. Her legs were flawlessly smooth, and as she had showered, Isabel had been alarmed to watch as the trimmed hair on her vulva slide away from her body, revealing utterly smooth skin underneath – so smooth, in fact, that it looked as though there had never been hair there in the first place. Her underarms were equally bare, and her eyebrows looked as if they had been professionally seen to.

"Well, I guess there's something to be said about beauty standards," Isabel murmured to herself, trying to dismiss the implications of her hairless body. She finished drying herself off and sat down on the edge of her bed, trying to decide whether or not she even wanted to get dressed.

Hours before – how long exactly, Isabel wasn't sure, since a clock was not one of the room's features – Gavin had told her that he had personal plans for her, and that they were somehow going to work together to free Oz. He had suggested that she would have to participate in a threesome in order to make that happen; and the part of Isabel's mind that was still mostly human--and tied to her previous life--couldn't quite believe that she would ever be so starved. Even though she'd managed to have sex with two men in the span of one evening, the thought of having sex with two men at the same time was beyond her. *On the other hand, my job is basically to be as big of a slut as possible,* Isabel thought, grimacing to herself.

As she considered the prospect of having sex with Oz and Gavin at the same time, Isabel couldn't deny that she felt the heat beginning to start up in her body once again, the sense of something akin to hunger beginning to stir inside of her. As she had progressed in her transformation, the stomach-gnawing feeling had started to subside, replaced by a deeper kind of hunger that she hadn't experienced since high school. Even at that, she thought, she didn't quite feel it in her stomach anymore; it made sense that she wouldn't--since she was more than capable of eating actual food, and since the source of the hunger wasn't her digestive system, but rather something else.

"One of these days," Isabel mused quietly to herself, "I will figure out everything there is to know about being a succubus, instead of having people only tell me as much as they want me to know about it." She sighed and looked around the room. It was difficult to prepare herself for some rescue attempt that Gavin might make when she had no idea what he might want her to do, or when he might come to spring her. She thought about the other vampire she had met, Portia, who had definitely taken the wrong approach if she had wanted to earn Isabel's trust. Isabel thought about the dark wings on the two vampires in her room and shuddered. Where

Oz's wings had been amazing – and somehow comforting – the darker wings of the vampires had reminded Isabel of predatory birds.

The door to her room opened and Isabel resisted the human urge to cover herself; instead she glanced in the direction of the noise and saw Portia walk in, with a man she had never seen before, looking almost drugged. "Thought you might be hungry," Portia said, smiling broadly enough to show the sharpness of her teeth.

In spite of herself, Isabel felt the jolt of arousal course through her at the sight of the man. The human part of her mind argued that the man wasn't even particularly attractive; he was maybe forty years old, with a flat stomach that looked as though it were starting to lose its tone, sunburned skin dusted with freckles and dark hair that had started to go gray at the temples. If he was mundane to Isabel, it was obvious from his immediate reaction to her that she was irresistible to him; the man's eyes widened, and he opened and then closed his mouth, speechless for a moment.

"God, I would pay my life savings to fuck you," the man told her. "You're probably tight as a virgin and wet as a slip-n-slide, aren't you?"

"This is Steve," Portia said, gesturing to the man. The door closed behind them and Isabel heard the lock click and thump into place. "He's a regular human, as you can see. His fantasies include being turned into a vampire and having two succubi service him at once." Isabel looked at the vampire sharply.

"I'm not hungry," Isabel said, shrugging. "Gavin took good care of me earlier." It was a lie, and Isabel knew that Portia was aware she was lying, but she'd had her commands from Gavin. Steve started towards her, seemingly transfixed. "Stay right there, bud," Isabel told him sharply.

He froze in his tracks. "Very good! You take to the mind control aspects of your new state better than some," Portia said with another smile. "We've had some difficulty getting some of our more ...

moralistic recruits to embrace that part of their nature."

"How do you handle that?" Portia shrugged.

"We starve them, and then feed them, and then starve them again, until they're at the brink of losing the ability altogether--at least, temporarily of course – and then only let them feed if they use the ability." Portia sat down in the only chair in the room and gestured to Steve. "He's one of our better trainers for that purpose. Just last week, he gave into a succubus' command to let her fuck him in the ass with a strap-on before she let him take her." Isabel glanced at Steve.

"Is that true? Tell me if it is," she said. Steve nodded.

"I'd let you do whatever you wanted to me, if I could get inside you," Steve told her. "Sure I can't come eat your tight, wet pussy for you?"

"That's enough, Steve," Isabel said. "From now on, you'll treat me with the same respect that you would your own grandmother." Steve frowned, obviously conflicted for a moment. Isabel flicked a glance in Portia's direction to see the vampire's amusement at the man's confusion.

"Okay," Steve said finally.

"Why don't you sit down, Steve?" Steve looked around for somewhere to sit and Isabel suppressed a grin; in a certain respect, the ability to bend men's minds was actually fun. "Sit on the floor," she told him. Steve obeyed without a moment's hesitation. Isabel turned her attention back onto Portia.

"They were right about you," Portia said. The vampire woman shook her head slightly. "I may not trust Gavin, but he certainly has an eye for recruitment."

"Wouldn't it be more Oz that had the eye? He did have sex with me first."

Portia shrugged as if the distinction didn't matter much.

"Whatever the case, you're clearly precocious," Portia said. "If you would just let us train you, let us teach you how to be the best you can possibly be ..." she smiled again. *Always smiling that one*, Isabel thought irreverently. "Then you could be a very wealthy, very powerful woman."

"And by that you mean, feed on whoever you bring me, and submit to your rules," Isabel said. She shook her head. "Not particularly interested."

"Gavin isn't going to be in the council's good graces forever," Portia told her. "You're going to need someone to handle you."

"I'm kind of full up on people commanding my life," Isabel said.

"Succubi on their own become self-destructive," Portia told her dryly. "Without guidance, without someone to make sure they're feeding safely ..." she shrugged again.

"And even if you got rid of Gavin, I'd still be here," Isabel pointed out. "It might have occurred to you that I'm not really keen on being controlled."

"No one is," Portia said. "But when it's inevitable, there's a certain joy to be found in having useful employment, as well as protection."

"Well, maybe I'll come around," Isabel said, glancing at Steve. "But right now, I'm not hungry enough to lower my standards."

"I'll bring you someone more challenging next time, then," Portia said with another insincere grin. "We have some college boys you might like; lots of stamina and no shame at all in them."

"I look forward to seeing what's on the menu," Isabel said brightly. She could feel the slick heat along her labia, the tightening of her muscles. If Steve was in the room for much longer, her self-control – motivated by Gavin's command – would start to crack, she knew it would. Even if Steve wasn't to her taste, the part of her that had already transformed into a succubus wanted him for what he had to offer.

"He won't get up until you tell him," Portia said, gesturing at the middle-aged man. Portia shook her head, giving Isabel an admiring look. "You've got better control than most of the succubi first coming into their powers. You really should reconsider your position." The woman stood and looked at Isabel expectantly.

"Why don't you stand up, Steve?" The man rose to his feet, his gaze still riveted on her, and Isabel couldn't help but feel a thrum of pride and desire, a jolt of hunger and a greedy thrill of need at the way he looked at her. "How much do you want me?"

"I would let her drink me dry if I could get a chance at your tight little pussy first," Steve said blandly. Isabel was torn between a cringe and a smile.

"What did I tell you about respect?"

"You asked!" Steve looked almost heartbroken. "I'm sorry, I didn't mean to disrespect you."

"It's okay, Steve," Isabel said, making her voice soothing. "I did ask. You can go now."

"But–"

Isabel scowled slightly at him.

"Go. You don't want to upset me further do you?" Steve shook his head and turned on his heel, nearly walking straight into the locked door in his haste to do her bidding. Portia snickered and followed the man, giving Isabel a quick, approving glance before she unlocked the door and stepped through it.

Chapter Thirteen

By the time Gavin came into her prison-room again, Isabel's whole body was on fire with need. "About time you came to see me," she said irritably as the vampire closed the door behind him. He smirked.

"Sit down," he told her firmly. Isabel, grumbling under her breath but unable to evade the command, threw herself down into the chair she had been pacing in front of. Gavin looked her up and down slowly, and Isabel felt a new flash of irritation at the amusement in his gaze, even mingled as it was with the desire she could see. "Portia came to visit you, offer you a treat?" Isabel nodded.

"Brought a guy named Steve for me to feed on," Isabel said.

"You didn't, did you?" Isabel raised an eyebrow.

"It's not like I had the choice to decide for myself," she said tartly. "You commanded me not to feed on anyone that anyone else brought to me. I'm so hungry I want to eat an entire fucking table."

"Or fuck an entire boardroom?" Gavin said. "Admit it," Isabel pressed her lips together, scowling at him.

"Fine," she said, glancing away from him. "If there *were* an entire boardroom of men in here, I would happily feed on them all."

Instead of saying anything, Gavin approached her. He reached out and pulled her from the chair to her feet, and brushed his lips against hers. "It's a good thing you're so hungry," he murmured, one hand cupping her breast in it, his finger and thumb closing around her nipple. "I may have an opening for us to spring Oz, but it's going to require you to be ready to feed."

"Okay," Isabel said, shivering slightly as Gavin teased her nipple into a firm nub. His other hand rose to cup and squeeze her other breast, and Isabel moaned against his lips as the heat that had been simmering in her body began to rise closer to a boil.

"We're going to have to work quickly," Gavin told her. Isabel nodded, biting her bottom lip as the cold feeling of Gavin's hands on her sensitive, hot skin sent tingles through her body. "But we have enough time for a little teaser."

Gavin's hands dropped down to her hips, and Isabel tried to shake off the bone-deep desire coursing through her body enough to think. Gavin kissed her lips hungrily, and slid one hand up between her legs, stroking against her slick, silken-skinned labia. "Your transformation is nearly complete," Gavin said, his fingertips finding her clitoris. Isabel gasped; just the barest touch from Gavin against her pleasure center was almost enough to make her come.

"Is ... is the hairless thing normal?" Gavin chuckled at her question.

"Yes and no," he said. He stroked her slowly, swirling his fingertips around the bead of nerves before beginning to rub up and down. Crackles of sensation coursed through Isabel's body. She felt herself getting more and more turned on. She hadn't realized that the intense arousal she'd had the moment Gavin had walked into the room, and the electric, desire that had propelled her from one end of her small room to another after Steve and Portia had left, had been almost nothing. Cold fingers slid along her labia, and Isabel moaned out as the fingers pushed into her slowly – achingly so. She marveled again at the fact that she felt so tight, her inner walls barely able to accommodate the thickness of Gavin's fingers.

"Y-yes ... and no?" Isabel struggled to focus on the conversation in spite of the hunger driving her thoughts. Images of Gavin taking her, pinning her against the chair and pushing into her, filling her up and pounding hard and fast inside of her until he came, and then lifting her up with her back against the wall and taking her again. Pushing her down onto her knees, pressing the tip of his cock to her lips and then past them.

"Not important right now," Gavin told her. "Tell me how hungry you are, little Isabel."

"Hungrier than I've ever been," Isabel said, her breath catching in her throat. "So ... so hungry I could take you five times and still want more. So hungry I could take you and two other people at the same time." Isabel started at the realization of the words that had left her mouth.

"Could you now?" Gavin said, his voice low and purring in her ear. His fingers worked her, pushing deeper, rubbing steadily against her g-spot as his thumb teased her clitoris, rubbing and retreating, making her whole body tingle with more pleasure, more sensation.

All at once his fingers retreated and Isabel groaned in dismay and frustration. "What the hell?"

"I told you – that was just a teaser," Gavin said, bringing his fingers to his lips and licking them clean. He smiled, looking pleased with himself. "Good to hear that you're nice and hungry, though."

"You do know that you're the single most frustrating person I've ever met, right?" Isabel scowled at him, irritable between the high arousal coursing through her body and the fact that Gavin could so readily manipulate her.

"Hungry women, all the same," Gavin said lightly. "You should get dressed." Isabel had forgotten that she'd never dressed after her shower.

"What's the deal?" Isabel went into the next room; along with the shower and a bath, there was a wardrobe with all of the clothes Oz had purchased for her, as well as a toilet and a vanity.

"Oz is in bad shape," Gavin said. "They've got him where they think they want him – and I said that it would be the perfect time for you to manipulate him."

"But my abilities don't work on either of you," Isabel countered.

"No, but Oz, as one of your makers and an angel, has a natural concern for your well-being."

"How about you?" Isabel peeked into the main room of her prison.

"That's not something they need to know about," Gavin said. "The green dress looks good on you, wear it."

"You haven't even seen me in it," Isabel protested.

"I saw it. I've seen you. It looks good on you." Gavin met her gaze. "Get dressed right now, Isabel."

Her hands began moving before she could completely process the command, and Isabel fought back the annoyance she felt at that particular aspect of her new existence. She pulled on the dress, wearing nothing underneath it. Then slipped on a pair of shoes that would coordinate. "Are we springing him tonight?"

"We are," Gavin said. "Which is why we're on a tight schedule."

"Am I going to lose all these clothes?" Gavin snorted.

"You spent the entire day naked without noticing," he pointed out. "Are you really going to miss clothes you haven't even worn?"

"I just feel bad ... Oz spent a lot of money on them."

"Oz would rather call it a loss and escape, I promise you," Gavin said. "Are you ready?" Isabel stepped out of the little room and into the main part of her prison suite. Gavin gave her an approving nod, and a raking, appraising look. "Remember: the only thing that should show on your face is hunger." Isabel rolled her eyes.

"I'm certainly hungry enough for that," she said.

"Don't be flip," Gavin told her. "Look hungry, and obey any commands that I give you." Isabel stared at Gavin for a moment.

"I can't disobey any commands you give me," she pointed out.

"Don't make any comments about commands I give you. You should look like you are too eager to feed to even think about anything else." Isabel could see that in spite of the vampire's confidence, he was tense. *Okay, so he's not sure we can pull this off, obviously.* Isabel took a deep breath and made her face carefully blank, before giving into the roiling, boiling sensation of need that she had struggled to keep at bay. "Good," Gavin said, smiling slightly at her.

He took her hand and led her to the door. The whole time that she had been in the room – the days, Isabel thought – she had not been able to imagine how it was that the vampires could come and go, but she couldn't even access the locking mechanism. She couldn't even recognize a mechanism for controlling the lock anywhere near the door. Gavin, too quickly for her to see, bit his thumb and pressed it to a particular spot on the door. The lock clicked and thumped, the door opened. Isabel filed that particular fact away in the back of her mind to ask about later; it was obvious to her that it would be against Gavin's wishes for her to speak on the way to wherever Oz was.

Gavin took her hand firmly in his and steered her out of the prison room, into a dimly-lit corridor. Isabel had barely been able to catch small slivers of the area behind her room, but she quickly realized that her cell had to be in a much larger building – and probably a very old one judging by the faintly dry, dusty smell she caught as she walked at Gavin's side. The carpet under her shoes looked worn, not quite matted, but its fibers had definitely seen better days – sometime in the past fifty years, at least. The walls were paneled halfway up, and then papered to the ceiling in print that almost looked Victorian to Isabel's eyes as they walked briskly through the hallway.

She followed Gavin, focusing on nothing more than the need to satisfy the hunger she could feel burning through her bones, coursing through her veins. If someone was watching – and based on Gavin's warnings, she was fairly certain someone was – it would look as though she were barely keeping up with him, Isabel thought. It would look like she was following in his wake, positively eager to go wherever he led. "Stop," Gavin said in a quiet, firm voice, and Isabel's feet froze under her almost too quickly.

He turned to another door, and once again cut his thumb on his sharp teeth, pressing the bloody digit to a spot on the frame. The door turned out to not be a door at all, but instead the entrance into an old-fashioned elevator. Isabel wanted to ask Gavin just what building they were in, where it was, how old it was, but she kept her face carefully schooled, and her lips pressed together to keep any words from tumbling out. "Come on," Gavin said, leading her onto the elevator.

As Gavin led her through the building, Isabel realized that every security measure was tied to the vampires; that it would be nearly impossible for anyone other than a vampire to leave the building unattended. Even if she had somewhere along the way been quick enough to get through the door of her room before it closed and locked behind one of her guests, she wouldn't have gotten beyond the corridor. They got off the elevator, went down another corridor, and then down several flights of stairs. Isabel thought to herself that the vampires within the building would have to have extraordinary memories to be able to reliably navigate the place.

"We are about to see your other maker," Gavin said, making his voice slightly derisive. "Are you ready to feast on him?"

"Yes," Isabel replied, looking up at Gavin with what she hoped was pure longing and desire on her face.

"You will feed exactly as I tell you to feed, is that understood?" Isabel nodded. "And when I tell you to stop, you will immediately stop."

"Yes," Isabel said. Gavin led her down another corridor and came to a stop at a door. It was more secure than the one she had been locked up behind, with panels made of some dark material over it; it looked doubly cruel, and the security for it was obviously more intense. Gavin had to bite his finger three times, and place it against three different hidden sensors, before the panels moved aside. And then he had to make himself bleed once again to get the actual door to unlock and open. Isabel took a deep breath, steeling herself for the next phase of Gavin's plan.

Chapter Fourteen

Oz's cell was darker and seemed smaller than the one Isabel had been trapped in. As she followed Gavin into the room, her eyes adjusted, and she looked around. She could smell the angel, a woody, warm scent under the odor of blood and sweat, but for a moment she couldn't see him. Then, as her gaze swept the room, she spotted Oz, and her heart stuttered in her chest.

He was crouched in a corner of the room, hunched over himself, hair lank and in his face. He was naked from the waist up, his jeans spattered with blood and other substances that Isabel couldn't and didn't want to identify. She shuddered at the sight of the angel, and shivered again when she realized his wings were out, their brilliance dulled. "Oz," Gavin said. "Not in as bad a state as I feared."

The angel looked up dully, spotted Gavin and then Isabel. His eyes widened. "Oh, are you on their side now, Gavin?"

"No," Gavin said. "Just a little play-acting before we spring you. Also, I thought you might appreciate the recharge." Oz half-smiled weakly. In spite of the angel's dire condition, Isabel couldn't deny the fact that it felt as though she had a hook embedded in her flesh, somewhere below her navel, and that she was being pulled towards Oz. Sharp pangs of desire jolted through her hips, and she felt her body reacting to the two men in the room with her— desire and hunger increasing by the moment. "It may not have escaped your notice that our offspring, here, is starving." Oz looked at her.

"Gavin promised to take care of you," Oz said. "I'm sorry I wasn't able to protect you, Isabel." Tears began to flow from his eyes, and Isabel stared in shock at the angel; she had never expected to feel pity towards the strong, powerful man, but somehow the flood of tears trailing down his face, even without any accompanying sobs, were the saddest thing she had ever seen. How could any of the vampires have been able to stand continuing to torture him?

"Go to him, Isabel," Gavin told her firmly. "Make him feel good." Even without the command, Isabel knew it would have been difficult for her to make herself hold back; but with the command from one of her makers, she found her feet moving even before she could consider the pathos of the image before her. Oz began to protest weakly, but Isabel's new nature rose to the top of her mind, taking over.

"Shhh," she murmured to the angel, letting her hips relax as she took the last few steps towards him. "Don't push me away, Oz. Let me help you." She sank down to her knees in front of him and reached for his face. Isabel brought her lips to Oz's and kissed him hungrily, tasting his lips and tongue. A new jolt of desire coursed through her veins as Oz began to deepen the kiss, his arms wrapping around her, drawing her close. In spite of the abuse the angel had taken, his body felt amazing as ever, pressed against hers, and Isabel felt the slickness along her labia increasing, her pussy starting to tighten in preparation for the angel.

She broke away from his lips and dipped down to the angel's neck, nipping and lapping at the skin there. Oz began to regain control of the situation, and his hands began to wander over her body, touching her through the fabric of her dress. Isabel could feel Gavin watching them, and some new sense she hadn't had the chance to experience yet told her that her other maker's arousal was increasing as Oz began to take over, slipping one hand up under the hem of her dress. "You're starving," Oz murmured. He sounded almost irritable, but as his fingers – by far warmer than Gavin's – began to slide against her slick folds, Isabel felt the tension in his body that told her he was becoming more and more aroused.

Oz stood unsteadily, lifting Isabel with him, and Isabel moaned as Oz's hands found the zipper on her dress. "As glad as I am that I bought this for you," Oz told her, tugging the zipper down, "It's annoying as hell right now." The fabric slid down over her skin with a whisper, and Isabel heard Gavin's chuckle behind her.

Oz pushed Isabel towards the bed, his eyes blazing in the room's dimness. "Tell me right now what you want, Isabel," he said firmly.

"I want you both," Isabel replied without hesitation. "I want you both to fuck me over and over again, every way you can think of. I want to taste your cock again, and feel you come inside my pussy, and then I want you to take me from behind while I suck Gavin off, and make you both come at the same time." Oz half-smiled.

"You work well, Gavin." He barely glanced at the vampire before turning his attention back onto Isabel.

"I've been keeping her on a diet," Gavin explained. "I didn't want her under anyone's influence but ours." Oz nodded absently and began to unbutton and unzip his jeans, hooking his thumbs in the waistband to tug them down over his hips. His cock sprung free of the confining material, and Isabel's mouth watered. Almost before she could even think of what to do, she sat up on the bed and nearly lunged towards him, reaching for the erection and wrapping her fingers around it.

"Definitely hungry," Oz said, amusement rippling through his voice. Isabel looked up at his face as she began to stroke him. She thought Oz's cock wasn't quite as burning-hot as Gavin's had been the times he had come to feed her, but it was larger, and she thought about the way that her body would adapt to him, according to Gavin. *Him and Gavin at the same time... oh.... oh.... fuck...* a hot-cold chill worked through her body with the image of both men taking her at once. She'd never in her life been in a threesome, and the idea of being penetrated by two men at once had never appealed to her, but she was so hungry that the thought of being trapped between the vampire and the angel, feeling them both inside of her body--filling her up, pushing against her tightness, hot and cold everywhere--was like seeing a three-course meal laid out on a table after spending a day not eating.

Isabel brought the tip of Oz's cock to her lips and closed her eyes, sucking and licking at the fluids that had begun to accumulate there. Oz's fingers tangled in her hair and Isabel took more and more of him into her mouth eagerly, moaning at the taste and feel of him; hot, silken skin against her lips, sharp-sweet taste, the spongy quality of the tip – it was as if she had been waiting all day for Oz's cock without knowing it. Oz groaned, his fingers tightening in her hair, tugging lightly. "I'd almost suspect ... that you're enjoying watching this," she heard Oz say; Isabel glanced up at Oz's face as she took as much of him into her mouth as possible. She could feel the tip of him brushing against the top of her throat.

"She's a greedy little thing, isn't she?" Isabel was so absorbed in pleasuring Oz with her mouth that she didn't notice anything else. "Look up at Oz," Gavin murmured. Isabel did as she was told, briefly disoriented as she struggled to keep moving and look at the angel at the same time. "Take your mouth off his cock and tell him how much you want his come inside you." Isabel pulled back, breathless with desire and need, and Oz's erection slid out of her mouth.

"I'm starving for it," she told the angel.

"Beg him," Gavin said firmly.

"Please ... please, Oz," she murmured.

Oz's hands on her head brought her mouth back to his cock. "If you want it, you'll have to work for it," Oz told her, mimicking Gavin's firm delivery. "*Show* me how much you want it." Isabel went to work once more, taking as much of Oz's erection into her mouth as she could, swirling her tongue around the sensitive flesh.

"You do realize, don't you, Oz, that we could do whatever we wanted to her like this," Gavin said, from behind her.

"I ... fuck, Isabel ... I don't have your proclivities," Oz said.

"A good little succubus like our girl here," Gavin said, "can get off just from sucking a man off. She barely kept herself from fucking a trainer.

Eager little thing. Think of what a catch she would be for the council."

"I'd rather not," Oz said, before groaning as Isabel reached up to cup his warm testicles in her hand and began to carefully squeeze and rub them against the base of his shaft.

"Izzy," Gavin purred. "You'd just love it if you had both of us in you at the same time, wouldn't you?" Isabel barely even registered the annoyance she normally felt at the hated nickname; the thought of taking both men at once spurred her to even greater effort, and she mumbled an affirmative with Oz's cock still between her lips.

All at once, Oz groaned, his hands tightening against her scalp, and Isabel felt the twitch of his cock, the telltale spasm through his balls as he came. She swallowed eagerly as hot, sticky-slick fluid flooded her mouth. Isabel's mind went blank as she devoured the gush of come, hungry for as much as Oz could possibly give her. She worked him with lips and tongue and hand, almost milking his erection, until Oz let out a sound somewhere between pain and pleasure and relief, pulling back from her unsteadily.

In an instant, his hands locked on her waist and he threw her down onto the bed. "My turn," he said, his voice almost growling in her ear. He pinned her down on her stomach, slipping between her legs from behind. "Beg him to fuck you, Izzy," Gavin commanded.

"Please, please fuck me, Oz," Isabel said, hearing the almost pathetic whimper in her own voice. She pushed her hips back, able to feel the burning heat of his erection against her skin; even without the command, it would have been easy to make her beg. She wanted to feel Oz inside of her almost more than she wanted to breathe, and the fact that he was still hard excited her more

Oz thrust into her all at once, ignoring the convulsive tightness of her body as it flexed around him. "Want it harder?"

"Yes!" Isabel lifted her hips and pushed back against him, scrabbling for a grip on the messy sheets of the bed, for some kind of leverage to give her the ability to take him deeper.

"Look at me," Gavin said. "Tell me how good his cock feels inside you."

"It feels ... fuck! God ... god it feels so good," Isabel said, looking at the vampire. Gavin's gaze was riveted on the sight of Oz taking her, his hips pressed flush against her buttocks. All at once, the burning, thick heat of it slid out of her and Isabel groaned in frustration.

"Do you want it in your ass, Isabel?" Her heart beat faster in her chest with a mixture of fear and need.

"We ... there's no lube," she said cautiously. Oz chuckled.

"*You* don't need it," he told her. "But I take it you've never done that before." Isabel shook her head. "Time enough for that, soon enough." Isabel moaned as he thrust into her again, moving hard and fast along her inner walls.

"She does seem greedy," Oz said. Isabel wasn't certain, but she thought the angel sounded better, stronger.

Pleasure tingled and crackled through her veins, along her bones, and Isabel gave herself up to the sensation, panting and gasping for breath, moaning as Oz slammed into her, deeper and deeper.

Oz groaned in pleasure, and Isabel bit the fabric of the bed sheets, moaning as a second – maybe even a third – orgasm began to rack her body, burning through her nervous system. Her climax intensified as she felt Oz's body tense against her, and then again, as she felt the first gush of burning-hot fluids beginning to flood her. Isabel heard herself screaming with pleasure, the sound barely muffled by the sheets as she buried her face against the bed. Her mind went utterly blank as

Oz's climax peaked, and she sagged against the sheets, for the moment satisfied.

Chapter Fifteen

"Oh, look: she's awake," Gavin said. Isabel turned over on the bed and saw both men watching her. Oz looked almost as powerful as he had been when she first met him. "We have fifteen minutes to get both of you out of here. Otherwise we're all fucked. And not in a good way."

"She's naked, is that going to fly?" Oz had put his jeans back on and somewhere he had found a shirt. Isabel pulled herself up, looking at the two men.

"Get dressed," Gavin said, picking up her dress from the floor and tossing it to her. Isabel found herself pulling the dress over her head, zipping it up, before she could even think about it.

"I'd like to know if there's any way I can get out of this 'obey any command your makers give you' thing," Isabel said, smoothing the fabric over her curves.

"Not that either of us is aware of," Oz said. "You're sure this will work?"

"My friends are where they need to be," Gavin told the angel. "But they won't be there long; the council will notice." Gavin licked his lips, looking almost nervous, and Isabel wondered just what Gavin had planned. "It'll be dawn by the time we get to the safe house."

"You have somewhere to stay?" Oz's expression echoed Gavin's concern.

"There at the house," Gavin said with a nod. "Okay." He looked at Isabel. "Remember, you're hungry, you're a thoughtless succubus who has no idea that anything out of the ordinary is happening." Isabel rolled her eyes but nodded, schooling her face into the appropriate expression.

She watched as Gavin went through the same rigmarole with the door as he had before, blooding himself to unlock the inner door and then the outer panel. Oz gestured for her to precede him, and

Gavin grabbed her by the hand, pulling her in his wake. Oz barely managed to get through the doors before they closed, and Isabel heard a low, seemingly subliminal trilling echoing through the corridor.

She almost tripped over her feet as Gavin pulled her through the hallway. When it was obvious that she couldn't keep up with his speed, Isabel gasped as Gavin lifted her off of her feet and into his arms, carrying her with apparently no effort.

Everything became a blur as Gavin and Oz moved through the winding, twisting hallways, down the stairs, and onto the elevator. Isabel closed her eyes, the speed of their movements making her dizzy. "We're almost there," Oz murmured, almost too quietly for her to hear. Isabel opened her eyes again as Gavin came to a stop.

"You'd better get under cover in the next thirty minutes," someone was saying. "And you'd better have an ironclad excuse."

"Don't worry about me, Kalima," Gavin said. "Just get this fucking door open and you won't have to think about me for at least a week."

Isabel felt a shudder and heard mechanical, lurching sounds all around her. Looking, she saw that what was opening wasn't precisely a door; it looked like the access to a vault, with steel rods that went into the ceiling, a seal on the edges of a circular piece of metal bigger than she was. Horizontal bars also apparently held it in place when it was locked, as Isabel saw them retreating into the mechanism of the door as well. All in all, she thought, if she wanted to secure a house of some kind, she couldn't think of anything better to choose.

Gavin carried her out through the entry into the building, and Oz, his wings disappeared from wherever they'd emerged, fell into step with them. "Car," Oz said briskly.

"Right over there," Gavin said, nodding. Gavin set her down on her feet and Isabel looked around while she had the few moments to do so; the building they had left looked more like a castle than a home or a prison of any kind. She supposed that she should have figured that out from the interior. The striking, gothic structure made Isabel wonder just how far she was from home.

The car waiting for them was a nondescript sedan with deeply tinted windows, and the doors to the back opened with no apparent cause. Certainly, there was no one in the back seat as Isabel climbed in, Gavin giving her a slight push on the small of her back. Both angel and vampire climbed in on either side of her, and the doors closed with the same, seemingly automatic movement. The car pulled away from the curb in front of the vampires' castle. Isabel looked up towards the front of the vehicle, only to see that there was some kind of solid metal or plastic wall – she wasn't sure – between the compartments.

"So," Oz said, settling into the seat next to her. "Where are we going, Gavin?"

"There's a group," Gavin explained. "Vampires, some of the shifters, even a few other super naturals, who want to stay mythological."

"How come I never heard about them?" Isabel looked at Gavin; the vampire smirked.

"Even when 'supes' agree with angels, they don't necessarily like them," Gavin pointed out. Isabel carefully stood, moving to the other seat in the back of the car, which she figured was some kind of limo, to be able to look at both men without craning her head.

"Whatever," Oz said. "So they're providing safety for us?"

"A safe house, outside of town," Gavin confirmed. "But we're going to have to move on at nightfall." The car began to pick up speed.

"The vamps will be on us before we even get there," Oz pointed out.

"I've got people cleaning up behind us," Gavin said with a shrug. "As far as anyone on the council will know, I took Isabel out here so I could give her some personal training."

"So you'll have to bring her back?" Oz raised an eyebrow. "Not sure I like that idea."

"I'll have to report back within a week," Gavin said. He shrugged as if the risks of that were unimportant. "But bringing her to you, feeding her with you after she starved herself earlier, that will work to my advantage." Gavin smirked. "You're going to be dead, Oz."

"I am?" Oz looked torn between amusement and concern.

"How … how were you able to get him out without anyone noticing?" Isabel had assumed that there were cameras in the corridors, watching eyes to go with the intense security.

"That is what Kalima, Harold, and Olivia are going to take care of," Gavin said. He smoothed his hair back from his face. "There's a record of the escape attempt, but it won't be tied to me; it'll look like Oz took advantage of a brief lapse in security for his chamber."

"So they'll be tracking him," Isabel said.

"They will," Gavin agreed. "Right up until evidence suggests that he's been murdered." Oz looked briefly stricken.

"And how is it going to suggest that?" Isabel felt her stomach lurch at the look on the angel's face.

"I will be bringing his wings to the council," Gavin said steadily. Isabel's eyes widened.

"What?!" she looked at Oz. "You're willing to …"

"They grow back," Oz said. He smiled. "It's one of the most painful things an angel can go through, but they grow back."

"Typically, the only time a vampire is able to get an angel's wings to present to the council as evidence is when they've killed that angel," Gavin explained. "As you might have noticed, angels and vampires don't tend to cooperate. The idea that Oz would willingly give up his wings in order to fake his own death won't occur to anyone." Isabel considered that.

"It might occur to Portia," Isabel said.

"Portia's not likely to be in a position to argue the point," Gavin said. His voice chilled Isabel almost to the bone.

"Why not?" Oz sounded almost eager. "What has happened to our dear Portia?"

"I informed the council that she was attempting to interfere with my plan to train Isabel myself," Gavin said. "As punishment, they've taken her fangs, and she was exposed to a UV lamp for twenty minutes. She should be sufficiently incapacitated not to bother anyone for at least a month." There was grim satisfaction in Gavin's smile, and for the first time, Isabel wondered if her initial impression of him – at least, the impression that she remembered – was at all accurate. Was he any better than the other vampires?

"Couldn't have happened to a more deserving person," Oz said. Isabel looked at him in shock. "Who do you think was in charge of torturing me, Isabel?"

"I'm just …" she shrugged. "I guess I'm not fully transformed yet. Torturing anyone seems …"

"She isn't tortured," Gavin said. "Just punished. As she should be. She would have tortured *you*." Gavin looked through the heavily smoked glass of the window. "We're not being followed. Good." He looked at Oz and smiled slightly. "At least you'll have our girl here to help you get through the pain."

Chapter Sixteen

The safe house looked almost as ornate as the castle they had left. As Isabel followed Oz and Gavin out of the car, she wondered once again whose side she was on – whose side anyone was on, in the complicated mess her life had become. The sky was lightening slightly in the east, and Gavin looked anxious to get inside of the building the car had taken them to. *Does sunlight actually kill them, or is it just bad for them?*

The door opened as they approached, and Isabel felt a shock of recognition, but as she looked more intently at the woman standing at the entry to the building, Isabel thought she had never seen her before in her life. "She's a succubus, like you," Oz told her. "Free – both of her makers killed."

"Get inside," the woman said. As Isabel passed her, she realized that the fact that the woman was another succubus was exactly what had caused her sense of recognition. The woman's blonde hair cascaded in perfect waves to her waist, and her ripe – almost overripe – body strained at the fabric of her clothes. Her ice-blue eyes glowed with a kind of supernatural heat, and her lips curled in such a way that Isabel could well imagine that any man who saw her would immediately picture himself pushing his cock between them.

Gavin and Oz both seemed to shudder slightly as they passed the woman, and Isabel was pleased to see that the magic – which she couldn't use on her two makers – wasn't something to which they were completely immune. She remembered Gavin telling her that with enough time spent in close quarters with a succubus, even strong vampires and angels would become susceptible to their abilities; maybe that was why they couldn't stay at the safe house for very long.

"There's a light-tight room at the end of the hallway," the woman told Gavin. "The rest of the house is more or less normal," she added to Oz and Isabel. The succubus smiled at Isabel. "Just finishing up your transition, aren't you?" Isabel nodded.

"I think I'm almost there," she admitted.

"Starting to get the little psychic vibes?" The woman looked at her intently. *Hear this?* Isabel's eyes widened.

"Wait, I can read minds?" The woman chuckled. Gavin left them, hurrying towards the light-tight room, and the succubus led Isabel and Oz towards a small, elegantly decorated living room.

"In a limited capacity," the woman told her. "Mostly, you'll be able to read – from a man – exactly what their deepest desire is. You'll get it like a feeling, or like a craving. You'll want nothing more than to suck them off, or hold your ankles while they plow you. But over time, it'll become clearer, especially if you spend a lot of time around other super naturals like your angelic maker, here."

"So when ..." Isabel looked at Oz, feeling almost suspicious. "When you asked me what I wanted ..."

"He was testing you, in more than one way," the succubus said. "I made tea if you'd like it." Isabel looked at the woman up and down, wondering.

"What's your name? And how are you able to live like this?" The woman laughed and sat down.

"My name is Moira," the blonde said. "And as to how I'm able to live like this, well, that much should be obvious." Isabel shook her head.

"It isn't," she told Moira.

"Think about it for a moment," Moira suggested. "I can give men everything they want – their deepest desires – and, as I'm sure you've already noticed, I can also convince them to pay whatever I want for it." Moira smiled. "So I've made a tidy little fortune."

"But how are you safe from the vampires?" Isabel looked at Oz; he hadn't given her any indication in their time together that she would be able to live independently.

"The current war between the angels – and some of the other supes – and the vampire council is pretty new," Moira said. "I became a succubus about ..." she frowned, lost in thought. "Four hundred years ago. By the time the vampires tried to round me up, it was pretty easy to show them that they couldn't contain me."

"They couldn't?" Moira shook her head.

"The longer you're a succubus, the more you'll be able to control your abilities," Moira said. "And the more powerful they become." Isabel shot an irritable glance at Oz, who hadn't specifically told her that. "On the other hand, the hunger grows, at least for the first two hundred or so years," Moira added.

"It grows?"

"At the peak of my hunger, I worked in a brothel and serviced twenty men per night on a regular basis," Moira told her. She laughed, almost to herself. "Back then it was the only way I could reasonably feed as much as I needed to. Now, of course, there are other options." She looked pointedly at Oz. "I have to admit, I envy you your makers."

"Did the vampires kill your makers, or something else?" Moira grimaced.

"They killed my angel," she replied. "Darius …" she shook her head. "He was always a risk-taker, always impulsive. Someone figured out what he was and took him out." Moira looked at Oz again. "Are you sure you're fully recovered from your ordeal?"

"As recovered as I need to be," Oz said, smiling. "Isabel's a prodigy."

"So it would seem," Moira said. "We have another twelve hours or so before Gavin can come out. Why don't the two of you relax a bit?" She rose to her feet. "I have a client I need to get to."

Chapter Seventeen

Isabel stared up at the bathroom ceiling in the room Moira had given her, thinking. Oz had gone to sleep, leaving her alone, and it was still hours until Gavin would wake up; but Isabel could already feel the hunger beginning to stir deep down in her body, the need mingled with desire that drove her feedings.

She pushed the prodding need out of her mind and tried to think. So much had happened in a week that Isabel wasn't entirely sure that all of it was even real.

Isabel absently scrubbed at her limbs, shifting in the warm, scented water of the bathtub. Obviously, Moira's story at least confirmed that the vampire council wanted to go public, and that they were pulling in succubi as some part of the plan to that end. The angels seemed to be – predictably – the "good guys," but Isabel thought that the common perception of angels was less than fully accurate. She shivered, remembering the rapt, intent look on Oz's face as Gavin had taken her, the comments that the two men had exchanged about how easily they could make her do whatever they wanted for their attentions.

But how do I know there aren't good reasons for the vampire council to want what it wants? Away from the direct influence of the two men, Isabel was able to question their motivation. Obviously, Gavin wasn't merely interested in keeping her from being tortured and manipulated into supporting and promoting the vampire agenda of going public; he had hinted more than once that he wanted her personally.

Isabel heard movement, and turned her head to see Oz walk into the bathroom. "Gavin will be up soon," Oz told her.

"How long have I been in this bathtub?" Isabel sat up and shivered as the water sluiced down her body, caressing her nipples on its way down. Everything had become even more sensitive, and she thought – somewhat grimly – that she could probably, under the right circumstances, get off even from literal torture, if the person doing it to her was a man. *Don't even think like that. You're going to be fine.*

"Gavin's an early riser," Oz said. "As long as he avoids the windows, he'll be able to leave the room. It's sunrise and midday that the vampires really need to stay out of; sunset isn't as potent."

"Everything is so complicated," Isabel said, knowing that she was whining and not caring.

"We're moving on to Paris, tomorrow," Oz told her. "I've made arrangements. Gavin will have to stay behind. He'll meet with us after he convinces the council that I'm dead." Oz looked her over slowly, and Isabel could sense the stirrings of desire from the angel.

"Is it really that painful?" Isabel pressed her lips together, cringing at the thought of Oz losing his wings. "You know …"

"Having my wings ripped off? You bet your perfect little ass it's painful," Oz said. "It's the most acutely painful thing an angel can go through."

"That ... that sounds horrific," Isabel said. She rose to her feet, and smiled to herself at Oz's lustful gaze on her body.

"Come here," Oz said firmly. Isabel stepped quickly out of the bath tub and nearly slipped, but caught herself instinctively, before closing the distance between herself and Oz. Oz pulled her onto his lap, reaching for a towel and wrapping it around her. "Even if you weren't mine, I would have had a hard time letting anyone else have you," Oz told her.

"Why is that?" Oz grinned, pressing a delicate kiss to the spot where her neck and shoulder met as his hands moved over her body, drying her and caressing her all at once.

"I chose you for a reason that night, and it had nothing to do with making a succubus," Oz said. "Even before you were supernaturally endowed, you were amazing." His hands cupped her breasts and

Isabel moaned softly. "You wanted to give yourself up, to be loved – or at least lusted after – with hunger as deep as someone's soul."

"I don't know about all that," Isabel said, feeling defensive in spite of the current of heat running through her spine, distracting her from human thoughts.

"You don't remember, do you?" Oz playfully nipped her shoulder – it didn't have the dangerous feeling of Gavin's sharp teeth, but it sent a thrill through her nonetheless. "I told you that you could only come when I said, and you …" Oz chuckled. "Your reaction to that was to try and make me come faster, so I wouldn't be able to deny you." Oz turned her around and kissed her hungrily on the lips, his hands holding her body tightly to his. "It was only a matter of time before someone chose you for this."

"It was?" Isabel could feel the hardening ridge of Oz's cock through his jeans.

"With the war going on, with vampires following angels to turn their conquests ... another angel would have found you, laid you, and another vampire would have completed the process. You're too good a catch to have gone unnoticed for much longer."

"Did you know it was going to happen?" Oz shook his head.

"Gavin kept himself pretty well concealed," Oz told her. "I didn't even smell him that night when you left. I saw him in the club, of course, but I thought he'd gone after another angel, another girl." He rocked his hips against hers, and Isabel bit her bottom lip, breathing in sharply at the jolt of lust the feeling of his cock gave her, even through the tough fabric of his jeans.

"So ..." Isabel shook her head, trying to clear it. "You just ... chose me?"

"I chose you," Oz said. "And I'd choose you again in a heartbeat." He smiled against her lips.

"So would I." Isabel started and looked over her shoulder at the direction of the voice. Gavin stood in the bathroom door, watching her and Oz intently. He had dressed in a new suit, and looked as gorgeous as ever. Isabel felt the hunger within her growing; she gritted her teeth, almost annoyed at the predictable surge of need, the images that flickered through her head of the two men taking her at once. "Don't feed her just yet, Oz," Gavin said. "You'll need her abilities."

"You just want to feed on her," Oz said dismissively.

"I need my strength," Gavin said, shrugging. "It's not easy ripping the wings off an angel."

"You're strong enough," Oz told the vampire.

"Do you have to rip them?" Isabel shuddered at the thought. Both Gavin and Oz nodded.

"If they're cut, it might open up questions," Gavin said.

"Not to mention he'd need to bleed himself a dozen times to hack them off with any blade," Oz added. "Ripping them off makes more sense, as painful as it's bound to be."

"But they'll grow back," Isabel said, making it almost a question. Both men nodded again.

"After about a week," Oz told her. "It takes that long for them to grow back." He made a face, rising to his feet and carefully putting Isabel down. The towel fell away from her body and Isabel caught the brief gleam of interest in Gavin's eyes. "In the meantime, my ability to heal others will be pretty severely diminished."

"So don't let anyone get hurt around you," Isabel said.

"You've got the tickets booked?" Oz nodded.

"They weren't able to freeze my alternate accounts," Oz told the vampire. "Isabel and I will be in Paris by tomorrow night."

"I'll meet you there by the end of the week," Gavin said. "I've given Sophia the codes." Isabel once more felt like she was profoundly out of her depth, but decided that – all things considered – it could be worse. *Definitely worth seeing if I can talk to Moira more before we go.*

"Okay then," Oz said. "Isabel, you'll probably want to stay out of the room until Gavin comes out with my wings." Isabel's stomach twisted inside of her, and she felt her eyes stinging with tears.

Isabel followed the two men out of the bathroom. "Go into the living room, Isabel," Gavin told her sharply. Isabel's feet took her in that direction, and cold chills worked through her, negating any hunger she might have felt moments before. She heard the two men walking in the direction of Gavin's room, and closed her eyes.

Moira sat on the couch, looking troubled but resolute. "Nothing you can do about it except take care of him when Gavin finishes," Moira told her. "If it makes you feel any better, you and Oz will be absolutely safe in Paris." Moira smiled slightly. "And there are plenty of men to feed on."

"I only want to feed on him," Isabel said.

"For now," Moira said. The blonde shrugged. "But where you're going – the safe space in Paris – is full of incubi and succubi, banded together to avoid the vampires. When you're with your own kind, you might find your loyalties … tested."

"Spurring each other to bad decisions?" Isabel remembered what Portia had said about succubi on their own becoming self-destructive.

"The best kind of bad decisions," Moira said.

From the other end of the house, Isabel heard a sharp, cutting scream. She sank down onto the couch, shivering at the pain she could hear in Oz's voice. "God ... that sounds ..."

"Oz will need you, for sure," Moira said. "Probably for the rest of the night." In spite of her anxiety and pity for Oz, Isabel could feel the hunger rising up in her again; she knew that however much Oz needed her, and for however long, she would keep feeding from him, and keep supplying him with the pleasure he needed to recover. "You'll get over it," Moira said blandly.

"I hope not," Isabel said. "I hope I never get over not wanting people to be tortured."

"You should spend more time with Gavin, once he's free," Moira told her. "You need balance, you need to learn how to be your full self." Another scream reached Isabel's ears from the other end of the house, and she closed her eyes.

A few moments later, she heard movement and looked up to see Gavin walk into the living room, two golden, feathered wings in his hands. "Go to Oz right now," he said. "We'll talk more once you're done treating him." Gavin closed his eyes, and Isabel saw the compassion in his face, so strange after the ruthlessness she had seen in him before. "Don't let him dismiss you until he's fully recovered."

Isabel walked past him, headed to where Oz lay in Gavin's light-tight room, and thought to herself that it would get interesting indeed when she, Oz, and Gavin were all together; both men were able to command her immediate, unquestioning obedience, and Isabel knew that there was no way the two men agreed on everything – or even, necessarily, on the most important things. She put the image of Oz's wings out of her mind, and knew that whatever else happened, she was committed to both the angel and the vampire, and that no matter what forces existed arrayed against them, she was fully born, fully transformed into her new state. She was going to take an active role in making sure the right people won the war.

END OF BOOK 1

Newsletter

This exclusive **VIP Mailing List** from Persia Publishing focuses on delivering high quality content to your inbox that will bring more passion, excitement, and entertainment to your life. Weekly insights, specials offers and free giveaways that you will love!

You are just one click away from getting exclusive access to the **VIP Mailing List**!

Click the "**Get Access Now**" link below to join today!

GET ACCESS NOW

http://www.persiapublishing.com/subscribe-to-romance-lucy/

LIKE US AT

https://www.facebook.com/LucyLyonsRomance/

CAN YOU HELP?

PLEASE leave a quick review for this book if it gives you any value. It provides valuable feedback that allows me to continuously improve my books and motivates me to keep writing.

Thank You!

Owned by The Vampire

The Vampire War: Part 1

Book 2

Lucy Lyons

© 2017

Newsletter

This exclusive **VIP Mailing List** from Persia Publishing focuses on delivering high quality content to your inbox that will bring more passion, excitement, and entertainment to your life. Weekly insights, specials offer and free giveaways that you will love!

You are just one click away from getting exclusive access to the **VIP Mailing List**!

Click the "**Get Access Now**" link below to join today!

GET ACCESS NOW

http://www.persiapublishing.com/subscribe-to-romance-lucy/

LIKE US AT

https://www.facebook.com/LucyLyonsRomance/

CAN YOU HELP?

PLEASE leave a quick review for this book if it gives you any value. It provides valuable feedback that allows me to continuously improve my books and motivates me to keep writing.

Thank You!

© Copyright 2016 by Persia Publishing- All rights reserved.

All rights reserved. No part of this publication may be reproduced, distributed, or transmitted in any form or by any means, including photocopying, recording, or other electronic or mechanical methods, without the prior written permission of the publisher, except in the case of brief quotations embodied in critical reviews and certain other noncommercial uses permitted by copyright law. For permission requests, write to the publisher, addressed "Attention: Permissions Coordinator," at the address below.

The information herein is offered for entertainment purposes solely, and is universal as so. The presentation of the information is without contract or any type of guarantee assurance.

The trademarks that are used are without any consent, and the publication of the trademark is without permission or backing by the trademark owner. All trademarks and brands within this book are for clarifying purposes only and are the owned by the owners themselves, not affiliated with this document.

CHAPTER 1

"Are you okay?" Isabel asked, placing a hand over Oz's shoulder. His body twitched as her fingers spread out slowly over his bony shoulder and then retreated to the back of his neck. Oz was still in pain, despite Isabel's untiring efforts to make sure he recovered.

"It's just not that easy," he said, his tired eyes fixated on the white floor tiles of the waiting room. The airport was buzzing with people, and Isabel had to admit she was terrified to be out in the public eye again, even though she knew she didn't have to resort to extreme measures to control her abilities. She didn't need to wear sunglasses anymore; she didn't even need to avoid eye contact with passers-by. All she needed was the will power to block out any outgoing signals from her end, and the truth was, she was getting pretty good at it. This morning, she slipped into one of the dresses Oz had bought her; black velvet, short with a plunging neckline. Isabel honestly felt great about herself. For once, she could dress up whichever way she wanted without having to worry about shit going down.

"Are you feeling a little bit better, at least?" she asked, playfully tugging at Oz's sleeve. Her compassion for him was growing stronger and stronger each day. Ironic as it was, she had developed a tender human connection with him, one that she didn't feel with anyone else, not even Gavin.

"Yeah," Oz nodded, raising his eyes to her. "Especially after last night... you know how to take care of me," he said, licking his lips.

Isabel felt a warmth radiate through her. *How the hell am I gonna make it through this flight?* "I'd let you take care of me, over and over again," she breathed. She caught Oz licking his lips again. *Trying to seduce an angel in the middle of an airport probably wasn't the smartest thing to do.* Besides, Oz could control his urges if he had to, which Isabel found incredibly frustrating.

"I think we should go now," Oz said, nodding towards the gates. Isabel got up, dusted herself off and headed for the sliding doors. "Here, let me get that for you," Oz said, grabbing the handle of her suitcase. Isabel felt that tingly sensation spread out through her body again.

This is crazy. His mere touch made her hungry. Isabel kicked herself for all the fantasies that were popping into her head. They were all so invasive, so intrusive that Isabel was finding it almost impossible to shove them out anymore. *You're going to get on this plane, and then you're going to sleep, no questions asked.* "Why, thank you," she said, batting her eyelashes. Isabel led the way across the asphalt, following the rest of the passengers onto the plane. "52H and 52J, that's at the very back," she said, trotting down the aisle. She could feel Oz's eyes on her, an instinct she had acquired through her transformation.

"And you think Gavin didn't do that on purpose?" Oz asked, raising an eyebrow at her.

Isabel froze for a second. "What do you mean?" she asked, turning to look at him.

"He knows people," Oz said, motioning for Isabel to take the window seat.

"Okay?" She tilted her head to the side.

"Don't worry about it right now," Oz said. "For now, let's just enjoy the ride."

Isabel smiled to herself. It had been a long time since she'd travelled someplace far away. She leaned back in her seat, wondering if Paris would be as she imagined. All her adult life she had listened to her wealthy girlfriends talk about how stunning Paris was, and never once could she ever imagine being in their place. She sighed loudly, staring out the window like a little girl, and it was only when she felt Oz's hand reach up her dress that she was brought back to reality. "Here?" she asked, rolling her eyes at him. But the truth was, Isabel was getting hungrier by the second. If it were up to her, she would let him take her right then and there.

Oz shook his head. "Maybe not here," he said, his lips curving to a smile. "But maybe..."

Isabel squinted at him. "Maybe?"

"In there," he said, cocking his head towards the bathroom behind them. Isabel could feel her heart drop to her knees. A million thoughts were racing through her mind; images of Oz fucking her in that tight space were starting to take over, and she couldn't help but let out a loud sigh.

"I don't know how I feel about that," she said, her eyes fixated on Oz's.

"You know you want to," he said, holding her gaze. Instantly, Isabel could feel herself succumbing to his orders. She couldn't resist the thought of him pushing her up against the wall, unzipping his pants and taking her from behind. She bit her bottom lip, her mind conjuring up images of pure lust. She brushed a hand through her hair and brought it to one side.

"I do," she breathed. "I really, really do." Oz flashed her a smirk, and it was only then that she became fully convinced of his fantasy. His fantasies were hers, too.

"We just got to wait until take-off, until everyone's asleep," he hissed. Isabel could feel her heart begin to race. She had never done anything like this before. Sure, she heard about it in the movies, but she didn't think you could actually do something like this and not get caught. It all sounded so surreal to her, as if she was caught up in one big simulation. But she couldn't resist the temptation; she couldn't let Oz down. After all, he needed her to take care of him, and she needed him, too. The hunger was gnawing at her, and she could feel that spark regenerate inside her once more.

"I can't wait," she whispered. Soon enough, the plane took off, and Isabel couldn't help but get lost in her own little world. She stared out the window, her eyes following the movement of the foamy clouds gliding across the sky. She flinched when she felt Oz's hand come over her shoulder.

"Sorry," she said. "I got distracted." She turned around to meet his gaze, and immediately felt an electric current rush through her.

"Shall we?" he asked, his head cocked to the side. Isabel laughed at how Oz tended to phrase his words as questions, when all they really were was a continuous series of commands.

"We shall," she smiled, her eyes darting from the empty aisle, to the bathroom door, and then to the aisle again. "I don't get it," she said. "Most people are still awake, this is a daytime flight... there's no way all these people will go to sleep at once."

"Oh, you underestimate yourself, Isabel," Oz said, glaring at her. "What did we say about your ability to control the minds of all men?"

Isabel paused for a second, confused. "Does that entail putting them to sleep?" she asked, raising an eyebrow at him.

"It entails shutting down certain parts of their brain so they're somewhat... sedated."

"And how do I do that?" she asked, suddenly nervous. "What if I end up putting the pilot to sleep or something?" Isabel had never been so disoriented. This was no joke: they were literally thousands of feet up in the air. What if she fucked up? Her body shuddered just thinking about it.

Oz chuckled. "You won't sedate the pilots, don't worry," he said, tilting his head towards her. "All you have to do is focus all your energy on the person you want to put to sleep... and remember, you have to look them in the eye."

"And what about the women?" Isabel asked.

"Don't worry, I've got it taken care of," he said, folding both arms across his chest.

Isabel nodded. She waited for the flight attendants to finish distributing the lunches, and then she got up and made her way down the aisle. "Excuse me," she said. "Can I just get a cup of water?"

"Sure," the woman said, staring at her for a moment before gesturing for her to go back to her seat. Isabel smiled and then turned around. She stood there for a second, inspecting the men around her. She made eye contact with one and then held his gaze. For a second his jaw dropped.

No, no, no, Isabel thought. This was no time for a passenger to be captivated by her, not in that way. *Okay, Isabel, just focus.* She took in a deep breath and let it out through her nose. Suddenly she could feel the energy surging through her. She didn't take her eyes off his, and then, slowly but surely, his eyelids began to droop.

"Ma'am, ma'am?" a woman's voice sounded from behind her. It was as if Isabel was caught in a trance; she wasn't moving, and neither were the men she tried to fixate. Suddenly they all dropped, one after the other, as Isabel finally pushed her way down the aisle. She averted her gaze to Oz, who just smiled at her, unaffected by the sedative power she had over everyone else. The flight attendant pushed past her, nose wrinkled, eyebrows furrowed.

"Yep, she definitely thinks I'm a freak now," Isabel said, shifting in her seat.

"Now, for the women," Oz said, clenching his eyes for what seemed like an eternity. Isabel watched as his entire body seemed to twitch. She held onto the back of her chair, her eyes darting from one woman passenger to the other, watching as their heads dropped like deflated balloons.

"What even?" Isabel said, turning to Oz. He opened his eyes again and looked at her, a wry grin settling over his face.

"Didn't I tell you?" he said. "Your transformation is almost complete, you just need someone to guide you through your abilities, because believe me, they're a lot."

Isabel couldn't resist him any longer. She could feel a warm sensation wash over her like a wave, and she reached down and touched herself, her fingers becoming soaking wet as she made contact with her panties. "Let's go inside," she whispered, her eyes fixated on Oz's.

Instantly, he got up, took her hand and rushed to the cabinet. It was already dark inside, and reduced to pitch black when Oz locked the door behind them. Isabel had always loved that feeling of utter and complete seclusion with him. He flashed her a little smirk in the darkness, calling her in closer, and instantly her hands found their way round to the back of his neck, her fingers slightly grazing at the base of his scalp. He pressed his lips to hers, and Isabel let the tip of her tongue rub up against the floor of his mouth in rhythmic, controlled motion. Once, twice, and a third time she slid her tongue all the way in, letting it collide with his in between her little moans and his brief gasps for air. When he was done tasting her, he slowly worked his way down the length of her neck, lightly sucking at the skin and exhaling fully in between. She cocked her head to the side, feeling her heart rate escalate and her body stiffen as he briefly slid his tongue into her ear. She could hear the little crackling noises his tongue made once his lips parted. She let out a sigh, and then she let her hands roam his chest, her fingers tracing circles around the buttons of his shirt.

CHAPTER 2

"D'you think they're awake now?" Isabel smiled against Oz's mouth.

"I think so," he whispered. "You go first. We probably don't have much time before they snap out of it; I'll sneak up behind you."

"Okay," Isabel said, unlocking the cabinet door and popping her head outside. She caught a glimpse of one of the flight attendants pacing the aisle, looking as though she had just woken up from a coma. The rest of the passengers looked disoriented as hell, and a part of Isabel felt guilty for what they had done. "Have we caused harm to any of those people?" she asked.

"Nah," Oz said. "Just some temporary memory loss, they should be okay."

Isabel felt her heart drop to her knees. "What do you mean?" she asked, blinking repeatedly. As soon as the sunlight seeped into the cabinet, Isabel winced, feeling a blind spot floating in her vision. "Oz, what do you mean?" she asked again.

"Ah, Isabel, stop being silly, nothing is going to happen to anybody," Oz chuckled. "They were just put to sleep, nothing more," he said.

Isabel breathed a sigh of relief. "I can't believe you did that to me," she said, shaking her head. She slowly slid out of the bathroom, making her way back to her window seat. Oz looked left and right, and then he followed her, the two of them sneaking back to their seats. They leaned back, panting, Isabel gasping as a drop of fluid trickled down her leg.

***

"Ladies and gentlemen, welcome to Charles De Gaulle airport. Local time is 10 pm, and the temperature is 1 degrees Celsius."

"Yikes, it's cold," Isabel said, wrapping her arms around herself. Outside she could see the city lights come into view, and the truth was, Isabel was pretty excited. All that apprehension she had been feeling was starting to fade away, and all she could think about right now was where Oz was taking her. The thought excited her, especially after their little episode inside the plane bathroom. Right now, Isabel felt ready to conquer: she felt ready to thrive and to be introduced to this whole new world ahead of her.

"Alright, let's go," Oz said, reaching his hand out to her. The two of them pushed their way down the aisle, and as soon as Isabel stepped out of the plane, she felt her lungs inflate with cold night air.

"Who's waiting for us here?" Isabel asked, holding onto Oz's arm as the two of them made their way through the terminal entrance. Isabel stood there for a second, utterly bewildered by what was going on around her: hundreds of people running around, dragging their suitcases behind them, people reuniting with their families, and their loved ones. Suddenly Isabel felt sorry for herself. There she was, having landed in a totally foreign country, standing amidst a sea of strangers, not knowing what her next step would be.

Oz looked distracted. It was like he was being bombarded with so many stimuli all at once, that he felt like he was all over the place. "Wait," he said, tilting his head to the side. Suddenly he pointed to an obscure point ahead of them, and Isabel found herself being dragged towards the exit. "Analise!" Oz yelled, raising one hand up in the air.

"Oz!" the woman said, standing on her tiptoes. She had some sort of French accent, which Isabel found endearing. "Oz!" she said again, meeting the two of them halfway.

"Analise, how are you?" Oz said, raising his eyebrows at the blonde, scantily clad woman. Isabel could recognize a fellow succubus when she saw one. She eyed her up and down, and, realizing she was being a bit too invasive, looked away.

"I'm alright, what about you? Ah! I see you brought her with you," Analise said, her green eyes boring into Isabel.

Isabel opened her mouth but no words came out. The truth was, she was star-struck by Analise. She was probably the most beautiful succubus she had ever laid eyes on, not that she'd seen many of them, but either way she was enchanted by Analise's flawless porcelain skin, short, choppy platinum blonde hair, icy green eyes, and pearly teeth. Isabel wondered how long she'd been around and how many men she fed on each day? It must be a lot. And they must all worship her. "Hello," Isabel said finally, feeling the insides of her cheeks dry up like prunes.

"She's beautiful," Analise said, flashing Oz a smirk. "It's a good thing you've brought her to us."

"She is," Oz nodded in agreement, wrapping an arm around Isabel's waist. She jumped at the sensation, but then settled down again, smiling at Analise.

"Hungry?" Analise asked, flashing Isabel a coy smile.

"Not at all," she lied, feeling Oz's fingers play at the very tips of her hair and down the length of her back. She thought back to what Moira had said about her loyalties being tested in Paris, and the truth was, she didn't even feel like feeding on anyone else but Oz. Her mind kept wandering, though. What about all those people— specifically men— she was going to meet? What if they end up starving her? What if they couldn't be trusted? A million thoughts were racing through her mind, but one thing was for sure; whether she liked it or not, she was going with this Analise.

"Well, I doubt you'll feel hungry ever again when you come with us," Analise said with a sincere grin. Oz didn't say anything. He just took Isabel's hand and squeezed it, as if to reassure her. "Well, then, I think we should get going," Analise said again. "There's a limo waiting for us outside."

Isabel had to pinch herself to make sure she wasn't dreaming. The car ride seemed to extend for an eternity. She couldn't keep her eyes off the road, following it ever so attentively, taking in all the details. The car took them up to the countryside, where Isabel would be staying. In the distance she caught a glimpse of what appeared to be a mansion, towering on top of a flowery hill. Even in the darkness, Isabel could make out the details of the forest-like landscape. One of the things she liked most about being a succubus was the night vision. She shifted in her seat and smiled to herself, thinking about how wild of a ride this was.

"So, Isabel, we're going to take you up to your room, in the tower," Analise said, pointing to the dome-like roof. The mansion was hidden largely in trees, their flowery vines dangling off the balcony of Isabel's assigned room.

"We're giving you the royal treatment," Oz said, flashing Isabel a coy smile. She smiled back, but the truth was, she really didn't get it. She had heard both Oz and Gavin talking time and time again about how special she was, how she was one of the best of her kind. But she couldn't really wrap her head around the reason behind it all. Soon enough, the limo pulled over in front of a big iron gate, and a bunch of guards opened it up to let them pass through. Isabel was growing more apprehensive by the second, but every time she looked over at Oz for reassurance, he always made her feel safe.

"You're awfully quiet, Isabel," Analise said in one of the sultriest tones Isabel had ever heard. She wondered if this was her normal way of talking, or if there was something more, something suggestive, about her tone of voice.

"Can you really blame me?" she asked, looking over at Oz. "I literally just landed in the most beautiful city in the world."

"Pretty fitting for a woman like you," Oz smiled. He and Analise exchanged brief glances, which Isabel could only interpret as consensus over her beauty. She basked in that for a moment before realizing they were pulling over again. "Alright, well, let's take you up to your room," Oz said, popping his door open and stepping out of the limo. Isabel looked up, star-struck by the architecture of the place; this place she would be staying for the unforeseeable future. She followed Analise up a marble set of stairs and just stood there while the blonde beeped away at a security monitor at the front door. Suddenly, the doors parted, inviting Isabel to step inside.

"Don't be afraid," Analise said, her pearly teeth showing through her smile. "Follow me." Isabel's feet moved in the direction of the entrance, her heels clicking against the hardwood floor. "Aden!" Analise said, her voice echoing all over the place. A young man stepped outside, looking Isabel up and down before his lips curved to a smile. He was broad across the shoulders, with short curly hair cascading down his forehead and freckles spread out over his face and nose. "Hello," he said, not taking his eyes off Isabel. "I'm Aden."

"Hi," she said, her eyes darting from Oz, to Aden, and then to Oz again.

"You go ahead, Aden's going to show you your room," he said, flashing Isabel a coy smile. Instantly, she could feel her feet taking her to where Aden was, the two of them starting up the stairs.

"So, Isabel, I've heard a lot about you," Aden said, glancing at her briefly in between steps. The tower was so high up Isabel could tell they still had a long way to go.

"What have you heard about me?" she asked, raising an eyebrow at him. Suddenly she could feel the hunger tugging at her insides. *No, now's not the right time,* she thought to herself. As they made their way up, Isabel caught glimpses of incubi going from door to door, rushing down the hallways, making beelines for each other's rooms. *Wow, this is totally the definition of torture,* she thought to herself, because the truth was, they were all gorgeous. Isabel let out a sigh, thinking about how hard living here was bound to be. She wasn't allowed to feed on anyone but Gavin and Oz, and that thought scared her, let alone the reasons behind it. She had grown used to not questioning them, to obeying their orders without much thought, but when something like this popped up, it messed with her head, nipping away at the logic she had structured in her brain. All these men were taking away her sanity. Isabel was going crazy just by the sight of them. Some of them were scurrying about the hallways naked, and she could swear she was this close to turning around and going in for the kill.

"I've heard you're one of the freshest, most beautiful succubi of our time," Aden said, turning to Isabel. He dropped her suitcases for a moment, dusted himself off and then picked them up again, gesturing for her to follow him down a red-carpeted hall. "You're also one of the most powerful ones of our time, too."

Isabel let out a polite giggle. "I don't know what to say," she admitted. "I don't feel all that powerful."

"Oh, but you are," Aden said with an all-knowing grin. He stopped at the end of the hall and climbed up another, smaller set of stairs. "We're almost there," he said. "Just hold on a little bit more."

Isabel sighed loudly. "Am I going to have to climb up and down all those stairs every time I need something?" she asked, her head cocked to the side.

"You're going to have everyone— including me— to serve you," Aden said. Finally, he stopped at a gold-plated door framed with velvet, and he unlocked it, letting Isabel into her room. She couldn't help but shiver. The room was beyond what she had expected. The furniture was all gold-plated, and she could've sworn she caught a glimpse of some rhinestones glittering somewhere on the walls. Aden turned to her, motioning for her to step inside. "Come on in," he said.

Although Isabel was utterly blown away by the setup, she still couldn't take her eyes off Aden. Her stomach was growling, and the hunger was taking over her, in all its forms. "Thanks," she said, pretending to fumble with her luggage. "You can go now, I need to change."

"Since when do succubi need to worry about that?" he asked, taking a step closer to Isabel. Slowly, he wrapped both arms around her waist. "Honey, with us, there's no such thing as overexposure." Suddenly, Isabel bounced back.

"No, I don't think I can do this," she said, despite the heat that was building up inside of her. It was like she had been programmed, made to believe that she belonged to no one else but her creators, and in a way, she was okay with that. "You're free to go now."

"Excellent," she heard a voice say. Isabel jumped when she saw Oz appear from behind Aden, a wide grin on his face. "You've passed the first test," he said, raising an eyebrow at Isabel. She shook her head in confusion, and then Analise appeared at the doorway, a cheesy smile patched to her face.

"I'd like to congratulate you, Isabel," she said. "I think you're probably stronger than you thought you were."

Isabel's eyes jumped from person to person, watching them as they watched her. "What was the point of this?" she asked, averting her gaze to Oz. He was pretty much the only person she trusted out of everyone.

"It's all a part of your training," he said. "I don't want you to worry."

Isabel nodded. But deep down, the hunger was still tugging at her. "Can I have something to eat?" she asked, almost robotically.

"Of course," Aden said, making a beeline for the bar they had set up for her. He stared at it for a second then started fumbling with the liquor bottles, picking up a small piece of crimson red satin cloth and polishing them clean. "Would you like a drink, Isabel?"

She shook her head. She didn't know what it was about alcohol that repulsed her. She never used to be like that, but maybe, Isabel figured, it was because alcohol had always been her number one go-to for when she wanted to charm someone. And now she didn't need to do that anymore. It took some getting used to, she admitted, but at the end of the day, she was living a whole new life, and with that, came a whole lot of changes. "I just really need to eat," she said in a low voice. But deep down, she knew it wasn't food she was craving. Isabel didn't need food to survive.

"Don't be ashamed, Isabel," Aden said, kneeling down and pushing aside a small, velvet drape. He grabbed the handle to a mini fridge, hidden away under the bar, and he pulled out an oversized bowl of fruit. "This is for you," he said with a smile. "We'll be bringing you your dinner in a little while. Pork chops, paella rice, string beans..."

"That sounds great," she said, turning to Oz.

"Alright, well, until then, do you want to leave the two of us alone?" he asked Aden, his voice firm.

Aden nodded, turned around and disappeared into the hallway. "Well, I guess I should be going, too," Analise said, flipping her hair back.

"No, can you wait, actually?" Oz asked, following her out the door. "I've been meaning to talk to you about something…"

Isabel rolled her eyes. "Well, this is going to be weird," she said to herself, turning around and making her way for the bar. The fruit looked nothing but ravishing, but Isabel didn't care to touch them. She knew that filling herself up with food would do nothing for the kind of hunger that was clawing its way up inside her. Suddenly she caught a whiff of Oz lingering in the air of her room. Instantly, she felt a current rush through her. "Oh, come back, already!" she yelled, stomping her feet.

"What was that?" Oz asked, popping his head in through the inched open door.

"Nothing," Isabel said, turning away.

Oz crept inside and closed the door quietly behind him. "You know you want me," he hissed, stepping in closer and closer to her. Isabel could feel the heat boiling up inside of her.

"I've been waiting on you all day," she said. "Why did you leave me hanging like that?"

"Didn't I tell you?" he asked, his head cocked to the side. "It's all a part of your training." And then he paused,clearing his throat. "And besides, Gavin will be here, soon."

Isabel raised her eyes to Oz. His stare was boring into her, penetrating her utmost, deepest desires. She knew what he had in mind, and, even though she was ashamed to admit it, Isabel felt the exact same way. She wanted them both so bad, and she wanted them both at the same time. "I can't wait," she said, smiling against his lips.

CHAPTER 3

Isabel woke up to the sound of birds chirping outside. She opened her eyes and blinked repeatedly, the room swimming in and out of focus. The light bounced off the gold-plated furniture, the rhinestones and the mirrored walls, illuminating the entire room. Isabel stretched out and rolled over, her eyes roaming over Oz's naked body as it shimmered in the light. His skin was so pale it looked like porcelain. She pulled the covers up to her chin, the chill in the weather making her entire body shiver. "Hey," she said, stroking Oz's cheek with the back of her hand.

"Hey," he said, opening his eyes. "Oh, it's too bright in here, could you maybe draw the curtains, Isabel?"

"Alright," she said, throwing her feet off the side of the bed. "I had fun last night."

"Oh, we're just getting started," he said throwing the covers off and clasping his hands behind his head. "We're going to go out into the city tonight," he said, eyeing Isabel as she skipped back in his direction.

"Oh, I'm excited," she said, her lips coming to a smile. "What are we gonna do?"

"You don't have to worry about that right now," Oz said. "All I want you to do is to kick back…" He leaned in close to her and pressed his lips to hers. "And relax."

The hunger was gnawing at Isabel, even more than before. "I'm looking forward to that," she breathed against his lips.

"But you gotta know something," Oz said, suddenly serious. "Whoever you choose to mingle with, you don't get to feed on them, ever."

Isabel nodded. "I know, and I'm okay with that," she said. "Is your back feeling better now?"

"It's a bit better, look, my wings are already growing back," he said, rolling over on his stomach.

Isabel squinted at the feathery trails running down Oz's back. "Are they supposed to be this black at the roots?" she asked.

"Yeah, it's just some clotted blood," he said. "When they grow out, they turn gold again."

"Do they still hurt?" she asked, her eyebrows furrowed.

"Like hell," he said with a smirk.

***

Isabel heard a knock at her door. "Who is it?" she asked. But there was no answer. She walked over to the door. *Please, God, let it not be Aden.* "Oh my God," she gasped. "Gavin!"

"Hey, Izzy," he said, wrapping his arms around her. "I see you've coped with being naked 24/7," he teased, spanking her lightly.

"Oh, don't do that," she said, turning around and walking to the bar. "Do you want something to drink?"

"Thanks," he said. "I just dropped by to check up on you. I heard Oz took really good care of you last night."

"As always," Isabel smiled. "I'm still trying to get used to the whole exile thing, though."

"Exile?" Gavin asked, almost offended. "Isabel, you're here because you deserve to live a good life; you're here because you're special."

"And I believe you," she said, undoing her braid so her thick curls were left unbound to tumble down to her waist. "You sure you don't want anything?"

"I do want one thing," he said, his eyes fixated on hers. He placed one hand on her hip and the other behind her back, and then he smoothed his way up the length of her spine. "You've got goose bumps, that's a good sign," he smiled.

"I'm always hungry for you," Isabel whispered. She could feel that jolt of arousal course through her again, so she tilted her head sideways and worked her way down Gavin's neck.

"Nuh-uh-uh," he said, cocking his head away from her. Isabel just stared at him, confused.

"We're going to have to wait until Oz is here," he said, a smug look on his face. Isabel rolled her eyes.

"Did you just bring me here to torture me?" she asked, her face drooping into a scowl.

"Don't say that," Gavin said, brushing a hand through her hair. "Your hunger is a good sign, it means your transformation is basically complete."

"Well, what if I don't want to wait until Oz is here?" she asked, grazing at the base of Gavin's scalp with her nails.

"You're practicing your abilities on me... not the smartest choice, Isabel," he said. "You'll never be able to control me, although you can try."

Isabel let out a sigh of frustration. She turned around and crawled under the sheets again. "I want to be alone right now," she said. A part of her was starting to wonder if she'll ever be free again. It was true that both Oz and Gavin were giving her what she wanted— her life depended on it— but what she didn't understand was why Gavin was holding back. She had been fantasizing about him ever since she got here, and having him pull away from her like that was torturous, even humiliating.

"Don't be like that," Gavin said, sitting down next to her. "Tonight, we're taking you out. You're going to see all the sights of Paris, all the clubs, all the nightlife. You're never going to want to go back home again." Isabel rolled over to her side and buried her face in her pillow. As soon as she caught Oz's scent in the satin pillowcases, she held back, getting up and making her way for the door.

"I know, I believe you," she said. "Now, if you don't mind, I'd like to take a shower now."

"Alright," Gavin smirked. "I understand your frustration, but it's only necessary. There has to be a balance," he said. "I'll see you soon, Isabel."

She nodded at him and then slammed the door shut. *Why's he doing this to me? And what's wrong with me? I've become a monster!* The truth was, she couldn't control herself anymore. It was like she was starving. Isabel was starting to think this was all one big game, a game of control. Her head was pounding, and she could feel a trickling sensation between her legs. She clutched her stomach with her hands, and then she worked her way down, her fingers dancing around her pelvis. "This is torture," she said out loud. Suddenly, there was another knock at her door. *Oz?*

She rushed over and found Aden standing in the doorway, a tray in his hands. "I brought you some coffee," he said.

"Come here," Isabel said, snatching the tray from him and setting it aside. "Shut the door behind you."

"Okay," he said, eyeing her as she undid her robe and let it drop at her feet. He stepped closer to her, his lips curving to a smile. Isabel couldn't wait any longer. She brushed a hand through his hair and pressed her lips to his. He wrapped both arms around her waist, pressing her up against him. Suddenly, the door swung open, and Isabel bounced back, instinctively picking her robe off the floor and throwing it back on.

"Isabel!" Analise exclaimed. "Aden, mind if I had a word with her?" she asked, nodding towards the door.

"No, not at all," he said, a smile plastered on his face. "I'll be back with your breakfast shortly." He pursed his lips and then turned to leave, and Isabel was left standing there, humiliated.

"Isabel, what did Gavin and Oz tell you about feeding on other people at the mansion?" she asked, her head cocked to the side. A kind of Cheshire cat grin was tugging at the corners of her mouth, and she spoke to Isabel in a way that could only be described as patronizing. "Isabel," she said again. "I won't tell Gavin any of this, only if you promise it will never happen again."

"They're letting me starve," she said. "I'm in pain."

"It's a test for you," she said. "It'll all pay off eventually."

Isabel nodded, but deep down, she wasn't convinced. "I can't wait for tonight," she said, falling back onto her bed.

"Oh, it's going to be quite interesting, for all of us."

***

Isabel was told to be ready by nine. She had a walk-in closet now, one that Oz had filled up with all the clothes he had bought her. Isabel had spent a good two hours trying to decide what to wear before finally settling on a shimmery champagne colored mini dress and a pair of matte crimson red pumps. "I look like a definite slut," she said to herself, twirling around in front of the mirror. "An elegant slut, that is." Isabel was starting to get used to looking at her own reflection and not being dumbfounded. And the truth was, it felt great. She had been waiting to go out for the past couple of days, and right now, all she wanted was for either Gavin or Oz to show up at her doorstep and take her away. She opened up her drawer and took out a bottle of foundation, squirting out a little bit of the latte colored lotion onto the back of her hand. "Gotta look a bit tanned tonight," she smiled to herself, spreading it all over her face and neck. She took out her blender and smoothed it over her face, adding just a little bit of highlighter to bring out her contoured cheekbones. "And just a little bit of perfume," she muttered, sprayed a little bit from the

Chanel no. 5 bottle Oz had bought her. "Alright, I'm ready to go."

Isabel made her way back into her room, sitting down over the edge of the bed and smoothing out the sheets with her hand. The door creaked open and she turned around, only to find Oz standing there, a smile on his face. "You look stunning," he said. "Have you had anything to eat this morning?"

Isabel nodded. "I'm starving though," she said, rather shamelessly.

Oz looked at her knowingly. "Just hold on a little longer," he said. "Tonight, everything falls into place."

"Alright," Isabel said. "Where will you take me?"

"We'll start off at the Eiffel tower, and then Gavin and I will take you to the underground scene."

Underground? "And by that, you mean?"

"Just some clubs, where you can meet new people," Oz said, nodding towards the door. "Now, let's go, the car's waiting for us outside."

Isabel nodded, throwing a black fur coat on and following Oz down the stairs that seemed to spiral forever. As excited as she was to "meet new people", as vague as that sounded, she was mostly looking forward to what Gavin and Oz had in store for her. Her mind kept going back to how hungry she was, but she decided she wasn't going to beg anymore. She trusted them, after all, despite their inexplicable behavior. "Oops, sorry," Isabel said, stumbling a few feet backwards. She had bumped into someone or something on her way down, and when she raised her eyes to look at who it was, she saw a black-haired girl with ashen porcelain skin, staring back at her.

"That's okay," the girl said. "Have I seen you around before?" A sudden wave of silence broke over the three of them. Isabel opened her mouth to speak, but when she realized the brunette wasn't paying attention to her anymore, she let her words slip back into her throat. " Never mind," the black-haired succubus said, shifting in her place for a bit before she squeezed past them, her head ducked down and her eyes fixated on the floorboards. Isabel was stopped dead in her tracks, staring at the back of her head as she floated down the stairs.

"What's wrong with her?" Isabel asked, hoping Oz could answer her. She couldn't see his face but she could tell he was smiling.

"She's just a troubled young girl," he said, almost to himself. Isabel shrugged, following Oz out into the courtyard.

That girl sure did look terrified. It was like Oz's presence threw her off balance, and she just ran off. Isabel ducked her head down and slid into the limo, only to find Analise sitting there, grinning.

"Good evening, Isabel," she said, patting the cushion next to her. "Come, have a seat. You're in for a wild ride."

***

As always, Isabel didn't get IDed when she walked into the club. In a way, she felt like she was in her element again. So many people dancing everywhere, flashing fluorescent lights, music blasting from the speakers. Gavin and Oz walked by her side, almost like bodyguards. "So, what are we doing here again?" she asked, turning to Oz.

"Well, there are lots of humans in here, as you can see," he said with a smile. "Gavin and I are looking to… recruit them."

"Recruit them?" Isabel asked, her eyebrows furrowed. "I thought only succubi and incubi were getting recruited?"

"Yes, and?" Oz asked, his eyes darting from Gavin, to hers, and then to Gavin again. Something about the way they were glancing at each other made Isabel uncomfortable. It was like they knew something she didn't. "Isabel," Oz started again. "How did we make you?"

Isabel wasn't sure if that was a trick question. "I had sex with the two of you in one night," she said.

"That sounded more like a question than an answer," Gavin said, amused.

"Just tell me what's going on, put me out of my misery," Isabel said, turning on her heel to meet Gavin's gaze.

"Well," Oz started. "We want to create more succubi, and we're going to start by tonight."

Isabel was stopped dead in her tracks. For a second, she couldn't really process what was being said to her. "So, what you're saying is that you're going to try and hook up with more people tonight?" she asked, her eyes darting frantically.

She could barely hear them over the sound of house music blasting in the background, but she was adamant she must know the answer. Isabel never really liked to admit it, but she was growing a true connection to not just one, but both of them. She didn't really want to see them sleeping around with someone else.

Oz nodded. "It's kind of our job, at this point," he said, rather coldly. "You understand that, don't you, Isabel? It's not like we want to do this, it's just the only way we could recruit more succubi to our cause.

"You know what, no, I don't understand," she said, stomping her foot against the floor. "You've been starving me all day, and now you want to go out hunting for other people to feed on while I stay behind?!" Isabel was so angry, she could feel the hunger eating her alive. She didn't know whether she really was developing an emotional connection with them, or if this was just the instinct talking. All she knew was that she really needed to feed on someone, even if that meant going up to a random person at a club in Paris.

Oz reached his hand out to Isabel. "Listen to me," he said. "You remember why you're here, don't you?" Isabel didn't answer. "We're here to summon as many of our kind as we can. To come together, as succubi, incubi and angels to beat the vampires at their own game. You remember that, Isabel, don't you?"

She paused for a second then, feeling Oz's eyes bore into her, looked away. "But I'm starving," she said again. Suddenly she could feel the power surge through her. It was such a foreign feeling to her, this feeling of utter and completely control; it was her instinct, manifesting itself in the form of unbreakable determination. She met Oz's gaze and held it, focusing all her abilities on trying to get him to give her what she wanted. He stared back at her, not blinking, and for a moment Isabel thought she had him like a ring around her finger. She smiled at him and tilted her head to the side. "So, Oz, are you going to feed me or no?"

Oz was caught in a trance. His hands were balled up into fists at first, but then they fell limp to his sides. His lips were slightly parted, like he was about to say something, but they were frozen that way. It was like Isabel had cast some sort of a spell on him. Gavin reached out and placed a hand on his shoulder, and then suddenly, Oz jumped. "Whoa, there," he said, his lips curving upwards. He let out a giggle, and then his giggle turned into uncontrollable laughter. Isabel shook her head, unable to absorb what was happening. Had Oz gone mad? "You think you can control me?!" he asked, his pearly teeth showing through his smile. "Isabel, my love, you're still a young succubus! You haven't mastered the skills to control vampires... or angels."

Isabel rolled her eyes. She was starting to hate him, little by little. But she knew she couldn't. It was like Oz had her on a leash, and it was hard to get away. She could feel his eyes piercing into her again, like they were infiltrating her consciousness, her deepest utmost desires. She knew what she wanted, but she still wasn't so brave to go out and get it. "This is all fun and games to you, isn't it?" she asked, folding both arms across her chest. "Anyway, just go out and do what you have to do... I'll be around, I guess."

"This is a test for you, Izzy," Gavin said, leaning in close to her, his face only inches from hers. "You're going to go out there and mingle, with the promise of not feeding on anyone else here. Now, if you'll excuse us, we've got some hunting to do... and soon, those people will be our allies."

Isabel nodded, as always. "This is going to be a long night," she thought.

As the night dragged on, Isabel was getting increasingly more drunk. She had been sitting by the bar for almost two hours now, reminding her more and more of what her life had looked like before she turned into a succubus. Except she was in Paris. A lot of men (and women) had tried to make advances on her, but the truth was, she was too drunk to respond. In her mind's eye, she knew she couldn't feed on any of those people, so what was the point? She was growing weaker by the second: her body felt like it might dismantle at any point. In a way, it felt like she was dying.

"Oh my God, what the fuck?" she heard a voice say from across the dance floor. Despite the loud music, Isabel could still hear the woman's shriek. She looked over to identify the source of the sound, and then her eyes landed on a pair of swinging doors that led to the bathroom. A red-headed woman had barged outside, pulling her coat together and throwing her handbag over her shoulder. She was holding onto her side, as though she was in pain, but despite her high-pitched shriek that seemed to echo all across the club, no one really paid her much attention. Isabel followed the woman outside.

"Oh my God, oh my God," the woman muttered to herself, fumbling with her phone. "Hello??" she yelled into her phone. "Amelie, you won't believe what just happened." Isabel smiled at how convenient it was that she was speaking in a language she could understand. "I'm pretty shitfaced right now," the woman said, slumping down on the sidewalk. "I met this really attractive guy, you won't believe how hot he was, but anyway, he lured me into the bathroom... it was pretty empty, and then we got into the stall and made out for a while... then it got more intense and the next thing I knew we're helping each other out of our clothes." She paused for a moment, cradling the phone to her ear. "And then he pushed me up against the wall and started kissing me... then."

Isabel moved even closer. *Stop eavesdropping, Izzy,* she thought to herself. Her inner voice was starting to sound a lot like Gavin. She shook her head, trying not to let her curiosity get the best of her, but there was something about that woman, something that made Isabel eager to know what she had to say.

"He was on his knees," the redhead said, her hand flying to her mouth. She was louder than anything else, and soon enough, Isabel didn't even need to eavesdrop. "And then, oh my God, Amelie, he looked up at me, and I swear, his eyes were red."

She flipped her hair to the side and started fumbling with her earring. "No, not bloodshot, just red! The whites of his eyes... and that's not even the worst part." She placed a hand on her hip again, this time, clenching her eyes. "Amelia, I don't know what kind of freaky shit he's into, but he bit me and I think I'm bleeding."

Isabel felt her heart skip a beat. She had to move in closer to make sure she heard right. "He fucking bit me, Amelia! It's not even funny... I think I'm gonna go to a doctor... well, not now, but first thing in the morning."

No, it couldn't be. But no matter how much she tried to dispel the thought, it was still nagging at her, and she had no choice but to believe it. Suddenly it all came back to her. It was true that Isabel was pretty drunk, but she had one hell of a photographic memory. That woman didn't run out of that bathroom alone. Isabel closed her eyes, and what she saw terrified her. Those broad shoulders, that stiff gait. In her mind's eye Isabel could see Oz staggering out of that bathroom stall, his hands stuffed into his pockets. "Oz? No, that can't be," Isabel said out-loud. She wanted to lie to herself that it wasn't him she saw coming out of that stall. She closed her eyes again but it was still him. What did he have to do with the bite marks on that girl's hip? Isabel needed some answers. Was Oz responsible for this? And if he was, since when did angels dig their fangs into other people? Since when did angels have fangs? "Goddammit!" She looked around and a couple of people outside the club were staring at her. "Great, now they think I'm crazy," she said again. She reached into the pocket of her coat and pulled out her cigarette pack. "It's been a long time." Suddenly Isabel felt uneasy, like something was nagging her to go back inside and confront Oz. She tried to resist the urge, but then the feeling got the best of her, and she broke the cigarette in half and crushed it in her hand. *Alright, I'm going back in there.*

CHAPTER 4

Isabel walked back in through the revolving doors. She looked around, her eyes scanning the place. It looked as though it had gotten darker somehow, and she cursed under her breath, squinting her way past the pivoting neon lights. "Where the fuck did he go?" she asked herself. She squeezed past the sweaty bodies gyrating on the dancefloor, only to find Gavin seated at the bar. He had been talking to a beautiful young woman with short raven black hair, and when his eyes met Isabel's, he flashed her a wide grin.

"Izzy!" he said. "Where have you been?"

"Where's Oz?" she yelled over the music.

"I don't know, he bumped into a pretty good looking girl over there, though," he said, pointing towards the swinging doors.

Isabel could feel the anger boiling up inside her. She felt like a clueless little child. Why did they drag her all the way over here if they were going to just release her in the midst of a drunken, good looking crowd? She had hoped they would give her what she wanted—

just like every time— but this time, they left her hanging. They just wanted to see how much she could take. "What did the girl look like?" she asked.

"I don't really know," Gavin shrugged. Isabel looked away. She was starting to feel ashamed again, ashamed of her instincts that were now so strong, so profound that they were driving her insane. "Isabel," Gavin said, getting off the bar stool. "I promise you, this will all be over in a couple of hours, and then everything will go back to the way it was."

"Hold on," Isabel said, catching a glimpse of Oz barging out of the club. "Oz, hold up!"

"Isabel, come join me for a smoke," he said, pulling out a pack of cigarettes and handing it to her.

"I've got my own, thanks," she said, turning away. The two of them stood side by side, Isabel trying to resist the urge to blow up in his face. The truth was, she felt like she could blow up in anybody's face, at this point. "I overhead this girl talking on the phone," she started. "She was sitting right there, and she was talking about-"

"Let's go back inside," Oz interrupted her. "I think we've kept you waiting for long enough." He took a couple of drags from his cigarette then threw it away. "Come on, follow me."

Isabel rolled her eyes and followed him back inside. This entire night had been a rollercoaster for her, and at that point, all she wanted was to end it on a high note. She knew Gavin and Oz wouldn't leave her to starve, but right now, it sure felt like it. She could feel the heat rising up inside of her like flames, and with every step she took, with every moment of eye contact she had with a random stranger, she could feel her core pulsate with sheer animalistic desire.

At that point the place was full of theatrical fog, and Isabel had a hard time seeing in front of her. The lights were shining through the dust particles in the air, and through the haze she could make out the back of Gavin's head. He was seated at the same spot, but this time, he was talking to a different girl. *How many girls was he planning on fucking tonight?* Isabel thought about asking if the two of them had succeeded in having sex with the same girl, but she figured she was going to find out anyway.

"Gavin," Oz said, placing a hand on his shoulder. Gavin turned to look at him, and when the two of them locked eyes, he rose to his feet, motioning for Isabel to follow them.

"Where are we going?" she asked, pushing her way through the people on the dancefloor. She was pretty drunk herself, and the truth was, she hated every second of it. This was nothing like the old days. It was like she was stranded. There she was, feeling lost in the middle of a club in Paris, and although her teenage self would've loved that, Isabel pretty much felt like the world was spinning around her. And not in a good way.

Gavin and Oz stopped at a red velvet curtain next to the swinging doors. Gavin stepped in first, and then Oz followed, the two of them hurrying down a long-hidden corridor. "We've booked a VIP lounge," Gavin said. "Just for the three of us."

Isabel felt her heart drop to her knees. She could feel that surge of energy surge through her for the millionth time that night. Were they finally going to give her what she needed? Gavin stopped at a red painted door at the very end of the hallway. He reached into the pocket of his jacket and took out a copper plated key, which he used to unlock the glossy looking door. "Oh," Isabel said, her eyes landing on the black leather couches inside. The lighting was dim with a bit of a warm feel to it. The music outside had boiled down to nothing but a dull, distant thud. "It smells like jasmine and liquor in here," she said, brushing a hand through her hair. "I need to be sober for this." She walked over to the bar and grabbed a water bottle, popping the lid off and chugging it all in one gulp.

"We're going to take care of that," Gavin said, slamming the door behind them. Isabel looked over and the two of them were staring at her hungrily. "Take it off," Gavin whispered, stepping closer to her. Instantly, Isabel could feel herself getting wet. She had been waiting so long for this, and when she finally found herself locked up with the two men she had been craving all day, it felt like time had stopped.

"What do you want me to do?" Isabel asked, raising an eyebrow at Gavin.

"Take it off," Oz said, coming up from behind her. The thought of being in a threesome had been hanging at the back of Isabel's mind for so long now, but she never thought it would actually happen. A million thoughts were racing through her mind, a part of her wondering if she could even handle it.

"Okay," she said, throwing off her stilettos. "I can't reach my zipper; will you help me?"

"You don't need that now," Oz said, smiling at Gavin. The angel placed both his hands on her shoulders and forced her down onto her knees, her line of sight directly at Gavin's crotch.

"You've been wanting this, haven't you?" Gavin whispered, gently rubbing a thumb against Isabel's cheek as her hands began to unbuckle him. She nodded, not saying a word, and worked his zipper. "Both of us, feeding you?"

Isabel pulled his pants down, reaching into his briefs quickly and pulling his hard cock out. Before she could do any more, Gavin grabbed her by the chin and lifted her so that she was looking directly into his eyes.

"Say it!" he said.

"I've wanted this so bad," Isabel quickly replied, trying to pull from his grip, but he held her fast. "I've wanted both of you. Now. Here."

Gavin chuckled and looked over at the angel. "I believe she's getting better at this," he said.

Oz grabbed Isabel by the hair and pulled her head back, but she kept her grip firmly on Gavin, stroking him. "There is so much we're going to do to you, Isabel," he said. "So much."

He let go of her, and Isabel immediately went for Gavin's cock, swallowing him into her mouth as deep as she could take him. His hand clutched her hair, and as her tongue swirled around his shaft, he began to move against her. He slid in and out, slow at first, then quicker, pushing his cock deeper down her throat.

"Look at me," he ordered, and Isabel's eyes shot up to his as he rocked his hips against her. She reached out and grabbed his ass, squeezing his cheeks, urging him deeper into her mouth. When he pulled out, she gasped for air, but kept her grip on him. Isabel leaned in, licking his shaft, her tongue flicking at the tip before she took him in again. She wanted more, so much more, and she quickly pulled her dress up around her waist to reveal her ass to Oz.

The angel bent down and smacked her, a quick slap that made her flinch and whimper in delight. She shook her ass at him, and moaned when his fingers reached around and into her panties, slipping between her pussy lips and into her wetness.

"She's ready," Oz said with a chuckle as his fingers continued playing, rubbing at her clit. She began to move against him, and when he slipped his fingers inside her, Gavin's cock slipped out of her mouth as she cried out in pleasure.

Gavin grabbed her head again and brought her forward, pushing back inside her mouth, rocking against her with faster and deeper thrusts. She felt like he was going to tear her throat apart, but when she looked up at his face and saw the way his eyes rolled back in ecstasy, she began to suck on him harder. Oz continued his assault on her pussy, and Isabel quickly succumbed to the orgasm that rocked through her body and sent shivers up and down her spine.

Gavin clutched her fiercely, and she braced herself as he exploded inside her mouth, filling her while she desperately tried to swallow it all. She squeezed his shaft, milking him for everything he had, wanting it all.

Oz pulled her away and guided her to the couch, quickly undressing and sitting down where she could suck him off next. Isabel didn't hesitate, scratching his thighs with her nails as she ran her tongue up from his balls to the tip, then took him in. The angel groaned as she began to work him, her hand pumping while she sucked.

She felt Gavin's hands on her ass, and with a quick motion, her panties were pulled down to her knees. "You want this, don't you, Isabel?"

Isabel only moaned, too busy pleasuring Oz, his cock deep in her mouth.

"Say it," Gavin ordered, and with surprising ease, tore her panties off and tossed them onto the couch next to Oz. "Tell me how much you want me to fuck you!"

Isabel pulled Oz's cock out of her mouth and looked over her shoulder, pushing her ass higher against Gavin's cock. He felt like stone against her, and in her mid, she already felt him tearing her apart from inside.

"Fuck me," she pleaded. "Fuck me, Gavin. Please just do it!"

Gavin's lips curled up in a wicked smile, and Isabel screamed out as he thrust his cock inside her with one quick motion. She grasped Oz's thighs hard, her nails digging into his skin as Gavin pummeled her, slamming against her harder and faster with every thrust, filling her and pushing against parts of her she never thought could be reached. Shocks of pleasure shot through her body, and she began to shake as he moved, shuddering with every thrust, her moans echoing across the room.

Oz grabbed her by the hair and brought her back to his cock, bucking his hips and sliding into her mouth, forcing her head up and down as Gavin continued from behind. Isabel felt like her entire body would explode with ecstasy, the feeling of two cocks inside her at the same time sending waves of unbridled madness through her. She was about to pull Oz out when she felt the twitch of his cock in her mouth, and he grabbed her by the head as he exploded, his groans rocking through the room.

His cock slid out of her mouth, his juices dripping down her lips and chin as Gavin slammed against her, rocking hard. Her eyes rolled back in their sockets, her mind overwhelmed by the sensations she was feeling all at once. Oz lifted her by the chin, gazing into her eyes with a satisfied smile and wiped his juices off her lips with her own panties. He was still hard, and she whimpered at the thought of having more of him, more of both of them.

Isabel's head snapped around in protest when Gavin pulled out. "Ride him!" he ordered, but she didn't need coaxing. As soon as the words were out of his mouth, she was on her feet and straddling Oz. She guided the tip of him to her wetness, rubbing it against her, and then slid down on top of him. She threw her head back at the feel of him inside her, and hardly noticed as Gavin unzipped her dress and pulled it over her head.

She began to grind, hard, fast, reveling in the feeling of him inside her and his strong hands against her waist. She leaned forward, presenting her breasts to him, and wrapped her arms around his head as he sucked her nipples and squeezed her ass. He began rocking her against him, and soon she was moving in quick up and down motions against his cock, in a full daze at how incredible he felt.

"Fuck him harder, Isabel," Gavin ordered from behind her, his fingers lightly caressing up and down her spine. "Show him how much you've been wanting this."

Isabel did as she was told, soon bouncing up and down on Oz's cock as he devoured one breast and then the other, sending bolts of pleasure through her body. She felt his hand snake down between her legs, and she screamed in pleasure when he found her clit. She grinded, his finger manipulating her until she was shaking and screaming in orgasm, before collapsing on top of him. He wouldn't let her stop, though, buckling up against her, harder and faster until she felt his entire body stiffen against her and his hot-gush of juices shoot out inside her.

Isabel didn't move. Her arms wrapped around Oz as she gasped for breath, her heart thumping like a rollercoaster against her chest. For the briefest of moments, she felt the world around her swim in and out of focus, as if at any moment she would drift away, satisfied and fulfilled. Still, a part of her wanted more, an inexplicable need and thirst that needed quenching, and she squealed in pleasure when Gavin pulled her off of the angel and threw her onto her back on the couch.

"We're not quite done yet," he growled, and Isabel couldn't have hoped for anything more.

He climbed on top of her, and she reached for his hard cock, stroking it as he looked into her half-shut eyes.

"Have you had enough, Isabel?" he teased.

"Never," Isabel managed between breaths, and she lifted her hips, pushing him deep inside her. She gasped as he filled her, stretching her out, and she wondered if seeing her riding Oz had turned him on so much that he had actually grown harder.

"That's exactly what I wanted to hear!" Gavin said, pulling out and then slamming into her again. Isabel wrapped her legs around him as he began to move against her, feeling every inch of him inside her, pushing against her, harder, faster. She rocked against him as he grabbed both her wrists over her head, his breaths hot against her neck, his other hand squeezing one breast before pinching the nipple and moving to the next. She was riding a high, every inch of her body tingling in pleasure as he moved.

"Tell him how much you love it, Isabel," Oz's voice came hoarsely from somewhere behind her.

"I love it!" Isabel screamed. "Fuck me, Gavin. Don't stop!"

Gavin growled, a deep rumbling from the back of his throat that only served to turn her on even more. Isabel felt like he would tear her apart with his thrusts, deep and hard, slamming into her with enough strength to send her into a frenzy of moans and screams. She didn't want him to stop. She wanted this to continue forever. She wanted more and more, and her thirst for it drove her mind into havoc.

Suddenly, Gavin tensed against her, pushing deep as he let go of her hands and grabbed her waist. Her hands grappled the sides of the couch as she steadied herself with her feet, pushing her hips up against him, forcing him in deeper as he exploded inside her. She felt her own body break into a series of shudders as her own orgasm burst through her, her screams muffled as she bit down hard on her arm.

Her hips fell onto the couch as Gavin pulled out of her and climbed off, and she immediately rolled onto her side. Her head was spinning, and as she closed her eyes, she fell into a deep abyss of blissful darkness, a satisfied smile on her face.

CHAPTER 5

Isabel opened her eyes and rolled over on her side. She stretched her body out and smoothed her hand over the bedsheets, feeling for Gavin's presence. The sheets were cold, and when she opened her eyes he wasn't there. She had spent an amazing time with him last night, and today was Oz's day. She was getting used to the whole alternating thing, and the truth was, she felt like her transformation was complete. She was more confident than ever; day by day, she felt like she was growing more powerful, more capable of controlling men's minds. She had noticed that the people in the mansion were multiplying, and she wondered if this was all the making of Gavin and Oz's late night endeavors. She had bumped into some attractive men and women, but she wasn't as tempted as she used to be. For now, either Gavin or Oz was enough for her, even better if it were both of them at once.

Isabel threw her feet off the side of the bed and just sat there for a few moments, brushing her fingers through her hair. It had grown longer, more luscious than it used to be. In a way, it felt like she had reached the peak of her beauty, with her breasts growing just a little bit larger and her waist getting just a tiny bit smaller over the past few days. Her hair was down to her hips, and she had grown used to having a long, cascading side braid that touched up on her breast and fell free at her stomach.

"Alright, let's get this day started," she said as she dusted herself off and stepped out into the corridor.

She hurried down the spiral staircase, the train of her dress floating behind her. "Good morning," she said to Analise on her way down. Isabel had gotten used to life at the mansion. It had only been a couple of weeks, but she had already gotten to know the people. She had come across a bunch of unfamiliar faces on the way, and she made a mental note to ask Analise who they were the next time she saw her. Tonight, Gavin and Oz had promised her a threesome, and she couldn't wait. The whole thing never seemed to lose its luster—Isabel figured it was just a product of mind control— but she didn't really mind it. She was having the best sex of her life with two of the most attractive men at the mansion; she wasn't complaining. The temptation to feed on other men was almost completely gone, and that had the power to both comfort and terrify her.

Just as Isabel was about to barge into the kitchen, she felt something tugging at the sleeve of her dress. "Yes?" she said, turning around. Suddenly she felt an unsettling feeling in her stomach. The woman tugging at her dress looked familiar. She had red hair, freckles, and wore a long-sleeved dress like her. *The girl from the club.*

"Can we have a moment in private?" the woman asked, her eyes wide. Isabel wasn't sure whether she should be scared or just roll with it. She definitely recognized the girl, but somehow, she looked different to when she had seen her outside the club. Her skin was paler, looking almost like porcelain, her hair had grown longer and her lips were extremely chapped. Isabel wondered if they were keeping her well-fed, because according to her own experiences, succubi weren't supposed to look like that.

"Sure," Isabel nodded, following her down the hall. The woman hurried past several rooms, looking right and left, before she stopped at one of them, dusting herself off before walking inside. She popped her head out the inched open door and cocked it to the side, motioning for Isabel to come in. Isabel hesitated for a moment, but then she remembered; no one could hurt her. Hell, she was the most powerful succubus in this mansion. She lifted her dress off the floor and walked inside, taking a seat at the makeup table. "What's wrong?" she asked, raising her eyes to the woman. There was something about the look in her eyes that was more fearful than anything else.

"My name is Ava," she said, her voice trembling. "I'm not sure why I'm here, but they brought me here... and I don't feel like myself." She paused for a moment, looking around her. Isabel watched as she paced the room back and forth. She was obviously confused. Her hands were balled up into fists, and when she seemed to have caught her own reflection in the mirror, she sprung back. "Can you help me?"

Isabel rose to her feet. A part of her didn't have a good feeling about this at all. "Listen, who took you and why?" she asked, her eyebrows furrowed.

"I... I don't remember," Ava said. "The last thing I remember is waking up and not recognizing myself in the mirror, and then I was told to come here."

"Who told you to come here?" Isabel asked. But she had a pretty good idea of who it was.

"This man," Ava said. "I don't remember what he looks like, but if I saw him I'd recognize him."

"Listen, Ava," Isabel said, her eyes fixated on hers. "Do you remember meeting that same man who told you to come here at a club, just a couple of weeks ago?"

Ava paused for a bit. Suddenly, her hand flew to her mouth, like she had just remembered something. "Oh my God, yes, I... I remember." Isabel watched her go through a chain reaction of realizations in her head. At one point, she was mouthing some things to herself, and Isabel couldn't wait, apprehensive as she was, to get something out of her.

"That man, Ava, what did he do?" she asked.

"I remember," the redhead said. "We hooked up in the bathroom stall of the club that night... I haven't been feeling well ever since."

"Did he do anything unusual?" Isabel asked.

"Actually," Ava said. "He... he bit me."

"He bit you?"

"He bit me. I remember I was really drunk that night, but the next day, I had bite marks on my right hip and it was bleeding."

Isabel couldn't believe what she was hearing. She just needed one more tiny detail to confirm her doubts. "And that man, are you sure you don't remember what he looked like?" she asked, hoping against hope that Ava would have something else to say.

She shook her head. "No, I don't quite remember what he looked like... but I do remember he was quite broad across the shoulders."

Isabel pursed her lips. "Okay," she nodded. "I'm going to talk to Analise right now... she knows more about how this whole place operates than I do," she said.

"No, wait," Ava said. "Don't leave me here, I have no idea where I am and what brought me here."

Isabel started pacing the room. Her brain was on overdrive. If Oz was the person that woman hooked up with, then how the hell could she have ended up with those bite marks? "Ava," Isabel said again. "Did you hook up with anyone else on that same night?"

"No," she was quick to recall. "Just this one guy... that's the only detail I remember out of everything that happened that night. I remember because he was pretty handsome... I even went out to call my friend, to tell her all about it."

Holy fuck, it's really her! At the beginning, she wasn't certain it was the same woman she had seen slumped down on the sidewalk outside the club, but that little detail confirmed it. Only question was, where did the bite marks come from? Oz had some explaining to do. "I'm going to ask you one last question," Isabel said. "And I don't want to sound too intrusive or anything... but did you go all the way with him?" she asked.

"No," Ava said. "I stopped him the second he bit me... he didn't seem too bothered by it. I don't remember him being rude or anything."

"Alright," Isabel said, folding both arms across her chest. She didn't know what it was that was making her so uncomfortable. It was like she was missing a piece of the puzzle. One thing was for sure: she needed to have a little talk with Oz. And she needed to have it straight away. "I'm going to get to the bottom of this," she said, stepping closer to Ava and looking into her eyes. The woman looked significantly weaker than the last time she saw her. "I'm going to talk to the man you met that night, he might have some explaining to do."

"How do you know him?" Ava asked, her voice falling to a whisper.

For a while, Isabel didn't say anything. She didn't know whether she should come clean about this whole thing, or whether she should come up with a more convincing story. This was her life now; this was her reality. But a part of her still held onto that time when she couldn't bring herself to believe any of it. And she knew that, if she were to bombard Ava with all of this information at once, she was pretty likely to go insane. Isabel had a hard time believing that she didn't go crazy, herself. And she didn't really want to put anyone else through it. But first, she had to make sure who this woman was, and if she really did hook up with Oz that night. Isabel could feel the hunger gnawing at her again, but this time, it blended in with a feeling of jealousy, of contempt. In her head, Oz was hers, and she was his. He had become such an integral part of her everyday life that it was literally impossible to survive without him. The thought of him going around sleeping with other women made her sick to her stomach, and she didn't know why that was. Was it because she was secretly afraid she would starve if he didn't make time for her? Or was there something else? Was it something deeper, almost like a connection that she felt for him? Or was it all just a game of mind control? Isabel didn't even know anymore, and she figured that, if she wasn't sure herself, then she shouldn't be putting anyone else through it, either. "I know him from around here," Isabel said finally, trying to gather her thoughts. "Alright, Ava, do you want me to get you something to eat?" she asked.

"Yeah, I'm starving," Ava said. "But I don't want you to leave me here, if that's okay."

Isabel nodded. "Alright, I'll take you to the main kitchen downstairs," she said, reaching her hand out to Ava. "I don't want you to be afraid. I know it's confusing, but everything will fall into place, it's only a matter of time." The truth was, she didn't know what else to say. The girl looked completely petrified. Every now and again, she would turn to look at herself in the mirror. She would run her pointer finger along her jawline, brush a hand through her hair and then start stroking the side of her face with her thumb. She would move in closer, inspecting her now flawless skin, searching for any pimples, any blemishes, anything to remind her of the girl she once was. Isabel just stared at her, and all at once she was reminded of that dark time in her life, when she didn't even know who she was anymore. She wanted so desperately to tell Ava that it was pointless, that her body would never go back to the way it was. But she couldn't. She decided she was just going to let her figure it out on her own. They stepped out of the room, Isabel taking Ava's hand as they walked down the hall and hurried down the stairs. On her way down, Ava was scanning the sea of faces around her, desperate to make out a face she knew. But it was useless. She was never going to bump into someone she knew in a place like this.

"I'm not comfortable," she said, her voice trailing off.

"What?" Isabel asked, holding onto her hand. She could feel Ava stop dead in her tracks, and when she turned around, she found her completely petrified, like she had just seen a ghost. "What's wrong?" Isabel asked, her eyes darting back and forth frantically.

"Good morning," Oz said, appearing at the stairway. He had an unusual glow about him, like he had been expecting to see Isabel with Ava. "I see the two of you have met," he said with a smirk on his face.

"I... I want to get out of here," Ava said, turning away and trying to squeeze past the people behind her.

"No, no, wait," Isabel said, trying to grab hold of her wrist. The girl stumbled a few steps, almost falling to the floor, but then she rose to her feet again and hurried in the opposite direction back to her room. "What was that?" Isabel asked, turning to Oz. "What did you do to her?"

Oz stared at Isabel knowingly. "Doesn't she remind you of yourself not so long ago?" he asked, his pearly teeth showing through his smile. Isabel almost found it disturbing, but she nodded regardless.

"She does," she said. "But there's something different about her... and besides, she said she only hooked up with you."

Oz's face drooped to a scowl. Isabel could sense that he was taken aback. "She was drunk," he said, clenching his jaw. "I don't think she remembers much."

"But so was I when I first slept with you and Gavin," Isabel said, shaking her head. "I woke up the next day and I remembered everything." She paused for a second, clearing her throat. "Well, maybe not *everything*, but I was at least able to recall that I had slept with not one, but two men."

Oz let out a sigh. "Isabel," he said. "Not everyone is able to regain full recollection when they're sober. You, of all people, should know that."

"Yeah," Isabel said, shrugging. But she still wasn't convinced. Despite Oz's great ability to control her thoughts, there was something about the way Ava reacted to him that made Isabel's stomach churn. "So, has she began her transformation into a succubus? Does she need Analise to brief her on what's gonna happen? I don't want her— or anyone in this house— to go through this alone... it can be a very scary process," Isabel said, sighing.

"She's begun her transformation," Oz said. "I'm going to call Analise to sit with her, just like she sat with you, and she's going to explain everything to her."

"I can sit with her," Isabel said.

"No," Oz shook his head. "Analise will take care of it." There was a pause. Isabel wondered why he was being so secretive about this, but she didn't want to start a fight. After all, she was getting hungry, and although she hated that her life practically depended on two people, she realized she basically had no choice but to roll with it.

"Alright," she said, her eyes dropping to the floor. "I'll come back to check up on her, though. She seemed pretty distressed."

"You can do whatever you want, Isabel," Oz said. "This mansion is your safe place, you're free to interact with the people however way you wish." Isabel thought she would talk to Gavin about this, but until then, she was going to keep a close eye on this girl.

***

The mansion was starting to fill up with unfamiliar faces. When Isabel first moved in, there was probably half the number or people— or succubi— that there were now. But there was something different about them. Isabel couldn't quite put her finger on it, but the way they looked, the way they dealt with each other, was foreign to her. She hadn't seen Ava in a while, and for some reason, she couldn't stop thinking about her. That horrified look on her face when she saw Oz, the way she was so sure that she hadn't even slept with another man on that night. Isabel still wanted answers, and she still didn't know how to get them.

Isabel was just starting her day. As always, she took a shower, threw her silk robe on and walked downstairs, eager to find Gavin. She had been closer with Oz lately, and she was starting to crave Gavin's company. "Oh, hey," she said, bumping into Analise on her way down. "I kind of wanted to talk to you about something."

"Of course," she said. "Anything you need."

"Okay, well, it won't take too long, but there's a girl here, she's new I think, and she... I don't know how to describe it. She seems a little off."

Analise pursed her lips. "And who would that be?" she asked, her head cocked to the side. For a moment, Isabel hesitated. Analise looked flustered, like she had somewhere to be.

"Her name is Ava?" Isabel asked.

"Ah, Ava!" Analise said, her lips curving upwards. "She's new here, what about her?"

"I don't know, she looks kind of traumatized, to be honest."

Analise let out a sigh. "You know, sometimes, new succubi don't cope that well at first. You of all people should know that, Isabel," she said, her eyebrows furrowed.

"I, I know that, but she didn't seem to be coping the same way I did. Like, at all," Isabel said, shifting her weight to one leg. "I'd like you to sit down and talk to her, the same way you talked me through my transition."

Analise stared at her knowingly, and when Isabel didn't seem to move, she let out a sigh, a grin settling back on her face. "Alright," she said. "I'm going to talk to her, I promise you."

Isabel flashed Analise a sincere smile and then walked away. In the back of her mind, the fearful look in Ava's eyes lingered, and she made a promise to herself that she would get to the bottom of this.

CHAPTER 6

The newcomers were still rolling in. Not a day passed by without Isabel waking up to the sound of people moving into the rooms below. She had made a routine of jerking out of bed, rushing downstairs to see who it was, and being absolutely taken by how different they looked to everybody else. But soon enough, the newcomers were everybody else, or at least they seemed to have outnumbered the people who Isabel thought were everybody else. They all had pale, almost white, porcelain skin, long straight dark hair and bloodshot eyes. The more Isabel looked at them, the more she realized they all looked the same. She had asked Gavin about it time and time again, but he never seemed to give her a definite answer. "It's all a part of their transformation, it's like when you're still an infant and your skin has that purple tinge to it, it gets better over time," he would say to her. What Isabel was worrying about, though, was Oz. There was something different about him. She couldn't quite put her finger on it, but it almost seemed as if he shifted characters whenever he was with her. He had developed a nervous tick that emerged whenever the two of them had sex, one that made his neck jerk violently to the side. Something was off. She had tried talking to him about that, too, but he never really gave her an answer, either. Isabel was starting to think that maybe life at the mansion wasn't as easy or luxurious as she thought it was.

"Good morning," she said, strutting down the hallway to check on the newcomers. But no one answered her. For some reason, everyone looked like zombies: unresponsive, pale-skinned, almost catatonic. In the distance, Isabel caught a glimpse of Analise, so she ran to her. "Analise, hi," she said, faking a smile. "How are you?"

"I'm good," Analise said, not looking at Isabel. "Hey, hey, this window's sealed shut, stop trying to open it, you'll break it, please," she snapped, diverting her gaze to one of the newcomers. *Sealed windows? That's new,* Isabel thought to herself. It was like they were treating those succubi like animals. Analise had her arms folded across her chest, gawking at the newcomers as they unpacked their things. "Whoa, whoa, be careful, over there," she said again. "Sorry, Isabel, I'm a bit distracted right now, can I meet you later?"

"Sure," she said, her eyes dropping to the floor. She turned around to leave, and then she remembered Ava. "Well, it looks like I'm going to have to resort to someone else for answers," she said to herself.

Isabel knocked on Ava's door and it swung open. She raised her eyes to the person standing at the door, only to realize it wasn't Ava. "Hello," Isabel said, tilting her head sideways. "Is Ava there?"

A tall, curvaceous ginger haired girl stared back at her with glassy eyes. "Do I know you?" she asked, almost robotically.

"No," Isabel shook her head. "I thought this was Ava's room?"

"I'm not sure," the girl said, narrowing her eyes at Isabel. There was something about her that made Isabel's skin crawl. She paused for a second, her eyes fixated on the hallway, darting from one passerby to the other. "Oh," she said again. "You mean the redhead?"

"Yes, the redhead," Isabel nodded. "She used to live here?"

"They moved her to another room, I think," the girl said with a low voice. "She stirred up some problems."

"Problems?" Isabel asked, worried. "What kind of problems?"

"I don't know," the ginger replied, shaking her head frantically. "I don't know, don't ask me these questions or they'll do to me what they did to her."

"Who are you talking about and what would they do to you if you talked?" A million thoughts were racing through Isabel's mind. She wanted answers, and she wanted them now. Suddenly, the door slammed shut, and Isabel was left with nothing but more questions. She could've sworn she saw a pair of black wings protruding from the hem of the girl's dress, but she thought it was all in her head. She just stared at the closed door, her mind blowing up with alternate scenarios. Who was this girl? And what have they done to Ava? Who were "they" to begin with? Isabel stamped her foot and hurried down the other end of the hallway, determined to find Analise again, but when she got there, Analise was gone. "This is one big ass mansion," Isabel said to herself. There was little to no chance she was going to find Analise again on the same day.

Isabel turned around to leave, only to bump into Gavin. "Whoa, you're in a hurry," he said, his pearly teeth flashing through his smile.

Isabel opened her mouth but no words came out. She decided she wasn't going to say a thing. If she was going to get to the bottom of this, then she was going to do it herself. "Sorry about that," she said, the corners of her lips curving upwards. "I'm just kind of in a hurry."

"Well, I hope we're on for tonight?" Gavin asked, raising an eyebrow at her.

"Sure," Isabel said, patting him on the shoulder and then squeezing past him. "I'll catch you later."

Gavin didn't like this. He didn't like this one bit. For the first time, Isabel didn't display any signs of uncontrollable hunger, and neither did she show any enthusiasm at the mentioning of sex. Was she growing immune to Gavin's mind control? Were they doing something wrong? Gavin took in a deep breath and let it out through his teeth. Something was going horribly wrong. Isabel wasn't easily tamed anymore, and soon enough, she would be able to resist mind control if they didn't stop her. Something had to be done. Gavin waited until Isabel disappeared around the corner and then he went after her.

"Um, hi," Isabel said to one of the newcomers. He turned to her, his ashen skin almost glowing in the light. "I was wondering if you've seen Ava? She used to live on this floor," Isabel asked, her eyes fixated on his.

"No, I don't think so," he replied, fumbling with a pair of dice. Isabel peered into his room, catching a glimpse of a bunch of girls sitting on the bed with some sort of board game spread out in front of them. She smiled when one of them got up and popped her head out the door.

"Hello," she said. "I think I know who you're talking about."

"You do?" Isabel asked, her eyes lighting up. "Have you seen her recently?"

Immediately, the girl's face dropped to a scowl. She stepped outside, motioning for her roommate to leave the two of them alone, and then she slammed the door shut, her eyes searching Isabel's. "Listen," she said. "I didn't want to say anything, but they took Ava, I saw it happen in front of me."

"Who took her? And what did you see?" Isabel asked, her eyes darting back and forth frantically.

"Ava was acting up... she found out what they're doing to us, so she spoke up. And then this woman, I think her name was Analise, came and took her."

Isabel's heart skipped a beat. A part of her wanted to ask more questions, to listen till the girl was done talking, but something told her that the more she listened, the more confused she would get. This mansion was all she knew, all she lived for, and now things were changing. Something was happening, something hideous, and Isabel was scared to uncover what it was. "Where did they take her?" she asked beseechingly.

"I overheard Analise talking about the chambers," the girl said, her eyes dropping to the floor. "They took her there, she was kicking and screaming, and they took her there…"

"Hey," Isabel said, placing a hand over the girl's shoulder. "Do you know where the chambers are?"

She shook her head. "No, but there is speculation… some say they're underground, some say that only one room has access to them… I really have no idea." She paused for a moment, inspecting their surroundings. "But I want you to be careful," she hissed. "You don't want them taking you there, it's an ugly place, I hear."

Isabel nodded, and then the girl retreated back into her room and slammed the door shut. "What the fuck was that?" she muttered to herself, turning around and making her way for the stairs. She had been skeptical of what was going on for a long time now, but it was only when Ava went missing that Isabel truly start to believe that something was horribly, horribly wrong. As she hurried down the stairs, she caught a glimpse of

Analise again. Isabel could feel her feet carrying her to where Analise was going, and she found herself following in zigzags between hallways and tiny little corridors that Isabel has never seen before. She was pretty careful, though. Every now and then she would stop for a couple of seconds, waiting for Analise to disappear, and then she would start following her again. Analise was pretty quick. She flew down the last set of stairs, and then finally, she disappeared into a dark hallway with cement walls. Isabel stopped dead in her tracks. She looked around her; all she saw were cement walls, part bare wire, part red brick. It was almost pitch black in there; a part of the mansion Isabel had never seen before. She let out a sigh, and when she felt a hand come over her shoulder, she jumped back, her heart feeling as though it would burst out of her chest.

"Isabel? What are you doing here?" Gavin asked.

Isabel didn't say anything. Her eyes were darting from Gavin, to the shadows dancing on the walls, and then to Gavin again. She could feel his eyes boring into her, his glare almost deadly. He tried to smile but it looked fake as hell, and Isabel would have made a run for it, if it weren't for the immense amount of control that Gavin was imposing on her. "I, I," she stuttered, trying to figure out what to do. Her brain was on overdrive. She felt like this was some kind of uncharted territory, somewhere she wasn't supposed to trespass. In a way, she felt like she had uncovered something, something that was better off left alone.

"How did you even make it all the way here?" Gavin asked. "Isabel, dear, you're not supposed to be here, only Analise and I have access to this place."

The more Gavin rambled on, the more Isabel became convinced that she had to get to the bottom of this. Something was off. There she was, namely the most powerful succubus of her time, and there were places in this mansion that she knew nothing about, hidden places. The very idea of there being an entirely different world underground made her stomach churn, and she figured that, if she was going to go on living the life she was living, then she had to be aware of everything that went on around her. Right now, it felt like she knew nothing. "Gavin," Isabel said finally. "Let me pass." She tried to squeeze past him but he stopped her, so she just stood there for a moment, straightening herself, trying to gather her thoughts. "Gavin," she said again, her voice firm this time. "I said, let me pass."

"Who do you think you are?" he asked, leaning in close to Isabel. His face was only inches from hers, and she could feel the warmth of his breath colliding with her skin. It made her sick. "You think you know everything?" he asked. "Izzy, my love, you know *nothing*."

Isabel stumbled a few steps back. Suddenly she felt out of breath, like Gavin was sucking the life out of her. His eyes were piercing hers, demanding that she take a step back. But she wasn't having it. "I'm not leaving," she hissed. "I'm not leaving until I figure out what the fuck is going on." Suddenly she could feel a gush of energy surge through her. She felt powerful, like something had stripped her of all her fear.

"You're still new to this world," Gavin whispered, brushing Isabel's cheek with the back of his hand. "It can get ugly sometimes, and it's still too soon for you to find out about the ugliness of this world... embrace your naivety, honey, *embrace it.*"

"Stop treating me like a child," Isabel said, pushing his hand away. At that point, she was just plain furious. She hated it when Gavin babied her; he tended to do that a lot. "Is Analise in there?" she asked, peering over his shoulder.

"Yes."

"Well, aren't you going to tell me what she's doing in there? I need to know what's going on or I'll go absolutely mad," Isabel said, trying to hold back the tears. Suddenly she felt weak again. The more Gavin exercised his powers on her, the weaker and more vulnerable she got. She thought she would get stronger with time. She thought she would be able to resist his powers. "Alright," she said finally. "I'm sorry."

Gavin nodded at her, and not long after Analise appeared again. When her gaze met Isabel's, she stopped abruptly. "What are you doing here?" she asked, her head cocked to the side. "You must get out, right now."

"Analise, where's Ava?" Isabel asked, pushing past Gavin and just standing there, not taking her eyes off the blonde. Her emotions were all over the place; one second she was confident, the next second she felt helpless, like the working of some impenetrable force was taking her over.

"Ava?" Analise replied, confused. "Oh, you mean the redhead?" In the distance Isabel could hear voices, like little cries for help. They echoed everywhere, and Isabel wondered if it was all in her head.

"What is that?" she asked, scanning the room around them with her eyes. "What's that sound?"

"What sound?" Gavin asked, his eyes darting from Isabel, to Analise, and then to Isabel again. "Izzy, you're not feeling well, let me take you to your room." For a moment, it felt like time had stopped. Isabel didn't know if it was Gavin who was making her feel this way, or the voices. Either way she felt like her head was going to explode; suddenly every muscle in her body felt fluid, her arms falling limp to her side.

Isabel's eyes dropped to the floor. Those voices were making her weak. She wrapped her arms around herself and started shivering, motioning for Gavin to lead the way. "Get me out of here," she hissed.

"Are you feeling alright, Izzy?" he asked, a smile settling back on his face. Isabel wondered if he felt any empathy towards her at all. It was like he wasn't half the man— or vampire— that she thought he was and that scared her.

"I'm okay," she whispered through her teeth. But in reality, everything was spinning. It was like Gavin had a tight grip on her, and she was finding it hard— almost impossible— to escape. Her powers were diminishing, and she felt herself shutting down. "I just need to lay down for a while," she said, turning around and starting up the stairs.

"Wait," Gavin said. "Analise, take her up to her room."

"Will do," she said, reaching her hand out to Isabel. The couple exchanged glances before Analise led the way up the spiral stairs. Isabel was slow— painfully slow— like she had taken a bullet to her knee. She could feel the strength of Gavin's powers penetrating through her, ordering her to back off, so she did. She followed Analise up the stairs to her room, and when they finally reached her floor, she could feel the insides of her cheeks drying up like prunes.

"I need water," she breathed.

"Are you out of breath?" Analise asked, placing a hand over her shoulder.

Isabel nodded. She unlocked the door to her room and stepped inside, sitting down over the edge of her bed and watching as Analise fumbled with some glasses on her bedside table. Her fingers tightened against the mattress edge; she knew Analise was hiding something, and she needed to find out what it was.

"Here," she said, handing Isabel a full glass of water.

Isabel inspected it for a moment before downing it all in one gulp. Suddenly she felt drained of all her energy, but she wasn't giving up. Deep down she knew that something was wrong, that she needed to find out who was down there. There was no way she was being delusional when she heard those screams; they were real, they were real and they were haunting her.

"Do you feel better now?" Analise asked her. "You don't seem very well... do you want me to call you a doctor?"

Isabel shook her head. "I'm fine."

"Alright, I'm going to get going now, I've got some matters to attend to."

Like what I thought I heard down there? Isabel nodded. "Okay, I'll see you soon," she breathed.

Analise flashed her a smile and then turned away, the train of her dress floating behind her as she left the room. Isabel buried her head in her pillow, hot tears rolling down her cheeks. "This is a nightmare," she mumbled under her breath. She felt sick, like someone had ripped her heart out of her chest. Finally, she lay down on her bed, staring at the ceiling for what felt like hours. The hunger didn't rise up in her anymore, but she knew it would strike again. Isabel closed her eyes. Maybe by sunrise she would feel better.

CHAPTER 7

The sunrise spawned a strange sense of confidence in Isabel. She jumped out of the bed and opened her door, only to find Aden standing in the next room. "Hello," she said, her lips curving to a smile.

"Isabel," Aden said, gawking at her with bloodshot eyes. Isabel stopped to look at him, and it was only then that she realized he looked hideous.

"Aden," she said, narrowing her eyes at him. "You look... tired."

"Listen, you've got to do something about this, they promised they would enable us... but I don't see it happening, not one bit!" he hissed, grabbing onto the edge of the bar. Isabel was pushed up against the marble counter, and for the first time, she felt like she was in danger. She could hear his nails clawing at the bar surface: it made her cringe.

"Do something about what?" she asked, obviously confused. "Listen, I've been going crazy since yesterday, I don't know what you— or anyone else— is talking about! I don't know anything!"

"Well I want you to know this," Aden said, his voice boiling down to a sinister whisper. "Gavin isn't trying to enable the succubi, and Oz isn't an angel either... they're both trying to control you, to distract you from what's really happening, and you're falling for it!"

"Oz isn't an angel? What are you talking about? Please, I don't understand," Isabel cried, trying to stay collected but failing miserably. "I haven't been seeing him around lately, I'm getting worried."

"Oh, you need to choose who you worry about," Aden snapped. "You better start with yourself." He turned around to leave, but Isabel stopped him.

"Please, just tell me where to look, you can't just throw that at me without explaining shit," she said, tugging at his sleeve.

"You know where to look, you know because you were told where to look... you were just there last night," he said. Isabel watched him run off, and so she followed him. She flew down the stairs, taking them flight after flight after flight, until she reached the basement. Surprisingly, there was no one around, not even Analise. She marched down the narrow path, the cement floors cold against her bare feet. Finally, she heard those screams again.

"Help, help!" one of the voices said. Isabel cocked her head to the side and listened. *Help, help!*

"Oh my God," she whispered under her breath. She held onto the iron bars blocking the entrance, squinting at the shadows playing on the walls. "Isabel, is that you?" a familiar voice called.

"Who is this?" she called out. "Speak up, I can't hear you."

"It's Oz."

Isabel froze. She looked around her, and when she was sure that no one was there, she turned back, trying to make out the source of the noise. She couldn't see Oz, but she knew he was there. "Oz?" she asked. "Are you in there?"

"Isabel, listen to me," the voice said. "You know me, I'm Oz, but the man you've been with for the past couple of months, he's not me."

"Then who is he?" Isabel asked, her voice trembling.

"He's a shape shifter."

Isabel could feel her heart drop to her knees. "A what?" she asked.

"A shape shifter," the voice said again. "Isabel, Gavin tricked you. He led you to believe that I would be the one escorting you to Paris, but he brought someone else."

"And who's that someone?" she asked, grabbing onto the iron bars.

"Mikael," he said, his voice trailing off. "He's one of the few shape shifters left of our time... his job was to replace me while I rot here."

"And what good would that do?" Isabel asked, feeling more lost than ever.

"Gavin, he's not on our side," Oz said. "He's on the vampires' side... he lied to you that he could reel you into joining his army! He's trying to control the succubi, all while recruiting more and more vampires to his cause."

"So Gavin's just going around turning people into vampires?" Isabel asked, her eyes wide.

"Yes, and it's not just him," Oz said. "It's Mikael, too."

"And you? What did he do to you?" Isabel asked, trying to hold back the tears. Suddenly she felt her entire world collapse. Everything she thought she knew was fading away, and she was only left with one distorted version of the truth. She wanted Oz to speak up, and she wanted him to do it right now. There were so many missing pieces to this puzzle; Isabel was done hearing lies. "Oz, what did he do to you?" she asked again.

"This whole thing about tearing my wings off, it was a lie! Gavin just ended up sedating me and throwing me in here while Mikael did his job. He went around convincing everyone—including you— that he was me."

Suddenly Isabel remembered Oz's wings, how they had been dark at the roots. It all came back to her, it all made sense. Something was off, and it had been off for a very, very long time. Mikael was a shape shifter, and he was going around in his vampire form, turning other people into vampires so they would multiply in numbers. That explained everything. It even explained why the newcomers at the mansion looked so different. Gavin's efforts at convincing Isabel that he was trying to build an army of succubi was just a pathetic attempt at buying himself some time. "And these vampires, what do they want?" she asked, shaking.

"Complete and utter destruction," Oz hissed. "They want to wage a war with humanity, they want us to be known."

And suddenly it all came back to Isabel. All this talk about vampires, about how they wanted to wage war against humanity, it all swam into view again before her eyes. It all made sense. Gavin was a liar, and Oz had fallen for it. And Analise? Who was she? "Analise," Isabel whispered. "How's she a part of this?"

"She's a succubus, just like you," Oz hissed. "Gavin birthed her decades ago with another angel, she's been under his spell ever since... she does everything he tells her to do. They've been running this place for a long time."

"And how do we stop them?" Isabel asked, tears gathering in her eyes. She felt hopeless, like she had gained access to this world when it was already too late. The vampires were taking over; Isabel already felt defeated. Who knew how much damage was already done? She had to find a way to stop this: it was her responsibility.

"This is why you're here," Oz said. "You're one of the youngest succubi, and the most powerful... it has been prophesized that you will come along and reverse all the damage that was done."

"And how will I do that?" Isabel asked, her grip around the iron bars tightening.

"You will have an ally," Oz said, his voice growing weaker, more vulnerable. "And he will guide you through it."

"And who's the ally? Please, I need answers!"

"I can't tell you who they'll be... I swore an oath but in time, you'll have all the answers you need."

"Oz, I don't know if I can do this," Isabel muttered. "I don't feel half as experienced as I'm supposed to be!"

"Don't you worry about that," he said, his voice frail. "With time..."

Isabel's mind was racing in all sorts of directions. Suddenly she didn't know who to trust anymore. If shape shifters were in the game, then how was she supposed to identify them? How would she know a shape shifter when she saw one? Isabel was going crazy. She wanted to ask Oz all sorts of questions, but she couldn't quite gather her thoughts to lay them all out in front of him. In the distance, she heard voices, and it was like they were calling out to her. She clutched the iron bars, her knuckles glowing white. Her hands felt like they were glued to the metal, like they would break it apart at any second. She felt a force rush through her, and then suddenly, without warning, she could feel the iron bars move apart, making way for her to enter. "Oh my God," she said to herself, her eyes fixated on the little passageway she has created for herself.

"It's only normal," Oz said, his voice coming to life again. "Your powers will intimidate you at first, but then you'll make peace with them, they will drive you."

Isabel could feel the power surge through her. Her desire to feed was manifesting itself in her strength, and for the first time, she felt like she could do anything. She wasn't just namely the most powerful succubus there is, but this time, she actually felt like it. "I've never felt so confident," she said, stepping in through the iron bars. "I'm going to get you out of here."

"No," Oz said. "A battle is brewing, you're not going to get us out in time."

Isabel turned around and she saw Ava, curled up in the darkness of her cell. "Ava, Ava," Isabel whispered, reaching out and touching her. She flinched awake, and when she realized it was Isabel, she smiled weakly. "What are you doing here?" Ava asked, crawling on all fours and resituating herself at Isabel's feet. Her black wings were clearly visible now, and they looked frail, almost broken.

"I'm here to save you," she whispered. "It's only a matter of time before I get you out of here," she said. There was a pause. "What happened to you, Ava?"

"I walked in on Gavin and Analise... I overheard them talking about a battle. When Analise turned around, I was there. I was shocked. I didn't want to be a part of this, and I think I made it quite clear. A "rebel", they called me, and before I could run away, they took me, and they brought me here."

"And what kinds of things do they do to you in here?" Isabel asked, scared. But no one answered her. She could tell by the looks on their faces that they were being tortured.

"The unspeakable," Oz hissed. "They starved us, and beat us. Isabel, they tore my wings off, don't you remember? And I went through all this pain because I thought they were doing it for the right reasons... but it turns out, Gavin really wanted me dead."

"And why didn't he kill you?" Isabel asked. "What does he need from you?"

"They want to control us," Ava said knowingly. "They want to starve us so bad that we'll do whatever they ask of us."

"How are they starving you?" Isabel asked.

"They don't give us any food, they don't allow us to feed on each other... what they created by putting us in isolation was a recipe for disaster."

Isabel knew exactly what hunger felt like. She had been starved so much by Gavin that, at some point, she felt like she couldn't even stand on her own two feet. The truth was, she felt for them, but she couldn't even begin to imagine what it must be like. "I'm so sorry," she breathed. "I don't know what to say... Gavin has been starving me for quite some time now, on and off," she said.

"Starving you how?" Oz asked, resting his head on the iron bars.

"You know," Isabel muttered. "They wouldn't let me feed...."

"They're trying to weaken you," Oz said. "That way, they have more control over you."

Isabel knew the jig was up. There was nothing left to hide, nothing to cover up. Isabel knew exactly what they're trying to do, and she didn't like it one bit. Everything was coming together now. "Ava," Isabel said again. "What did Oz, I mean Mikael, do to you that night at the club?" she asked.

"He bit me... he shape shifted into a vampire, Isabel, and now I'm on my way to becoming one."

There was a pause. "And how will we know who the vampires are, and who the shape shifters are?" Isabel asked. The realization only made her stomach churn.

"We don't," Oz said. "That's the disturbing part… we don't know unless we go up against them, but until then, it's just a dirty game of trial and error."

Isabel could feel her energy running low again. She crouched down on the floor and started crying, the weight of her realizations finally taking their toll on her. At that point, she had no idea where to start, or what to do. Was she just going to wait until the vampires took over? Or was she going to show them she was onto them? So many questions were racing through her mind, and a part of her just wanted to drop everything and run away. But she knew she was never going to have her old life back; from the second she laid eyes on Gavin, she knew nothing would be the same anymore. She hadn't been in touch with her family for months now, the very image of what her life used to look like turning into a distant memory in her mind. "What's my next step, then?" she asked, her eyes following things that weren't there.

The silence of the cells rang in her ears. She could feel their desperation, their hunger; it was seeping into her. She felt starving, herself. She knew she had no choice but to feed on Oz— the real Oz— sooner or later. She knew something was off about Mikael. Her mind kept going back to his pale skin, his bloodshot eyes and his death glare. Oz was never like that. She should've known something was up since they came to Paris. "I'm so stupid," she muttered, raising her eyes to Oz, who had his eyes closed. "Oz?" Isabel said before she realized he had drifted off to sleep. He looked weaker than she had ever seen him; his wings had grown back, except now, they had a dull shine, like gold turned into copper. Isabel looked closely and she could see dark patches growing near the roots, like something was cutting off the blood supply to certain areas of his wings. She cringed at the sight, and she promised herself she would do anything to beat the vampires at their dirty game. Only problem was: how was she going to tell them apart? She was still new to this world; so naive, so inexperienced that even the boldest of signs weren't enough to tell her what to do.

"The prophecy," Ava whispered, her voice throaty and dry. "It says you're going to meet someone, someone brave… he's going to help you fight, to conquer."

"And then what happens? What happens after we go up against the vampires?" Isabel asked, eyeing Ava as she struggled to stay awake.

"The vampires will vanish, and then we'll all be free. The only ones left will be the succubi, the angels and the rebels," she said. "Isabel, if you don't conquer the vampires, they're going to take over, you're going to be like a ring around their finger. Then and only then, will they truly control you, all of you."

"What do you think their next step will be?" Isabel asked. A part of her didn't even want to know the answer.

"I haven't been around for long... but I hear things. They think that just because they've got us in here, that we're unaware of what's happening around us," Ava said, shaking her head. "Well, little do they know... we can hear every word of what they're saying. They think we're oblivious, just because we're starving, but, Isabel... we've never been more awake."

"And what did they say? Do you remember anything, anything of importance?"

"They're going to build an army... they're going to go around recruiting people, people like me," Ava said, her eyes dropping to the floor.

"Like you how?" Isabel asked.

"Vulnerable. Mikael took advantage of me because I was drunk, and then he did what he did. You know, you would think that the standard definition of "taking advantage" would be to have sex with someone while they're drunk," she scoffed. "Turns out it means digging their fangs into your skin, turning you into a vampire."

"And now they're going around clubs turning people," Isabel said, shaking her head. She didn't know what to tell Ava. For all she knew, they were both in deep shit. Oz was snoring, and Isabel could just tell he was growing weaker and weaker every day. Suddenly, she heard a loud crash. "I think I need to go now," she said, bouncing to her feet. "But I'll come back, I promise."

"Don't be long," Ava said desperately. It was like she was calling out to Isabel, begging for her help. "I'll be waiting," she said.

"I promise, I'll do something about this," Isabel said, turning to leave. In the distance she could hear voices, so she turned around again and rushed past the cells. *There has to be another way out of here.* Suddenly she found another stairway and took it, floating up the steps until she came across a little red door at the end. *What is this, Alice in Wonderland?* She turned to knob on the door. What she came across astonished her. She walked into a bedroom, fully furnished in gold plated furniture, and when she looked around, she realized it was Analise's room, but it was empty. "I thought I saw this room before," she said to herself. Everything made sense to her. Analise was in charge of the cells, and she wouldn't be surprised if Gavin's room was connected to that dungeon, too.

"Well, I think it's better if I just got out of here," Isabel said as she staggered out of the room. She was back out in the hallway again and, judging by the looks on people's faces, she wasn't supposed to be there. She stuffed her hands inside her pockets and made her way upstairs again, to the tower. She needed to go back to her room. She needed to start planning.

CHAPTER 8

Isabel was restless. She was tossing and turning in bed, her head spinning with what Ava and Oz told her about the vampires. A battle was brewing, and she still had no idea how she was going to stop it. She thought about visiting the cells again, but then she decided it was too risky. Isabel sat up, dangling her feet over the side of the bed, contemplating her next move. Her staying up all night resulted in nothing but more nerves, more questions. She decided she had to snoop around if she was going to take matters into her own hands. She got up, threw her robe on and stepped outside, wandering about aimlessly until she heard Analise's voice. Isabel felt her skin crawl. She looked around, but there was nothing.

"You don't understand, someone broke in there last night, I don't know how the hell it happened!" she heard the voice say. Isabel cocked her head to the side, and when she realized she was standing right outside Analise's room, she moved in closer, trying to listen in on what was happening.

The walls were thin, a bit too thin, and Isabel knew that all this talk was about her. The thought made her sick.

"What do you mean "broke in"?" another voice said. Isabel immediately recognized it as Gavin's.

"I went down there and I literally saw the iron bars, they were pushed apart, like someone had broken in," Analise said. Isabel could just feel the tension radiating through the walls.

"And who do you think did this?" a third voice asked. Isabel squinted, trying to identify who it belonged to; it was a strange voice, an unfamiliar one, but there was something about it that made Isabel curious. A part of her felt like she heard this voice somewhere before, and yet she felt like it belonged to a stranger.

"Who do you think?" Analise asked, rather sarcastically. There was silence. "Tell him, Gavin."

"It was Isabel," he said after a long pause.

"Wait, has anyone gone missing?" the unfamiliar voice asked.

"No, I checked. Everything's in its place," she said. "That's not the point... now that she knows where the place is, not even a lock can stop her! She's too powerful, you don't understand, this is dangerous."

There was a pause. Isabel could just feel the tension building up inside the room. *Of course they would find out I did it,* she thought. She contemplated running away, but then decided against it. There was a pretty good chance they were going to say something useful. "Gavin," Analise said. "Did you lock my room the other night?"

Another pause. "Yes," he said. "I'm pretty sure I locked it."

"So she must've used the stairs, like last time," she said. "Gavin, you need to keep an eye on her more, she can't just roam around like that."

"What do you want me to do, tie her to the bed?" he asked.

Another pause. At that moment, Isabel felt like she was this close to running away. Her feet were itching, as if enticed by some invisible force. She had never been so scared in her life. Ever since Gavin saw her down there, she had been having trouble keeping it together. No matter how much she liked to deny it, even to herself, Isabel knew they were going to find out that it was her, and they were going to come after her. "Isabel," she heard Gavin say. She could feel her heart drop to her knees. Were they going to come out looking for her?

"What the fuck's that supposed to mean?" Analise snapped. "You just let her roam around like that?"

"Well, I suppose you think you could've done a better job? Listen, here, Analise, don't forget your place."

The tension was oozing through the paper-thin walls. "I have a lot on my plate, Gavin, and you know that!"

"Hey, I think you need to calm down, what if the newcomers hear us?" the third voice said.

"He fucked up, Mikael," Analise said. "He needs to get it together, or our plan's bust."

Isabel took a step back. *Mikael.* She wondered what he looked like in real life, but for now, his identity remained unknown, behind the closed doors. Isabel wished she could just barge in and tell them she was on to them. She wished she could get rid of them. She had contemplated using her powers to demolish Analise, but the funny thing was, she didn't even know if that was possible. How was killing a vampire even possible? Did it involve a wooden stake to the heart, like what you see in the movies? Isabel didn't know. The tougher question, though, was how was killing a shape shifter possible? She needed to do her research. There was no Internet access, not much technology and very few resources to get through to the outside world. If she was going to find out information about vampires that didn't involve watching modern day soap operas, then she had to start digging. "Alright," Analise said again. This time, her voice was calmer. "Did Isabel see anything she wasn't supposed to see?" she asked.

"She didn't," Gavin said. "She can't do anything, I've got her under my control." Isabel stomped her foot just hearing that. "What was that?"

Isabel took off. She could feel her feet taking her to the far end of the corridor, but before she could round the corner, she heard Analise's vicious voice call her name. "Isabel, can I have a word with you for a second?" Isabel turned around and walked back. She couldn't let them know she heard anything.

"Hey!" she said, faking a smile. "How are you? I was just going to get something to eat, you want to join?" Isabel could feel Analise's eyes boring into her. Her eyes were like daggers, and they were piercing into her soul. Suddenly, Isabel didn't feel safe. Something told her to make a run for it, so she did. Seconds later, she felt a pair of claws grab her from behind, and then another hand came over her mouth, shutting her up completely. She could feel herself being lifted off the floor, and she was kicking at the air with her feet, trying to break free from their grip. But it was no use: whatever had a hold on her was extremely strong. She could only see the ceiling, but she could tell the hallway was completely empty, like everyone had disappeared into thin air. Isabel twisted her neck around, the sound of feet clicking against the hardwood floor echoing in her ears. Where was everyone? "Let me go, let me go!" she mumbled under Gavin's hand. Suddenly she felt an incline, like her body was being carried down the stairs.

CHAPTER 9

"Where are you taking me?" Isabel yelled, struggling to free herself. She could feel her captors' grip tightening around her ankles and wrists, but she couldn't quite tell who was at each end. Her stomach churned at the sensation of being carried down the stairs, the floors too many to count. She knew where they were taking her, wasn't it obvious now? "Please, just let me go!" she cried again. The sounds of their clothes rustling echoed down the stairwell, and Isabel could almost smell Gavin's breath on her face. She didn't know what it was about his smell, but she could almost always recognize it. She looked around and all she saw were cement bricks, and it was only then did she confirm that they were taking her to the underground cells. The panic was rising up in her; what were they going to do to her in there? She thought about Oz, and how weak he looked. Isabel wasn't very optimistic. Suddenly she felt her body become perfectly horizontal again, but she was still floating in midair.

"Alright, did you do this?" Analise asked. They lowered Isabel back down, and the first thing she saw were Gavin's piercing eyes. They were fixated on something behind her, and when Isabel turned around, she saw the iron bars, pushed apart as if done by some kind of animal, and the animal was her. "Isabel," Analise said again, leaning in close to her. "Did you do this?"

Isabel could feel a lump form in her throat. She took in a deep breath and straightened herself; she was getting in trouble either way, so she might as well just tell the truth. "I did," she breathed, her lips curving to a smile, a smile so menacing that it made Analise flare her nostrils.

"And you did this, why?" she asked, folding both arms across her chest. Isabel felt like she was back in high school again, and that Analise was her bitchy math teacher.

"I heard voices," Isabel said, almost robotically. "They were calling out to me, telling me to save them."

Analise just stared at her. She turned around to look at Mikael, who was nothing short of the scariest man— or shape shifter— Isabel had ever seen. He was about seven feet tall, his legs resembling flag poles, and he was broad across the shoulders. He had reddish stretch marks all over his skin, making it look like some invisible force had tugged it at. Isabel deduced that it was a shape shifter thing. What blew her mind, though, was how he looked nothing like the real Oz. How is it possible for someone to change so much? Isabel looked over and saw that Analise hadn't taken her eyes off her. "Who did the voices belong to?" she demanded.

Isabel hesitated. The last thing she wanted was to get Oz and Ava into trouble. She opened her mouth to speak, but before she could say anything, she heard a throaty whisper coming from inside the cells. "The voice belonged to me," it said. "I did it." Isabel turned around, and it was Oz. His skin was paler than ever, and she could see him crawl on his hands and knees, eventually settling down next to the cell door. His voice was raspy— Isabel deduced that he was dehydrated— and the corners of his lips were chapped to the point where it hurt to look at them. It seemed as though every time he opened his mouth, the corners would bleed a little. Isabel cringed at the sight. "We're on to you, you think we're not on to you?" Oz hissed.

Analise walked over to his cell, eyeing him up and down before she started kicking at the iron bars loudly. They vibrated in their place, their ringing echoing all across the cemented cell floor. Oz rolled over and covered his ears with both hands, his body rocking back and forth violently. Isabel felt helpless. She tried to move but it felt like her feet were cemented to the floor. *They're doing this on purpose, it's all a part of the mind control.* She averted her gaze to Gavin, and when their eyes met, she realized he had been staring at her, holding her in place. If she was going to rebel, then she had to find a way to overcome Gavin's powers. She closed her eyes and tried to focus all her energy on what was happening. She could feel an invisible force, something intangible, and it was taking over her mind and soul. Bit by bit, she began feeling detached, like her soul had escaped her body, and she was watching everything and everyone from afar. She had a will, a free will, to do whatever she wanted, and to act however way she wanted. Suddenly she felt more powerful than ever. She fantasized about breaking into those cells and freeing everyone that was in there, but then she felt her arms falling limp to her side again, her ability to focus diminishing altogether. She wondered why this tended to happen without warning, and she cursed herself for not being to gain control over her own life and body.

"Stop, Stop!" Oz yelled, folding both arms above his head. He was curled up in a fetal position, his body shaking to the rattling of the metal bars. "Please, for the love of God, just stop!"

"This ought to teach you to mind your own business!" Analise snarled. She stepped back and turned to Gavin. They exchanged brief glances, and then suddenly, Gavin grabbed Isabel and pulled her towards him. She tried to wiggle away from him, her body arching all the way back, but then his grip on her wrists tightened, and she could feel herself being pulled towards Gavin again and then shoved into the cell with Ava. Her body slammed against the wall and she fell to the floor, crawling on all fours in an attempt to get out. "Don't even think about it!" Analise hissed, kicking Isabel so she fell back again. "You're going to regret this... do you want to get yourself killed?" she asked, glaring at Isabel.

"I want to get out, get me out!" Isabel yelled, rising to her feet and trying to push past Analise. She felt her body being pushed back again, and she ended up right back where she was. Ava was lying there on the ground, her eyes following them as they came at each other like animals. She tried to get up but her body failed her. She couldn't even stand on her own two feet. Since they locked her up in there, she hadn't been feeding on anyone, and it made her weak. She and Oz were locked up in separate cages. If they had been able to get through to each other, they could've fed off of each other. But instead, one watched the other all day, their lives turning into this endless cycle of desperation.

The truth was, Isabel was their last hope. They both knew how powerful she was, but she just had to believe in herself. Ava opened her mouth by no words came out, and with every breath she sucked in, she could feel her throat dry up like sandpaper. She reached out to Isabel, but then Analise kicked at her hand, and she fell back, howling in pain. "Why the fuck did you do that?" Isabel asked, shoving Analise.

"Gavin, are you just going to stand there and watch?" Analise asked, turning to him briefly before she realized Isabel had slapped her across the face. "That's it," she snapped, taking her claws out and attacking Isabel.

"Wait," Gavin said, placing a hand over Analise's shoulder. "This isn't how you're supposed to handle things."

"Oh, and you're the expert at it?" Analise asked, rolling her eyes at him.

Gavin gently pushed Analise aside and stepped closer to Isabel, his eyes locked on hers. Suddenly she could feel the hunger rise up in her again. This time, it was fierier, more intense than it ever was in the past few days. She clutched her stomach with her hands, trying to control that tingling feeling, that warmth, which was slowly spreading out through her. "Analise, I'd like for you to step out," Gavin said, nodding towards the exit. Analise narrowed her eyes at him, her face drooping to a scowl. She stood there for a moment, as if waiting for Gavin to change his words, but when he didn't she let out a sigh and turned around, making her way back upstairs.

"Sometimes I wish I was a free woman, but I'm not, now, am I?" she muttered, her voice growing more and more distant as she climbed up the stairs. Isabel cocked her head to the side, listening to Analise's footsteps as they moved further and further away. In her absence, Isabel found peace. And now, she was left with Gavin. She squirmed in the corner of her cell, trying to stay as far away from him as she possibly could.

"Isabel, why so scared?" he asked. There was something about the way his teeth protruded through his smile that made Isabel shiver. He wasn't the old Gavin anymore, but he was something else, something more menacing. Isabel looked over and Oz had his eyes closed; he was almost completely out of it. Ava was slumped down on the floor, her body curved into a wobbly L shape. "Well, that just leaves the two of us," Gavin said, raising an eyebrow at Isabel.

She tried to resist it, but Gavin's eyes ignited a spark inside of her. She hadn't fed on anyone in days, and as much as she had liked to push back the feeling, it always seemed to pop back up. Her hunger was something she couldn't control, and it seemed to her that it had reached its breaking point. Just looking at Gavin made her feel desperate, like an electric current was zapping through her, and no matter how hard she tried, Isabel knew she wouldn't be able to resist. "Please, just stay away from me," she said, holding up both hands in front of her. "I don't want to do this."

"Oh, you don't?" Gavin asked, crouching down in front of her. He got down on his knees so his eyes were level with hers. "Look at me," he said. Immediately, Isabel raised her eyes to him, like some invisible force was pulling them up. "Look at me and tell me you don't want me," Gavin continued, licking his lips. Isabel's lips were slightly parted, and she could feel the desire gush right through her.

"I, I-" she muttered.

"Shh," Gavin said, leaning in close to her. She could feel his warm breath against her face; she couldn't resist it anymore. Isabel dove in and kissed him hungrily, their tongues intertwining.

She closed her eyes, letting the feel of his hands on her ignite the fire inside her, and despite how she felt about him, couldn't deny how much she needed this. She could feel her body reacting to his touch, the feel of his lips against hers, and she knew that whatever false bravado she had put up only moments before was gone now. All she wanted was to feed, and a part of her tried desperately to close off the notion that she was getting what she wanted from Gavin.

She wrapped an arm around his neck as his hands slid under her robe and cupped one of her breasts, instantly sending waves of desire through her. The touch of his fingers against her nipple only made her want him more, and without any form of control, she was undressing him just as quickly as he was disrobing her.

Gavin brought her to her feet and pushed her against the cell wall, clutching her by the neck as his eyes took her in. She could see the hunger in them, and she wondered if his matched hers. With a swipe of her arm, she pushed his hand away and pulled him to her, her hand immediately grabbing his cock and stroking. Their eyes locked, and she shuddered at the smile he gave her.

"Turn around," Gavin ordered.

Isabel hesitated for the briefest of seconds before he grabbed her by the shoulders, turned her around and pushed her against the wall. She could feel the cold stones against her body, but the warmth of his hardness pressed against her bare ass was enough to make her ignore the momentary discomfort. Besides, it was just as well that she wouldn't have to look into those eyes.

She began to rotate her hips against him, urging him on, letting him know that she was ready. She felt his hand snake in between her thighs and press against the softness of her, his fingers easily finding her clit and making her shudder and moan.

"I bet you're hungry, aren't you, Isabel?"

Isabel only whimpered, and when she reached back to grab him and guide him into her he slapped her hand away.

"Please," she moaned as his fingers sent shock waves through her. "Please, just do it already."

"I thought you didn't want this," Gavin teased, and she hated herself for being in this situation, at his mercy. "You said so yourself."

"I was wrong," Isabel sighed. "Gavin, I –"

He didn't wait for her to continue, obviously just as eager to fuck her as she wanted to be fucked. He quickly pushed her legs open and thrust inside her, without any warning, forcing her to scream as he penetrated deep inside her. She felt her insides being torn apart, and when she tried to move, his pushed her harder against the wall and stopped her.

Gavin began to thrust against her, hard, slamming his cock deep inside with every stroke, her screams of pleasure mixing with pain. He picked up the pace, and within seconds her ass was smacking against his hips as he rocked against her. She placed her hands against the wall, trying to keep balance as she felt her legs go numb with his intensity, his cock filling her up.

Gavin leaned against her, pushing deeper inside, and Isabel pushed her hips against his, urging him in further. She forgot that it was Gavin drilling her, and when she closed her eyes, she replaced him with a multitude of other faces as she screamed in pleasure with his every thrust.

He suddenly dug his nails into her waist and pulled her to him, pushing even further inside, and with a loud grunt, exploded. She felt his warmth gush into her, his cock pulsating inside her as he emptied himself. She tried to catch her breath, feeling her own muscles twitching, and when he pulled out she slid silently to the floor. She closed her eyes, and pulled her knees to her chest, and let her mind float away.

CHAPTER 10

"Well, that was nice," Gavin whispered, running a finger down Isabel's bare back.

"Yeah, it was," she said, almost robotically. She felt numb, violated, almost, but she couldn't bring herself to admit it, even to herself. Gavin still had the power. A part of her believed that he always would, and that saddened her more than anything. She was done playing the victim, and she was done being irresponsible. She couldn't let the hunger get the best of her; she had to find a way to overcome her own shortcomings. "Gavin," she said suddenly. "I want to be alone."

"How are you feeling, Isabel?" he asked, brushing his fingers through her hair. Isabel grabbed hold of his wrist.

"Please, just leave me alone," she said again, her voice stern. Gavin narrowed his eyes at her. He didn't like this, not one bit. Isabel was gaining control over her own life, or at least she was trying to, and to him, this was a major threat to their system. She was like a means to an end; he didn't want her wandering here or there. He needed her to stay put, to obey his orders without fail.

"You never used to kick me out like this," he said, a serious look on his face. "What's the matter?"

"What's the matter? What do you mean "what's the matter"?" Isabel asked, pulling her robe together. For the first time, she didn't feel good after a night with Gavin. The feeling was like being bloated after a big meal, but nowhere near satisfied. Something was changing, and Isabel had to figure out how she was going to cope with it. It was all so overwhelming.

"Isabel, we have an amazing time together," Gavin said. "What changed?"

What do you mean "what changed"? Oh, I have a pretty good hunch it has to do with the fact that I'm locked up in a dungeon, Oz is dying and there's a shape shifter on the loose pretending to be him?

"I, I don't know," she said, looking away. But deep down, she knew their plan was backfiring. Isabel was getting stronger, more in control. Gavin repulsed her. It was true she needed him to feed, but that feeling of exclusivity, or relying on him and him only, it completely vanished. Isabel didn't know what it was that led to this progression, but it sure was working. And she couldn't let Gavin know that was the case. This time, she was going to play it smart. "I think I was just scared, that you were going to pull away again," she breathed, smoothing the hair off her forehead. "I was scared you would leave me hanging again."

"I'm sorry I left you hanging, Izzy," Gavin said, tracing circles over her bare arm. Isabel felt her skin crawl at contact with his fingers. "Are you okay? You seem cold."

"You're just making me hungry all over again," she said, her lips curving to a smile. The truth was, Isabel had outdone herself. She didn't know she could lie like that, to be able to turn her disgust into pleasure. "You're making me want you all over again."

"In time," Gavin whispered. "I won't be long."

"You better not be," Isabel mouthed. Inside, she was glad he was leaving. She hoped he would leave her alone for good, but she knew this wasn't an option. She wrapped her arms around herself and let out a sigh, her eyes locked on Gavin's. "I'll be waiting for you here," she hissed.

"You want to go back up to your room?" he asked, rising to his feet. "I know I can talk Analise into taking you back there."

"No, I think I'll be good here," Isabel said. "I don't feel so well, I better not take the stairs."

"Alright," Gavin nodded. "I better go now, but I'll be back."

Isabel smiled to him, and as soon as he turned around to leave, her face drooped to a scowl. "Well, that was definitely disgusting," she muttered to herself.

"It sure was," Oz said. Isabel looked over and he had pushed his body up against the wall. He was sweating, his skin glistening under the dim lights. "Now, who's a better performer in bed, him, or I?"

Isabel chuckled. "Oh, God, I hope you didn't see anything," she said, her hand flying to her mouth. "You missed out on quite the threesome, though," she said, rolling her eyes.

"You wish that was me instead of Mikael," Oz said, folding both arms across his chest. Isabel thought he looked weaker than ever, and yet, she was so attracted to him right now. A part of her just wanted to pounce on him, to revive that fervor they once had. Oz was her one chance at revival, and with him, she felt like she could do anything.

"I do," Isabel said, rising to her feet. She walked over to his cell, which, in her haste, Analise had left unlocked. She sat down next to him, brushing his hair with the back of her hand, and when he looked up at her, Isabel felt something inside of her shake. She had missed Oz, the real Oz, and with Gavin, a part of her always felt like there was something wrong. "I think, I think we should join forces, you and I," she said, her eyes roaming his face and neck. "We can beat the vampires at their own game, together."

Oz wrapped his arms around her and pulled her close. She placed her head on his chest as he cradled her, and for the first time in a while, she felt safe. It was ironic, she thought, that the safest she felt in weeks was in a prison cell. But with both Oz and Ava around her, she knew nothing would happen to her. Isabel let out a sigh, not knowing what her next move should be. She looked up at Oz, and his eyes were fixated on the cement floor. She wondered if he was strong enough to do this with her, to face up to the enemy. But by the looks of it, they weren't even close.

"Oz," she said, taking his hand and squeezing it. His fingers were so cold and bony, but he squeezed back with just enough pressure to indicate that he was still awake. Isabel wasn't really hopeful. "Do you want to do this together?" she asked.

"It's not a matter of wanting to, it's a matter of needing to," he replied. "If I don't do anything about this, I'll die. I've been starving for a while now... they're just giving me enough to keep me alive," he said.

"Oz," Isabel said again. "Why are they keeping you alive?"

"Because I help them," he replied. "They starve me, Isabel, sometimes I have no choice but to give them what they want."

"Do you give them information?" she asked, raising an eyebrow at him.

Oz nodded. "I tell them what controls you, what makes you tick," he said. "They're studying me like a lab rat so they can go on creating this image, this replica. They want to use me to get to you, Isabel."

"Well, now I know the truth," she said. "I knew it right from the start, that there was something wrong about this Mikael... he wasn't like you."

"Funny you should tell the difference," Oz said, the corners of his lips turning upwards. "When they brought Mikael to you, they made sure that everything matched. They made no mistakes."

"I don't know, something just felt... off," Isabel said. And she knew it was true. She had grown so attached to Oz, that a part of her felt like she couldn't survive without him. And then it came to her; Gavin had made a huge mistake by leaving them together. "We can make each other strong," Isabel said, leaning in close to Oz. "We can feed on each other."

"But if they catch us, it'll be a disaster," he said. Isabel opened her mouth to speak but no words came out. Suddenly, they heard voices coming from upstairs. "Quick, go back to your cell," Oz whispered.

Isabel bounced back to her feet, retreating to the tiny box that was her cell. She crouched down on the floor and pretended to be asleep. "Let go of me, God!" she heard a voice say. She cocked her head to the side and listened. The voice sounded familiar. In the distance she could hear footsteps, interrupted briefly by the sounds of people whispering. "Can you just let go of me?" the voice said again. Isabel shook her head, immediately recognizing the voice as Aden's. She remembered the last time she saw him, how weak he looked and how distraught. Something must've happened.

"Lock him up in there," Analise said, appearing in the doorway. Gavin dragged Aden into the cell next to Isabel. He flashed her a smirk before he pushed him inside, his body slamming against the wall. "Gavin, did you lock her in the cell last night?" Analise whispered, nodding to Isabel.

You think I don't hear you, bitch?

"I did," Gavin lied. Isabel wondered what was going on inside his head. In any case, she knew he couldn't stop thinking about their night together. She fixated her eyes on him as he went about the place. Suddenly, he turned to look at her, and when his gaze met hers, his lips slightly parted, and he couldn't take his eyes off her.

"Gavin, I think we need to go," Analise said, her hand coming over his shoulder. Gavin flinched. He could feel her fingers tightening around his skin, and she rolled her eyes, taking them off Isabel and turning to look at her again. "What are you doing?" Analise whispered. "Don't let her control you, you're letting her control you!"

Gavin nodded, following Analise back upstairs. It took a lot of time and effort to bend him, but she knew she was getting there. She turned over to look at Aden, who was sweating profusely. "What did they do to you?" she asked, clicking her fingers together so he would look at her.

"I let them know I was on to them," he said, his right eye slightly twitching. "Pretty stupid, huh?"

"Yeah," Isabel said. "It is pretty stupid." There was a pause. Aden's eyes were bloodshot and his voice was groggy, like he had been crying for hours. "What did you find out?" Isabel asked, slamming the iron bars with the back of her hand so Aden doesn't fall asleep.

"Well, for starters, my roommate went missing," he said. "I looked everywhere for her, and then I overheard Analise talking over the phone. It was all in French, but I concluded that they shipped her off somewhere."

"Like where?" Isabel asked, her eyebrows furrowed.

"The other mansion."

"There's another mansion?" she asked again. "What do you mean?"

"What I mean is that… there's somewhere else, somewhere they're keeping the rebels," Aden said, his voice boiling down to a whisper.

"Why are they keeping you here, then?" Isabel asked, tilting her head sideways.

"Because there are people worse than us, there are bigger threats," he said.

"And what are they threatening to do?"

"They're plotting something at the other mansion," Aden said. "And we're going to find out what that is, very, very soon."

"Are you in contact with the people in there?" Isabel asked, holding onto the iron bars while she stared at him.

Aden nodded and then looked at her. His eyes darted back and forth, as if checking to see if anyone was listening, and then he got closer to her, trying to fit his head as far between the bars as he could. "They send me letters," he hissed.

Isabel looked around and everyone else was asleep. She wondered how much time they had left until they dropped dead. The very thought of something happening to Oz horrified her, but she knew that, if she was going to pull them all out of this mess, she couldn't rely on just him. She had to work with what she had. "What do they tell you in these letters, can I know?" she asked.

Aden looked left and right, and then he stuffed his hand into his pockets. He pulled out a folded piece of paper, and then he handed it over to Isabel through the metal bars. She reached out and grabbed it, keeping an eye on the door. "Come on, unfold it," Aden hissed. Isabel sighed and spread it out in front of her, and then she realized it was a map. "Wait, what is this?" she asked, her eyebrows furrowed.

"It's a map of how to get to the mansion," Aden said, his lips curving to a smile. "The succubi sent it so we know exactly how to reach them," he continued.

"And those people at the mansion, are they all succubi?" Isabel asked.

"Some are succubi, some are angels, some are rebel vampires," Aden replied, a serious look on his face. "We can't have intruders, intruders like Gavin and Mikael," he said.

Isabel nodded. Suddenly, she saw shadows dancing on the wall. "What the fuck is this?" she heard Analise say right before she appeared at the doorway. Her eyes went straight to Isabel, who had the map spread out in front of her. Isabel felt her heart drop \. Analise barged to her cell, swinging it open and snatching the map from Isabel's hands. She read it carefully, her eyes going up and down the squiggly lines, and then she scrunched it up in her hand and held so tightly onto it that her knuckles turned white. "Answer me," she hissed, her eyes darting from Isabel, to Aden, and then to Isabel again.

"I gave it to her," Aden said. "It's mine."

Analise diverted her gaze to Aden, who stared back at her challengingly. "That's it, you need to go," she said. "Gavin, guards!" Suddenly, Isabel could hear the sound of feet scurrying down the stairs again, and then she saw Gavin, who squeezed past Analise and ambushed Aden in his cell. The guards, whom Isabel had never seen before, cornered Aden, and it seemed to her like they had swallowed him up, because he disappeared. "Aden, Aden!" Isabel yelled, getting up and rushing to the door. She could feel herself go crazy at the sight of him being carried away, kicking and screaming. She knew he was never coming back, that the only way she could see him again was to go over there herself. Were they taking him to the other mansion? What sorts of sick things do they do to the people in there? Isabel could feel her stomach churn just thinking about it. But she knew she had to do something. Ava and Oz rose to their feet and protested at the gates, but nobody blinked an eye. Isabel yelled for Aden, but it was too late. They had already taken him away. She sank down to her knees, feeling around for the map in the darkness of the cells. But Analise had already taken it away. *Stupid, this is all stupid!* Aden shouldn't have taken that thing out in the first place. Now Isabel was never going to find out where they took him.

"Fuck, how are we going to get to him now?" she asked, turning to look at Oz. He looked surprisingly lively for a person who had been starving for days. He looked out into the distance, like he was thinking about something, something troubling.

"We're going to join him and the rebels at the other mansion," he said knowingly.

"And how are we going to do that?" Isabel asked, her eyebrows furrowed. For some reason, she always trusted what Oz had to say. The real Oz, anyway.

"This place isn't fit for us anymore, it's filling up with vampires and shape shifters, we need to get on the other side," he said, ignoring Isabel's question.

"How can we reach them?" she asked. "Aden said they sent him letters?"

"They did," Oz said. "But it's too risky."

"Do you think Aden will reach out to us from over there?" she asked.

"Maybe, it all depends on security," he replied. "I guess we'll just have to wait and see."

CHAPTER 11

The days dragged on. Isabel stretched out her arm in front of her and all she saw was a streak of white extending out into the darkness of the cell. She was getting just as weak as the rest of them. She looked over at Oz and he was chugging down some water from a rusty can. He set it down next to him and stared at her with glassy eyes. "This is taking too long," he said.

"What is?" Isabel asked, blinking repeatedly as Oz's face swam in and out of focus. "Are they going to bring you any food?" she said, her eyebrows furrowed. Suddenly, a beam of light slashed in through the doorway and Gavin stepped inside with a tray full of food. Isabel squirmed to the front of her cell, holding onto the iron bars as Gavin lay down the food in front of them. He diverted his gaze to Isabel and clenched his jaw. She stared at him as his eyes darted from her, to the bread, and then back at her again. She nodded to him, and then he rose to his feet and walked away. "What in the world?" she mumbled, toying around with the bread. She took it apart but there was nothing, and then she grabbed the other loaf and took it apart as well. "Oz, Oz, take a look at this!" she whispered.

"What, what is that?" he asked, his eyes fixated on the piece of paper.

"It's a letter," Isabel hissed. She checked to see if anyone was still there and then unfolded it, her eyes going up and down the lines of writing.

Dearest Isabel,
This is to let you know that I've crossed over to the other side safely. This letter isn't meant to be read by anyone except Oz, Ava and yourself. Gavin has agreed to cooperate with me to deliver this letter to you... only because you have charmed him. Believe in yourself, Isabel! You have just as much power to control him as he does you, if not more. The enemy are nothing but fools! If only they had the slightest idea what kind of chaos is brewing in the other mansion, if only! Locking us all up in one condensed space without much security or

surveillance isn't the best idea, now, is it? I just want you to know that I'm well, and that soon you'll be joining us, all of you.

Yours Truly,
Aden

Isabel looked up from the letter and averted her gaze to Oz. The corners of her lips curved to a smile. It all made sense now. She was glad to hear that Aden was okay, even more glad that he has some sort of plan. Aden seemed so sure of himself, and Isabel had to admit, it made her nervous. What kind of war was brewing in the other mansion? And has it already begun? How does Isabel fit into all of this? She had so many questions that were left unanswered, and it was all up to her to decide which path to take. "It's from Aden," Isabel mouthed.

"Can I read it?" Oz asked, reaching his hand out to her.

"Not right now," she said, crumpling it up and stuffing it into her pocket. She cocked her head towards the door, just as Analise came marching in with a smile on her face.

"Hello," she said. "How are my little succubi and angels doing today?" she asked with a smug look on her face.

"Bitch, don't talk to us like that, we're onto you! We're onto you!" Ava snarled.

"Guards," Analise yelled, cocking her head towards Ava. "Take her to solitary confinement, that *bitch* needs to learn her lesson," she said. Isabel opened her mouth to speak but no words came out. She watched as the guards took Ava away. Why did she have to do that? Does being trapped in a dark cell for weeks on end do that to a person?

It probably does... But she knew Ava was smarter than that, she knew she must have some sort of plan. She waited until Analise was gone, and then she looked over at Oz. "What was that for?" she whispered.

"She's doing what we're all supposed to be doing at this point," he said with a smile on his face. "She's trying to get them to move her to the other mansion."

"The more, the merrier, I guess?" Isabel asked. "What's it like there?"

"There's only one way to find out," Oz said with a smirk on his face. "But we need to wait, or else it'll look suspicious."

"You're right," Isabel said. She raised her eyes to Oz and, realizing he had already been staring at her, she flashed him a smile. "I've missed you," she said. "We're all alone now."

"It's too risky," he said. There was a pause. The two of them exchanged brief glances, interrupted by their sighs of yearning, and then suddenly, Isabel crawled to the front of her cell, holding onto the iron bars and pulling them apart. Slowly but surely, they started moving. Little by little, Isabel began to muster up enough strength to create a dent in the prison door, one that was wide enough for her to fit her whole body through. She slowly rose to her feet and shouldered her way through the dented bars, and then she crouched down on the floor, her eyes fixated on Oz's.

"I want you so much right now," she whispered.

"I can tell," Oz said with a smirk on his face. He eyed her as she wrapped her fingers around the metal bars, holding onto them for a second before she pulled them apart with as much effort as would be required to draw some drapes. Her muscles flexed as she did this; Oz thought it was the sexiest thing he had ever seen. "You're getting stronger," he said. "I'm proud of you."

Isabel crawled inside. "The sun just went down, I think," she said. "I can't really tell anymore."

Oz chuckled. "I think it did, the night shift guards will be out soon, though," he said. "We don't have much time left… come here."

Isabel crawled over next to him. Her lips found his instantly, and she eagerly pushed him onto his back as his arms wrapped around her. She sighed against his lips, feeling like she could stay in this exact position forever, his strong arms holding her close, his lips intertwining with hers, the heat of their body mixing in a way that made her want him more and more.

She broke away from their kiss, only to let her lips explore the rest of his body, undressing him as she moved. His hands quickly opened her robe, and he gently pulled her towards him. He took her breasts in his hands, and she lowered herself so that one nipple found its way into his mouth. He sucked hungrily at her, and she clutched the back of his head, sighing in pleasure. She caught a moan before it escaped her lips, careful not to alert the guards, and closed her eyes as his mouth worked.

She felt a rush of cold air against her skin, only then realizing that Oz has opened her robe completely. She adjusted her position, moving so his cock was between her legs, and lowered her hips against him. She gasped as she felt him between her wet lips, and bit her lip when his eyes rolled back at the pleasure of feeling her against him.

She moved, gently grinding, and kept her eyes locked on him as she slowly slid him inside her.

"Oh, Oz," she moaned gently against his ear as he filled her up. His hands grabbed her by the hip, guiding her, supporting her as she moved against him, slowly sliding him in and out of her in long and deep strokes. She felt his hand against her, a finger rubbing her clit, and she shuddered at his touch. Sitting up, she let her robe fall off her shoulders, smiling as he took her naked body in, and increased her pace.

Within minutes, she was riding him fervently, his thumb pressed against her clit sending one wave of orgasm through her after the other. She lost complete track of time, all worries about the guards and everything else slipping to the back of her mind as she reveled in the now. The feel of him inside her, the touch of his hands on her skin, his beating heart against the palm of her hand, it was an overwhelming mix of pleasure and desire.

She let out an involuntary moan when she felt his hips push up against her and his hands pull her against him, allowing him to push in deeper as he grunted and exploded inside her. She felt her own body shake in orgasm, shivering in the darkness, scratching at his bare chest.

They collapsed onto each other, breathing hard, heartbeats racing, and she allowed herself a small smile as he wrapped his arms around her and held her close.

**

"That was…"

"Fantastic," Isabel said. "You know, I've always felt like there was something a bit off whenever Mikael and I were together... it makes me wonder."

"Isabel, you've always been special to me," Oz said, brushing his fingers through her hair.

"And why do you think that is?" Isabel asked, raising her eyes to him. "When you found me, you had a job to do, nothing more, nothing less."

"I think you're underestimating how emotional supernatural creatures can be," he said with a smirk. "It's true I was on a mission the day I saw you at the club, but, Isabel, I couldn't stop thinking about you the minute I laid eyes on you."

Isabel could feel her cheeks getting red hot. Somehow, she just couldn't get enough of him. A part of her was convinced that she was falling for Oz, and that scared her. What if he isn't the person she thinks he is? What if this is all a game of pretend? Isabel could feel her mind going off in all sorts of directions. She felt like she couldn't trust anyone, not even Oz. But she knew she had to trust *someone*. A battle was brewing; Isabel needed to pick a side. She wondered if Oz was just using sex to get to her, she wondered if Gavin was doing the same. But it didn't work with Gavin; Isabel was growing more disgusted by him every day. She thought she would be able to tell by now if she was being used, but that wasn't the case at all. "D'you think angels can fall for succubi?" she asked, resting her head on his shoulder.

"Aren't we a living example of such a case?" he asked, wrapping his arm around her and pulling her close. "Isabel, I'm sure you've seen stranger things than two people falling in love."

"But we're not "people", Oz," she said, raising her eyes to him. "I don't know why I can't come to terms with that, I always feel the need to say it out loud to believe it."

"Sometimes I regret feeding on you, I think a part of me always will." he said. Isabel didn't say anything. Suddenly she found herself diving into deep contemplation about her life and what it has come down to. She tried to think back to what everything looked like before her transformation, before she even came to this mansion. But she felt nothing, and she saw nothing. Her previous life had become just a blank slate, one that was tarnished, almost blackened, by her current life. Maybe Oz was right: maybe he should've never fed on her that day. Maybe they should've never met.

"I think about that sometimes, too," Isabel said, trying to hold back the tears. "I don't know if I'm meant for this."

"You're special, Isabel," Oz said, smoothing her hair back. "I don't want you to forget that."

"Everyone keeps saying that, I don't get it," she said. "I don't have a special power, I don't understand how this world works, then how do you expect me to accept my fate as some kind of legendary mythological creature?" she asked. "It makes no sense to me!" Oz shifted in his place. He opened his mouth but no words came out. "What's wrong?" Isabel asked, tilting her head sideways. "You're hiding something."

"I'm not hiding anything," he said calmly. He stumbled for a while before his lips parted again, the tip of his tongue quivering between his teeth. "It's just that... centuries ago, the vampires and the angels were on the same page, they didn't really disagree on anything," he said. "At that time, the vampire council decided that they were going to pick one succubus and one incubus every century to be the chosen ones."

"Chosen to do what?" Isabel asked, furrowed little panicked.

"To run the council," he said. "Well, at the time, there was only one council for all supernatural creatures, you know, back when they all agreed... and when the vampires rebelled, nothing was the same again."

"So they picked me to be the succubus of the century?" Isabel asked with a smirk.

But Oz wasn't laughing. "They did, and now that vampires are on one side, and the rest of us are on another, you're going to get tugged at from all sorts of different directions, and it's up to you to find your way in the end," he said.

"That's the thing, how do I know who to trust?" she asked. "For all I know, you could just be another shape shifter," she said.

"That's why you're special, Isabel," Oz said. "You were born with this special skill, this ability to filter out stimuli, so you better use it," he continued.

Suddenly Isabel felt pressured all over again. This was a nightmare for her. Then she remembered something. "You said the vampires pick one male and female, right?" she asked. Oz nodded. "Who's the incubus?"

"You'll find out soon enough," Oz said with a smirk. Suddenly, Isabel heard a loud crash. She bounced to her feet and snuck back into her cell. The shadows were dancing on the walls again. Somebody was here.

CHAPTER 12

"Oz, what's going on?" Isabel asked, her eyes darting back and forth frantically. Something was going on outside. She hopped back to her feet again, clutching the iron bars, bracing for action. Something told her there was more to what was happening outside than just a guard brawl. Suddenly, she heard another loud crash, and one of the guards came tumbling down the stairs. Isabel eyed him as he lay there, motionless, drowning in a puddle of his own black blood. She looked over at Oz and his face was expressionless. He nodded to her.

"A storm is coming," he mouthed. Isabel could feel her heart beat out of her chest. Was Analise coming for her? Were they going to take her away to the other mansion? Another loud crash. Analise's dead body came rolling down to the bottom of the staircase. Isabel's hand flew to her mouth.

"What's happening, what's happening?" she turned to Oz again. But he didn't look at her. He just held onto the metal bars, his knuckles a screaming white. He was begging to come out. One guard flew down the stairs and landed on his feet. He was quickly followed by a silver haired ghost -he seemed to have come out of nowhere- and he started throwing punches at him. The first punch glanced the guard's chin. He noticed too late that it was a feint, though, when the second punch doubled him over and expelled the last bit of air from his fat belly. He had the wind knocked out of him, and he fell to the ground, motionless. Isabel couldn't believe what she was seeing. Has this man— or creature— single handedly knocked out every single guard up there? No, it couldn't be. She watched as a red-haired girl rushed downstairs, hauling the bodies off the ground, making sure they were dead.

"What, Ava?" Isabel asked. She waited for the girl to turn around so she could make out who she was, and when she did, Isabel realized that those piercing eyes belonged to Ava. "Ava!" Isabel yelled.

The girl stared at her knowingly, and then she motioned for her to stay where she was. Isabel sank to her knees, her nose poking out of the gap between the metal bars. She felt helpless, like she should be doing something and she wasn't. Suddenly she felt a rush of energy surge through her. She shouldered her way out of her cell, pushing past Ava and making her way up the stairs. What she saw astounded her. The entire mansion was on fire. In the distance she could see shadows dancing, people throwing punches at each other, chairs flying through the fumes. All hell was breaking loose.

"Well, if it isn't you, Isabel?" she heard a voice say, a voice belonging to none other than Gavin. "I didn't think you'd make it out of there," he said.

Isabel turned around, only to see Gavin climbing up the stairs. He looked as though he had appeared out of nowhere. "The succubi have revolted," she hissed. "It's already happening, you might as well just give up!"

"Oh, is that so?" he asked, tilting his head sideways. He cleaned his teeth with his tongue. Isabel cringed at the sight. "You're the chosen one, Isabel, I suppose you already know that, by now."

Isabel didn't say anything. She felt as though she was pinned to the floor, transfixed by Gavin's spell. She had to break out of it. She had to join the other side. He stood straight, eyes bulging with rage, and stared at his opponent, who had her hands balled up into fists. Without thinking, Isabel charged towards him. She threw a punch at him but it felt too sluggish. She knew the second she launched it. Gavin ducked under it, and before Isabel could register the dodge, another body shot, this one to his ribs, sent fresh ripples of pain through his torso. Isabel took a step back, eyeing Gavin as he sank to his knees in pain. She looked around, and Ava was still throwing punches at one of the guards. Before Isabel could do anything, Gavin wrapped his hands around her neck, and she sank to her knees, feeling the last bit of air being squeezed out of her. She felt like she was dying.

"This ought to teach you," he snarled. Isabel looked at him, her eyes wide, and when she finally felt like she would slip out of consciousness, Gavin gasped and his grip on her loosened. She coughed violently, her throat burning, but she could breathe again. Gavin slumped onto the floor beside her, the wooden leg of a chair pierced through his back and protruding from his chest.

Isabel looked up and saw the silver-haired ghost. He was staring down at her. She instantly felt herself being hauled off the ground and onto a softer surface.

"It's all over," the ghost said. Isabel blinked repeatedly, the man's face swimming in and out of view. She felt her lips curve to a smile when she saw Oz standing right next to him. "I'm Preston," the man said.

"Isabel," she replied, scanning the place with her eyes. Utter and complete destruction. The crystal chandeliers were swinging back and forth, the bodies of guards and vampires were lying around everywhere, people were trying to put out the fire.

"How about we get out of here?" he asked, reaching his hand out to her.

Isabel grabbed his hand and squeezed it. "Lead the way," she said.

She looked around and the flames didn't seem to hurt her eyes anymore. For the first time, she felt free, like the weight of the world had been lifted off her shoulders. This was the start of something new, and the truth was, Isabel couldn't wait.

Newsletter

This exclusive **VIP Mailing List** from Persia Publishing focuses on delivering high quality content to your inbox that will bring more passion, excitement, and entertainment to your life. Weekly insights, specials offers and free giveaways that you will love!

You are just one click away from getting exclusive access to the **VIP Mailing List**!

Click the "**Get Access Now**" link below to join today!

GET ACCESS NOW

http://www.persiapublishing.com/subscribe-to-romance-lucy/

LIKE US AT

https://www.facebook.com/LucyLyonsRomance/

CAN YOU HELP?

PLEASE leave a quick review for this book if it gives you any value. It provides valuable feedback that allows me to continuously improve my books and motivates me to keep writing.

Thank You!

Owned by The Vampire

The Vampire War Part 2

Book 3

Lucy Lyons

© 2017

Newsletter

This exclusive **VIP Mailing List** from Persia Publishing focuses on delivering high quality content to your inbox that will bring more passion, excitement, and entertainment to your life. Weekly insights, specials offers and free giveaways that you will love!

You are just one click away from getting exclusive access to the **VIP Mailing List**!

Click the "**Get Access Now**" link below to join today!

GET ACCESS NOW

http://www.persiapublishing.com/subscribe-to-romance-lucy/

LIKE US AT

https://www.facebook.com/LucyLyonsRomance/

CAN YOU HELP?

PLEASE leave a quick review for this book if it gives you any value. It provides valuable feedback that allows me to continuously improve my books and motivates me to keep writing.

Thank You!

© Copyright 2016 by Persia Publishing- All rights reserved.

All rights reserved. No part of this publication may be reproduced, distributed, or transmitted in any form or by any means, including photocopying, recording, or other electronic or mechanical methods, without the prior written permission of the publisher, except in the case of brief quotations embodied in critical reviews and certain other noncommercial uses permitted by copyright law. For permission requests, write to the publisher, addressed "Attention: Permissions Coordinator," at the address below.

The information herein is offered for entertainment purposes solely, and is universal as so. The presentation of the information is without contract or any type of guarantee assurance.

CHAPTER 1

"He's still breathing."

"Should we kill him?"

"I don't know."

Isabel crouched down next to Gavin's motionless body. He looked transfixed, as if put under a spell, but when Isabel pressed two of her fingers to his neck he still had a pulse. She looked to her side. The chair leg was still there, staring back at her, begging to be driven into his chest, not only once, but tens of times more. Gavin had to be demolished; he needed to be wiped out. "I think... I think we should let him live."

"What good would that do?" Presten asked, his eyes darting from Isabel to Gavin's limp body and back again. "The whole house is in flames, we need to move fast."

"Let's take him to the other mansion."

"The other mansion? Where the rest of us are?" Presten asked, furrowing his eyebrows. Smoke filled his view as he looked around, then a bright glint of orange. The fire screamed and Isabel held back a sob as she watched the house being swallowed up in engorging flames. All they could hear was the crackle of the white paint chipping., It was only then that they realized they needed to get out of there, and they needed to do it now.

"Quick, grab him by his legs," Isabel said in a panic. They carried his motionless body along the flaming shards of wood that were thrown all over the place. The entire time, Isabel felt invincible. She felt like she could conquer anything. There she was, all partnered up with a man she had just met, and they were fighting evil together. Nothing could beat that feeling, the feeling of sheer empowerment; there was no turning back now.

"The entrances are blocked. I think the ceiling might collapse at any second," Presten said, his eyes darting back and forth frantically. The tethered draperies had all caught fire, and they were blocking the windows, the only escape they had left.

"Wait— over there!" Isabel said, cocking her head towards a crack in the wall that she knew was part of a secret passageway. They exchanged brief glances before they charged for the entryway. Presten dragged Gavin's body across the floor. Isabel ducked and held her hand out to him. They crouched down as near to the floor as possible and scurried outside. "We're almost there," Isabel said. "Just keep your eyes on the light at the end of the tunnel."

"There is no light, Isabel," Presten said.

"But there is."

Suddenly the bluish hue of the night swam into view, and they found themselves out in the woods again. A cool rush of fresh air came over Isabel and caressed her face; she felt whole again. Presten stood by her side. Gavin's body was spread out over the muddy grass. They knew they had no choice but to make their way to the other mansion.

"What do you think we should do with him?" Presten asked, turning to look at Isabel.

"We're going to use him to our advantage; we're going to make him ours," she replied, staring out into the distance. Presten eyed her admiringly. He'd known before he'd even met her that she was the bravest succubus of their time, but seeing her in person was a whole other thing.

"Do you think we control him by now?" he asked, scanning the area around them. The fire wasn't dying down, and it seemed like the place would eat away at itself until it turned into ashes. In the distance, Isabel could hear a chattering sound and as she turned around she thought she saw Ava, her red hair resembling the fire itself.

"Most definitely," hissed the voice.

Presten jumped and turned around, his eyes wide. "Who's there?" he asked.

"It's Ava," the voice said. She stepped closer to them, her face swimming into view. "Listen, Presten, you did the right thing by letting Gavin live," she said, staring down at his motionless body. He seemed lifeless. Ava bent down to take his pulse and nodded to confirm that he was in fact still alive.

"He's under our control now," Isabel said again, her voice even more confident than before. "We bent him, so we might as well use that to our advantage." Isabel caught a glimpse of something else lurking in the distant darkness; she knew it was Aden. "I wasn't worried about you," she said, her lips forming a smile as she called into the darkness.

"And I wasn't worried about you," Aden replied. "Let's get this son of a bitch to the other mansion, the rest of the vampires can rot in hell."

"Wait, what was that?" Isabel asked, cocking her head to the side to listen. Beyond the crackling of the fire they could hear rustling sounds. Was there yet another person lurking in the darkness?

Suddenly, something jumped out at Isabel and she was knocked to the ground.

"I'm going to kill you," a voice snarled, a voice Isabel immediately recognized as Analise's. Isabel quickly rose to her feet and attacked with a strong right overhand punch. Analise stepped out of range, but before she could bring her hands up in defense, Isabel drove her shoulder into her chest, and she fell back, howling in pain. The rest crowded around her, throwing punches and making sure she would never be able to get back up again.

"Come on, we need to go… we don't know how many of them are still out there," Presten said, pulling Gavin's body off the ground and started to make his way downhill. The rest followed, leaving Analise behind. Isabel tried to stop her mind from going off in all sorts of directions. She couldn't believe what had just happened. She had never felt this strong. Was it true that Presten had given her this strength? Better yet, was it true that they fed off each other's strength? It was all an enigma to her; she needed time to get used to it.

"Wait," Isabel said, suddenly freezing in her place. "Where's Oz?"

All four of them stopped suddenly, like a flock of sheep that had been transfixed by some force of nature. "I'll go," Isabel said, her eyes locked on Presten's. "The rest of you keeping going... we can't all risk going back there again."

Presten hesitated. "I think it would be better if you and I stuck together," he said. Isabel thought about it for a second before realizing he was right. "Okay, but the rest, head for the other mansion... Presten and I will meet you there."

"We'll take Gavin with us," Aden said, nodding. "Take care."

"Alright, let's go back," Isabel said, her eyes following the rise of the flowery hill. It was pitch black, to the point that Isabel felt like the darkness would swallow her alive. But she soldiered on, smiling at Presten every now and then to give him strength. With him, she felt invisible, but that didn't mean she couldn't conquer the dark alone. Oz was right, she really was powerful, and when Presten was with her, she felt even more so, like she could take over the world. They ran up the hill, as if pushed by some supernatural force. "Wait," Isabel said, stopping dead in her tracks. "I smell something."

In the distance Presten could hear footsteps pushing through the crunchy leaves. He froze in his place as well, trying to listen for any unusual noises. "What is it?" he asked, his head tilted sideways.

"It's Oz," Isabel said, a smile settling over her face when she noticed his wings in the dark. He was limping in their direction; his body looking as though it would collapse at any second. "Oz!" Isabel said again, hurrying to him. She had never been so relieved to see someone in her life. "I'm— I'm so sorry," she said, her voice trembling. "Tell me, are you okay?" An immense amount of guilt washed over her. How could she have left Oz in there to die?

"No time for apologies," Oz said, his voice firm. "We all need to get out of here... what happened to Gavin?"

"They're taking him to the other mansion," Presten said knowingly. "It's the best that we could do right now; he needs to remain under our control."

"There are still people in there," Oz said, pointing to the flaming ball of fire on the very top of the hill. "We need to get them out." Suddenly, Isabel heard footsteps again, but this time, there were many of them and they sounded like they were charging towards them. Her first instinct was to run the other way, but she remained pinned to her place; something told her she shouldn't be running away.

"Isabel! Isabel!" the voices yelled from a distance. As the lurking figures came closer, Presten looked like he was ready for battle, but when he realized that they were succubi, he breathed a sigh of relief.

"They made it," Isabel said, rather to herself. She found herself drifting closer to the sea of people and they welcomed her in their arms. She took a closer look: they were all covered up in dust and ash, and some of them had cuts and bruises all over their bodies. There must've been at least twenty of them, and Isabel could recognize them all as the people she had grown close to during her days at the mansion. "You made it!" Isabel screamed, leading the way back down the steep hill. The others followed her and in the background, she could hear some murmuring about an impending victory.

"They're gone," a voice said from behind her. "They're all gone."
"We burned them."

"Stuck a wooden stake to their hearts."

Isabel smiled to herself as she and Presten led the way downhill. The vampires were diminishing, but the battle was still far from over. They still had to head down to the other mansion, gather their allies, and work towards building a proper army. "I would say we've done a pretty good job, all of us," Isabel said, flashing Presten a smirk.

"Succubi are strong, Isabel, there's a reason why you and I didn't have to go around rescuing each and every one of them from the fire," Presten said knowingly. Isabel knew he was right. She wondered who was still in there and if any of the succubi hadn't make it out alive. Her heart skipped a beat at the very idea of losing one of them, but she knew she had to soldier on if she wanted to make it to the mansion on time. It was almost dawn; they needed to hurry.

***

"Move away," Isabel said, her eyes fixated on the guard's. For a moment, it felt like time had stopped. Isabel had an entire army of succubi backing her; the guards didn't really have that much of a choice. The air was tense and Isabel wondered if she needed a little bit more than an army to get through the gates to the mansion. "Alright, then,

I'm going to say this one more time. Let me through." She looked so deeply into the vampire's eyes that he wouldn't dare deny her. This was the first time Isabel had experienced full control over a vampire; the feeling was exhilarating. Without saying anything, the black winged guard opened up for them, and like an army of soldiers, they marched, pouring into the castle from all corners.

"Guards, what is this?" one of the vampires said, as he flew down the stairs. He froze when he saw Isabel standing in front of him. At that moment, he knew what she had come for. He knew who she was. "Step back," he said, shaking his fist at her. "Step back! Guards!"

But they didn't do anything. They were all transfixed, as if Isabel and Presten's very presence was enough to keep them sedated. "Don't move," Isabel said, averting her gaze to the vampire standing at the bottom of the stairs. He froze in his place, as if trapped behind some sort of electromagnetic field. Every part of him was still except his eyes. Isabel and Presten remained focused on him but when more vampires appeared behind him, Isabel's energy weakened and she found that she was unable to control all of them at once.

What was that? Isabel thought to herself. She felt the ground beneath her shake and when she turned to look at Presten, his eyes were fixated on a trapdoor hidden away under a rug at the far end of the room. The door shook, and then, without warning, it burst open, body after body lifting itself up and crawling into the room. Isabel felt her heart rise in her chest. *The rebels.* One by one, they climbed out, joining Isabel and Presten until they formed an army so large that all the vampires in the mansion combined couldn't stop them. Together, they charged towards the vampires, pushing them aside and scurrying up the stairs. The sight was horrific. Isabel drove her shoulder into one dark winged vampire after another, wrestling them to the ground until they lay there, motionless. Nothing could stop them now; the vampires were severely outnumbered.

"Lock them up in the cells!" a voice yelled. "Give them a taste of their own medicine!"

Isabel watched on as all hell broke loose. The succubi were dragging the vampires down the trapdoor, throwing them into the cells and locking them inside. There were so many of them that they had to really cram them inside. Presten threw Gavin into one of the cells, too, but this one was secluded. He didn't want Gavin mingling with anybody else. He was especially dangerous. The mansion was shaking underneath their feet; everyone was throwing punches at each other. Presten was battling with five vampires at once and Isabel was fighting off some shapeshifters that seemed to have sprung up on her out of nowhere. At one point, it became difficult to tell who was on whose side, but Isabel stayed focused on the wings. The battle continued on for what felt like an eternity, until the vampires were all locked up in cells, crammed in with no breathing space.

Isabel was left breathless. She scanned the dungeon with her eyes, trying to take in the scrunched-up faces of those locked inside. She spotted Gavin in solitary confinement and she flashed him a smirk when he stared at her hungrily.

"You're not going to get away with this," he mouthed to her. It sent chills down her spine.

***

CHAPTER 2

Isabel stayed over at the mansion. It took a lot of guts, but she knew she couldn't be away from the prisoners for too long. There were too many of them, even though they were locked up tight. The succubi took nightly shifts to make sure the vampires couldn't find their way out and by the end of the night, they were all passed out. A hand on her shoulder woke Isabel. "What, what's going on?" she flinched, blinking repeatedly as the room swam in and out of focus. "Oz?"

"Hey," he said, sitting down next to her. She had fallen asleep on a couch outside, right next to the trapdoor. She looked up and saw Oz's face, and the truth was, she had never felt so relieved. He always had this way of making her feel safe; she didn't know what she would do without him. Even last night, when she felt her most powerful, she knew she still needed him by her side. He had slept over next to her, as had Presten, and in a way, Isabel had never felt safer. But she still needed to know what Presten's deal was; until now, she only knew a little about him. If they were going to work together, then she needed to find out more. That would have to wait until later.

"Hey," she said finally, stroking Oz's face with the back of her hand. "How are you feeling?"

"Like shit," he said, his lips curving to a smile. That smile she adored. She knew the real Oz when she saw him.

"Come here," Isabel said, getting up and motioning for him to sit down at her feet. He gave his back to her and she ran her hands along his neck and slid them down to his chest, massaging them as she moved downwards. "I think you just need to relax, this'll all be over soon."

"Oh, it's just begun," Oz said, closing his eyes.

"Are you always this pessimistic?" Isabel asked, rolling her eyes.

"I'm just being realistic… you've got tens of vampires trapped in there, Isabel, and the vampire council doesn't even know it yet. Do you realize how dangerous this is?"

"I do," Isabel said, her voice trailing off. "But what were we supposed to do? At least now we've got them all in one place and we can control them to keep their mouths shut."

"They're too many to control," Oz said. "We don't have much time: they'll break out eventually."

Oz always made Isabel nervous. She knew he's been around for way longer than she had and she felt powerless around him sometimes. "I think we should hold a meeting, all of us," she said after a long pause.

"I was going to propose that we do that," Oz said, grabbing Isabel's hand and squeezing it. "We need to call Ava and Presten, now."

"We're right here," Ava said, coming down the stairs. She looked surprisingly cheery for a girl who had been battling vampires the night before.

"Good morning," Isabel said, motioning for Ava to come sit down. "Hey, Presten."

"Hey, I overheard you talking about holding a meeting," he said, sitting down next to Ava. "I stayed up all night thinking. I might be onto something." There was a pause. "We need to get some information out of our guests' downstairs in that cellar," he said, raising an eyebrow at Isabel.

"Think we should torture them?" she asked. *Do you hear yourself?* Suddenly Isabel didn't feel like herself anymore: since when was she that kind of person? Had being a supernatural being caused her to turn into a monster? She shook her head and looked straight ahead, trying to avoid making eye contact with anyone else.

"Yes," Oz said solemnly. "We need to try and get them to confess to what's happening," he continued.

"Vampires usually don't respond well to UV light," Ava said, brushing the hair off her forehead. "We can use that to get them to talk."

Isabel nodded, but deep down, she hated the monster she had become. It was true those vampires would probably eat her alive given the chance, but she hated the way she tended to resort to the most violent action to protect herself. "So, we're going to extract information about the council?" Isabel asked, her eyes darting from Ava, to Oz, and then to Ava again. All three of them nodded collectively.

"We're holding them hostages. The council's going to find out sooner or later," Ava said coldly. "We're going to need to try and get them to talk before the council sends out a rescue mission to find them."

Isabel nodded and looked away. She found herself in deep contemplation about her life again. Has she always been this aggressive as a person? Or were supernatural creatures different? Isabel thought she knew the answer to that. The movies were right about one thing; vampires were scary. She would be more than happy to demolish them, although she had no idea if their plan was foolproof. At that point, she just knew they had to move forward if they wanted to accomplish anything. "Alright, I think we should go check on the hostages now," she said after a long pause.

All four of them rose to their feet and made a beeline for the trapdoor. It was oddly still, and it stayed that way throughout the entire night. Isabel had almost slept with one eye open; she had no idea if the vampires would try to escape. After all, there were so many of them down there; a collective effort on their part would've been disastrous. "I'm so fucking apprehensive," Ava said, clenching her jaw. "What if they're plotting something down there?"

"If we think like that, we're screwed," Presten said, glaring at Ava. "Oz, open up the trapdoor, why don't you?"

Oz pulled the trapdoor open forcibly, all four of them climbing down to the cellar. "Wait, let me go first," he said, motioning for Isabel to stay away. She wondered whether he still cared about her like she did about him, and deep down, she knew he did. Oz landed on his feet in the cellar. His nose crinkled at the smell, which must have resulted from the vampires being in there for so long without having a bathroom. Oz's eyes darted from one ashen face to the other, and it was only then that he realized trying to question these fallen creatures was a lost cause. "Hey, check this out," he said. The others landed on their feet next to him, their faces drooping to a scowl as soon as they caught the stench that was slowly diffusing to the top floor.

"That's nasty," Isabel said, her wrinkling her nose. She spotted Gavin in the corner. He looked just as tired as the rest of them. Asleep on his back, his wings were spread out to his sides. Isabel caught a glimpse of his chest slowly rising and falling and she breathed a sigh of relief. He was still alive. The fact that she felt such relief, though, made her question everything; it scared her shitless. Did she still care about Gavin? If he belonged to the enemy, then why should she care if he lived or died? The thoughts were driving her crazy, but right now, she knew she had to stay focused. "I don't think we can question them right now," she murmured to the others, watching as the vampires winced at the soft rays of light coming in through the trapdoor. "We're just making them weaker... we can't kill them, that's not what we want. We want information."

"You're right," Presten said, nodding. "I think we need to get them fed— that is, if we want to get something out of them."

"I'll go get it," Ava said. Isabel walked over to Gavin, not taking her eyes off him. *Oh, how the times have changed,* she thought to herself.

"I heard that," Gavin said, opening his eyes. Isabel froze. "I can still read your memory, you know... I created you, remember?" Suddenly she felt her heart drop to her knees. Was she never going to get rid of him? Even at his weakest moment, Gavin was still menacing, still annoying. Now Isabel just wanted to see him dead, as cruel as that sounded. She pretended not to hear him, but he was persistent. "You're never going to get rid of me," he said, smiling slowly. He closed his eyes and froze in the same position as before, not caring to roll over. He had been lying on his back since the night before; his lips were chapped and his face was an ashen white. Isabel wondered how much longer he still had to live. She fetishized starving him to death; at that point, Gavin was just a menace, something that reminded her of how weak she was, how incompetent. But she couldn't let him get to her. She couldn't let him win. She stomped one foot against the floor and looked him in the eyes.

"I'm going to block you out, you won't know how to get to me anymore," she said, her jaw clenched. Gavin just stared at her and grimaced. "You look like you want to say something," Isabel said, leaning in close to him. Gavin didn't threaten her anymore, or at least, she was getting used to the idea that she was hundreds of times stronger than he was.

"I, I," he breathed. The corners of his mouth looked as though they had been glued together and he was left mumbling words that even Isabel could not understand. He closed his eyes and stiffened back into his initial position. A smile settled over Isabel's face; she was in control again.

"I'm back," Ava said, her legs appearing through the trapdoor. She carried three trays of food, not nearly enough to suffice for the number of hostages trapped inside the cells. She walked over to Isabel, trying not to drop anything. "This should get 'em talking," she said, her lips curving to the contended maw of a wolf after feasting on a fallen elk. There was a sudden movement in the cells. It was like the vampires could smell the food and they flinched awake one by one, trying to sniff for anything to eat. They gawked at Ava hungrily, their eyes darting from her face, to the plates of food, and then to her face again. If she wasn't mistaken, they looked like they were about to bite her face off.

"I think we're going to need more food than just that if we're going to feed them all," Presten said matter-of-factly.

"I don't see you moving," Ava said bitterly. "The kitchen's up there."

Presten smiled to himself. "You're a sassy one, aren't you?" he muttered. "Isabel, would you like to come with me?"

"Sure," she said, averting her gaze to Oz, who nodded at her. Presten hopped out of the basement first, reaching his hand back to Isabel so he could pull her out with him. "Do you know exactly where the kitchen is?" Isabel asked, staring somewhere over Presten's shoulder. The place was totally unfamiliar to her, which, in some ways, she found to be extremely unsettling.

"Ava said it's a few floors above," Presten said. "I guess we're going to have to find out." They made their way up the stairs, which seemed to spiral forever. It was awfully quiet and Isabel thought something would jump out at them at any second. "So, I've been meaning to ask you... how old are you?" he asked, breaking the silence.

"Twenty-four," Isabel said without giving it much thought.

"No, how old are you?" Presten asked, popping his neck forward.

"Oh," Isabel said, her eyebrows furrowed. "In succubus years?" Presten nodded. "Around six months," she smiled, brushing the hair out of her eyes.

"Me, too," Presten said, tilting his head sideways. Their heels clicked against the hardwood floor, the silence of the halls even more smothering than before. Isabel opened her mouth to speak but no words came out; a familiar feeling was trickling through her, the feeling of hunger. This past week has been nothing but overwhelming for her and for the first time in days Isabel was able to bask in the silence. It wasn't like she didn't want to make conversation with Presten, but she was exhausted. "We're both pretty new to this, I would say," he said again, turning to look at her.

Isabel noticed his eyes. They were deep, electrifying, even, and for some reason she couldn't stop staring at them. "I would say we are," she said, holding his gaze for a second before she looked away. "How did you feel when you first found out?" she asked.

There was a pause. "I found it to be quite hilarious, to tell you the truth," he said. "It was Rene, my maker, who told me. My first reaction was; I fuck two girls on one night and I get this?"

Isabel chuckled. "I felt the same way," she said. "Although, I felt like something about me was different… I knew something was terribly wrong."

"Terribly wrong… or undeniably right?" he asked.

"You know, even after all this time, I really can't tell you," Isabel said, shaking her head.

"You're a very special creature, Isabel," Presten said. "You're the type they hear about in legends."

"And so are you, I'm assuming?" she asked, her head cocked to the side. At that point, they were just pacing the halls. Isabel wondered if Presten had forgotten about the task at hand.

"No," Presten shook his head. "You're different. In mythology, women are portrayed as goddesses, because they are." Isabel could tell he was flirting.

"You flatter me," she said, fluttering her eyelashes. Presten couldn't tell if she was being sarcastic.

"You're really hard to tap into, you know that?" he asked. There was a pause.

"You know, in this world, it's really hard to know who you can trust," she said. "Don't get me wrong, I know I can trust you, or else we wouldn't be here... but I've been through hell trying to figure out who was on my side and who wasn't. So I'm careful now."

"You have every right," Presten said, his eyes roaming her face and neck as they walked. "It's hard to tell who you're talking to, let alone figure out who's on your side."

"Yes!" Isabel jumped. "The shapeshifters, Presten, oh, the shapeshifters!"

"Have you encountered any recently?"

"Let's just say... I've spent a considerable amount of time sleeping with the enemy without even knowing it," she said, raising an eyebrow at him.

Presten shook his head. "That sounds horrible," he admitted. "What if I told you Rene, my maker, turned her back on us all and joined the vampire council?"

"What?" Isabel asked, her eyes wide as a set of plates.

Presten nodded. "She's really close with... the King vampire, if you've heard of him."

"I've heard stories," Isabel said. "But I'm not sure—"

"Oh, hey, there's the kitchen," Presten said, sprinting for the door. He pushed it open and flicked on the lights, his eyes travelling up and down the black decaying walls. This mansion was nowhere near as fancy or luxurious as the last one. Isabel stepped inside, and could immediately feel the cold air envelope her entire body. Splotches of the original paint hinted at the house's former prosperity; has this one caught fire, too?

"Well, this is definitely spooky," Isabel said, her arms folded across her chest. The windows were covered with grime and dirt, and a large jagged hole dug through the wall as though daring anyone to enter. "Let's just get this over with," Presten said, walking over to the fridge door and swung it open. Oddly enough, it was filled to the brim with food. Together, they took out some fruit, a jug of water and some leftovers, and soon enough, they were on their way back down. As they walked, Isabel became more and more certain that the mansion was filled with secrets, and she was adamant she would find them out. The corridors seemed to stretch out indefinitely, and she knew that if she were to unlock a single one of the doors, she would be opening up the gates to a never-ending maze of halls and passageways. "Do you want to come back and check this place out?" she asked Presten, a smirk on her face.

"Do you really think we should be loitering around here?" Presten asked.

"Come on, where's your sense of adventure?" Isabel asked, strutting down the hallway. "Seriously, though, we kind of need to figure out the anatomy of this place if we're ever going to carry on this battle."

There was a pause. "You're absolutely right," Presten said. They climbed down the trapdoor leading to the cellar. "This should last them the night," Presten said, setting the food down on the floor in front of the hostages. They eyed him hungrily, as if ready to pounce at any second.

"I think you're going to have to go back for more," Oz said.

Presten opened his mouth to protest but before he could, Isabel stopped him. "We're on it," she said, cocking her head to the side. She and Presten exchanged brief glances, and it was only then that he realized Isabel wanted to go on an adventure.

"We'll be back in a second," he said with a smirk.

CHAPTER 3

"So, do you know anything about this mansion?" Isabel asked, looking around curiously once they were alone.

"I've been here quite a lot," Presten said. "It was never the most pleasant experience... they tried to hold me hostage here, more than once, but I always managed to escape."

"Do you think Analise and Gavin have rooms in here?" she asked, ignoring his moment of triumph.

"They do," he said mischievously. "What, you think you're the only one here up for an adventure?"

Isabel smiled and followed him. He took a right and headed down one of the corridors, surveying one decaying door after the other. "I don't know everything in this mansion, but this, I know," he said, standing in front a pair of swinging doors at the far end of the hallway. Isabel pushed one of them and they begrudgingly creaked open. A musty, dank stench travelled up her nostrils. The house was dead silence except for the intermittent creaks and moans that echoed everywhere as they walked across the floorboards. Black and brown mold dotted the ceiling in clusters, evidence of rain seeping through the roof. "So, what are we looking at?" Isabel asked, her nose wrinkled.

"Gavin's room," Presten replied.

Isabel felt the hair on the back of her neck stand up. Finally it settled with her that Gavin had this whole other life, a life she knew nothing about. She walked across the suite, looking at the musty walls. "This room's too shabby to be Gavin's room," she said, rather to herself.

"I wasn't allowed to enter," Presten said. "I only caught glimpses."

Isabel stopped when she noticed a closet at the far end of the suite. She walked over to it, swung it open and started searching through Gavin's clothes. Suddenly her sleeve got hooked on something and she let out a gasp. It was a doorknob. "Presten, check this out," she hissed, motioning for him to join her. Presten crept up behind her, and as soon as she felt him brush up on her back, an electric current flowed through her.

"What is it?" he asked, leaning in close to her ear. Isabel would have liked to let him take her right then and there, but she was wise enough to know that this little discovery of hers was much, much more important.

"It's a doorknob," she said. "But the door's locked." The both of them sighed in frustration, and then, desperately, Isabel started searching for the key in the pockets of Gavin's clothes. "It's not there," she said, clenching her eyes. "What do you think it is?"

"I don't know," Presten said, his eyebrows furrowed. "I think we might find the key somewhere around here," he continued, looking around the room. He probed near the bedside table, pulling its drawers open and searching inside. Nothing. "Gavin probably has it," he said.

"No, it might be lying around here," Isabel said, her voice stern. "We need to find it, who knows what could be in there?"

They must have spent an hour searching. Isabel flipped the mattress over, crawled under the bed and ripped the pillow sacks apart, but still, she found nothing. She rose to her feet and clasped her hands behind her head. This was hopeless. "Oh my God," she said. "I've never been so frustrated in my life."

"Hey, come look at this," Presten said. Isabel jumped to where he was, and when she realized he was holding a pair of books, she snatched them from him. "I see you're excited," he said, rolling his eyes at her. He was beginning to think Isabel was a little controlling. She realized it herself, not that she was apologetic about it.

"Oh my God," she said, flipping through the pages. She closed the leather-bound book and stared at its cover. "No title," she said, opening it up again and beginning to skim through its pages. What she saw shocked her. "Hey, Presten, d'you think this is Gavin's handwriting?" she asked, her eyes darting from Presten, to the squiggly pen lines, and then to Presten again.

"I am absolutely certain of it," he said.

"How can you be so sure, though?" she asked, raising an eyebrow at him.

"Isabel, we're in Gavin's room, this is his study," Presten said. "Who else's handwriting would it be?"

"Yeah, that makes sense," Isabel said, her eyes fixated on the lines of writing. They were awfully hard to decipher. "Alright, this is going to need some looking into," she said, closing the book and tucking it under her arm. "Let's save it for later."

"Are you sure you wanna do that?" Presten asked, raising an eyebrow at her. "I, personally, have never been more curious."

"I'm even more curious to see what's behind that door," Isabel said, ignoring him. She scanned the room one last time before she pounced on the bed again and started tucking her hands underneath the mattress.

"We've already looked there," Presten said, heading for the coatrack. "Maybe it's in one of those pockets," he said.

"Did you find anything?" Isabel asked impatiently as he finished searching the pockets.

"No, nothing."

"This is hopeless."

Isabel clasped her hands behind her head again and started pacing the room. Deep down, she knew they wouldn't find anything. Gavin was smarter than that; he wouldn't leave an important key lying around like that for anyone to find. He must've taken it with him. She thought about ambushing him in the cells, but she knew that was a horrible idea. He would probably resist with so much force that even Isabel wouldn't be able to stop him.

"I think we should call it a day," she said finally.

"I think so, too," Presten said, his eyes fixated on the chipped walls. "Besides, this room is giving me the creeps."

"Let's just head back down," Isabel said. "But we're going to come back, and we're going to find that key."

"Tomorrow morning?" Presten asked. Isabel nodded. "Just remember to take those books with you."

"I will," she said, flashing Presten a smirk. "You don't think I'm that forgetful, do you?" They headed for the door, but when Presten reached the end of the corridor, he was alone.

"You gonna come with me, or?" he called back to Isabel.

"I think we should assign ourselves rooms, first," she said. "Because by the looks of it, we're gonna be here for a while."

"Alright," he shrugged. "Where would you like to stay?"

"Well, when I was staying at the old mansion, the vampires were sure to assign me a room in the tower… they said they wanted to make me feel special or some shit, and, of course, I fell for it." There was a pause. "Turns out they were just trying to isolate me from all that was happening. How could I have been so blind?"

"Don't beat yourself up," Presten said, stepping back along the hallway. "We've got the entire mansion to ourselves, we can pick whatever room we want."

"That's true," Isabel said, smiling. "I think we should look for a room a couple of floors down... just so we're closer to all the happenings."

Presten led the way downstairs as they strutted down the corridor, their eyes darting from one bedroom door to the other. "I find this door to be quite appealing," Isabel said sarcastically. Besides Gavin's room, they all looked the same. "I'll just stay in here," she said, picking out a room at random. She swung the door open and stepped inside. She had started to feel the hunger gnawing at her and thought it might be best if she and Presten parted ways. "Would you like to stay in the room next to me?" she asked.

"I would very much like to," he replied, the corners of his lips curving upwards. Isabel knew what he was thinking. She'd be lying if she said she didn't think the same. But she knew she had to resist it; any imbalance could possibly cost them their lives. After all, Isabel had been warned time and time again not to feed on anyone else but Gavin and Oz, and even though she now knew that all she had learned was bullshit, these ideas were still engrained in her mind. The truth was, Isabel was having a hard time unlearning the things that were once so integral to her being. She was lost, like a little girl trying to find her way. One thing was for sure, though, she was free to have sex with whoever the fuck she wanted.

"I guess I'll see you tomorrow, then?" she asked, eyeing Presten as he retreated into the room across from hers. He nodded, flashing her a coy smile before he closed the door behind him. Isabel stepped back into her room, her mind spinning with images of Presten and what he could possibly do to her. She could feel herself getting wet, but she shrugged it off, trying to distract herself with anything else. "Maybe if I go out, I can get my mind off this," she thought. But where would she go? She couldn't leave the mansion right now; that was her responsibility. So she just wandered around the corridors, opening up random doors to see what was inside.

"Hello, Isabel," a voice said, as she opened a door. It took her a second or two to realize that the voice belonged to Oz.

"Oz, what are you doing here?" she asked. "Weren't you guarding the vampires?"

"Well, you guys were taking too long, so I thought I'd check up on you," he said. Isabel knew he was up to something. He was spread out over the bed, as if waiting for her to barge in there at any second. Was he jealous of Presten?

"I appreciate that," Isabel said, staring down at her feet. Seeing Oz always seemed to make her feel better.

"Why are you standing all the way over there? Come here."

Isabel's feet steered her in his direction. After all this time, Oz still had the most control over her; he was her weakness, the one person she knew she would never get over. It had occurred to her that maybe he had the most power over her because she loved him so much, but then she dismissed the idea, thinking that succubi don't fall for angels, they don't fall for anyone. "Are you going to stay in this room?" she asked, sitting down at the edge of the bed.

"Yeah, it's about time I get some rest from the cold hard prison cells, don't you think?" he asked, wrapping his arm around her. Isabel moved in closer. He was reeling her in. Her head was on his chest and she could hear the sound of his heartbeat.

"I missed that sound," she said, burying her head in his chest. All at once, she took in his smell, that smell she had missed so much. She had been away from him for so long; all she wanted right now was to be one with him. He pulled her even closer to him.

"I missed you," he whispered. She leaned in and pressed her lips to his, and they made out in rhythmic, synchronized motion. She found herself lost in his arms, and everything around her seemed to melt, everything but him. He was the only one she saw, the only one she knew she wanted. Her memory of anyone else just melted away; his touch was the only touch she craved. His hands spread over to her thighs and he squeezed them lightly. Instantly, she could feel the fluids trickling down her leg. She had never been so drawn to someone in her life, and deep down, she knew no one else would measure up to him.

"I want you so much right now," she said against his lips. And suddenly, he rolled up on top of her, pressing his entire weight against her.

"Just the way you like it," he hissed. Isabel closed her eyes and freed her mind. She knew she wouldn't be craving anything or anyone else in a long, long time.

CHAPTER 4

"So, what are you thinking?" Oz asked, brushing a hand through Isabel's silky brown locks.

"I'm thinking how much I've missed you," she said, raising her eyes to his. He planted a kiss on her forehead and continued to stroke her hair. "What, don't you miss me?" she asked, her eyes boring into his.

"It's not that... I'm just speechless," he said, staring back at her. "Isabel, I don't think you realize how beautiful you are."

"And I don't think you realize how much I love you," she said after a long pause.

"I love you, too," he said. They sat in silence. It had occurred to Isabel that maybe this was the first time she had ever been in love. When she was with Oz, all her doubts seemed to disappear, to dissipate into thin air. She felt safe with him and only him. "You know, the hardest part of all of this was having to be away from you."

"It was hard on me, too," Isabel admitted. "It was really scary, seeing you in the state you were in... at one point I didn't know if you would live or die."

"I didn't know, either. Isabel, you have no idea how much I've suffered without you. You've given me strength." He paused for a second, clearing his throat. "When Mikael decided to replace me, they locked me up in this room... and they tore off my wings and threw me into the cell. I thought it would be worth it, but it turns out, I was an idiot."

"There was no way you could've seen that coming," Isabel said, her eyes swelling up with tears. The truth was, she couldn't stand to see Oz get hurt. She knew how much he had suffered in those cells, and as much as she wanted to listen to him, it still hurt like a bitch. Somehow, she felt responsible for all of this. Was there anything more she could've done to prevent this? Were there any red flags she should've paid attention to? Of course there were. She knew from the second she saw Mikael that something was wrong. She knew he didn't have Oz's spirit in him. But she stayed quiet about it, thinking that maybe she was wrong. "I'm the one at fault here," she said, sniffing. "I should've paid more attention, I should've known that something was wrong."

"Hey, there was no way you could've seen that coming," Oz said, his lips curving to a smile as he repeated her words back to her. "I think we should both just give ourselves a break," he continued, stroking her face with the back of his hand. "From now on, promise me you won't worry about anything."

"I can't guarantee you that," she said, taking his hand and squeezing it. "I won't rest until we end this, all of this."

"And we will," he said, his eyes locked on hers. "You just need to believe in yourself, and in Presten."

"Right, Presten," she smiled. She didn't know what it was about the mention of his name that made her uneasy. Perhaps she wanted to feed on him just as much. Perhaps she would, someday.

"Isabel," Oz said, brushing his hand under Isabel's chin. "Don't let me hold you back. We have a great time together, but that doesn't mean you can't feed on anyone else."

Isabel opened her mouth to speak but no words came out. She wanted to tell Oz that she loved him more than anyone, that there was no one else she would rather feed on or be with, but she held back. Oz made her weak, and she didn't like feeling weak, not anymore. "You're right," she said after a long pause. "You're not holding me back... I want to be here right now, with you."

"Well, I was just making sure," he said, brushing the hair out of her eyes. "I want you to forget everything you learned while I was away... I want you to start over."

"And I will," Isabel said, raising her eyes to him. "I promise."

"We need to meet up, all of us, to plan our next move. Isabel, are you with me?"
She looked at him with the determination of a thousand warriors. "I'm with you."

CHAPTER 5

Isabel woke up with a strange sense of contentedness. Her nights spent with Oz always seemed to recharge her, to make her feel whole again. She was ready for that meeting. "Hey, hey," she whispered into his ear. He shifted in his place before he drifted off to sleep again. "Hey, Oz."

"What?" he jumped. "Is it time for our meeting?"

"I would say so," she smiled. "Come on, let's call the rest... we need all the time we can get."

Not long after all four of them were back around the round table next to the trapdoor. Every now and again, Ava would climb down, leave the hostages some food and then climb out again, a weary look on her face. "They don't look so good," she said, shaking her head. "They're in really bad shape."

"Word's going around that the vampire council's out looking for them," Presten said, rising to his feet and beginning to pace the room. "One of the hostages threatened me last time I brought them food... he said the vampires would come for us. I'm surprised they haven't, yet."

"They must be plotting something," Isabel said, looking a little frantic. "You can never really predict their next move."

"They're going to come for us, we just need to be ready for when they do," Oz said. There was a pause. "Holy shit," he said suddenly. "We're missing something."

"What, what do you mean?" Isabel asked, her eyebrows furrowed. "Oz, talk to me." He leaned back in his chair and clasped his hands behind his head. He clenched his eyes shut, and for a moment it looked like he was mumbling to himself.

"They're rebuilding the old mansion," he hissed, his eyes fixated on the wall behind Isabel.

"They're trying to find another headquarters, and they're leaving us to plan here like idiots!"

Isabel felt a lump rise in her throat. "This's crazy," she said, shaking her head in denial. "Do you think a lot of them made it out alive after the fire?"

"Right before the fire, the vampires had reached their peak; there were more of them at the mansion than we could count," Oz said. "Gavin had already recruited tens, maybe hundreds of them… the hostages we have down there are nothing compared to the rest!"

Suddenly it hit Isabel that they were all severely outnumbered. Gavin had managed to round up so many vampires while Oz was away. It was unbelievable he had gotten away with it. Isabel kicked herself for never questioning him, for letting all of this fly past her. She felt stupid, but right now, she knew how to recognize a vampire when she saw one. "But they're still going to come for them," she said finally. "They're going to reassemble their army and attack us here. We need to act, fast."

"I know what we need to do," Oz said, his eyes darting from Presten, to Ava, and then to Presten again. "You two need to go visit the mansion."

"What, are you crazy?" Isabel asked, slamming her hand against the table. "This is insane, do you want to get the both of them killed?"

"Do you seriously think I would suggest such a plan if I thought it would backfire?" Oz asked, suddenly agitated. "Isabel, let me convince you on this."

"Why don't we just let them speak for themselves?" she asked, nodding towards Presten and Ava, who were seated across from them.

"I think Oz has a point," Presten said. "A lot of the vampires don't even know who I am or what I look like... they may know me by name, or that I'm the chosen one, but very few of them have actually seen me." But Isabel wasn't convinced. She shook her head in protest; were Presten and Ava about to throw themselves into the fire?

"What about Rene?" she asked, tilting her head to the side. "What if she sees you?"

"We'll be careful," Ava said, leaning across the table. "Isabel, you don't have to worry about us... I know the old mansion like the back of my hand, nothing bad can happen."

"Then I'll go with you," Isabel said.

"See, now that's crazy."

"If you can go, then I can go, too."

"Isabel, no," Oz said, jumping to his feet. "This isn't going to happen; do you realize how impulsive you're being?"

"These people know you, they've been after you for months now," Presten said, his eyes locked on Isabel's. Suddenly it felt like an intervention. The three of them were hunched over and staring at Isabel; they were going to talk her out of it if it was the last thing they did.

"And what am I supposed to do, stay behind?" she asked, suddenly furious.

"No, you're going to come with me; we're going to have a little talk with Gavin," Oz said, raising an eyebrow at her. The sound of Gavin's name sent shivers down Isabel's spine; he was always there, at the back of her mind, taunting her. The very idea of having to face him made her skin crawl. "You and I, we can't be at the other mansion, but what we can do is this: we're going to go down there to the cellars and you're going to try and get as much information out of Gavin as you possibly can."

"And what about you? What are you gonna do?" Isabel asked, tugging at the tips of her hair.

"I'm going to come with you, but I'm not going to be in the picture," Oz said. "Gavin's more likely to trust you, to talk to you. I'm going to hide, and whenever you feel like he's not giving you enough information, the information you need, that's when I come in."

Isabel wondered what that meant. She knew she could bend Gavin, or at least she thought she could, but that didn't mean she couldn't use some help. She and Oz made a great team; with him, she felt like she could do anything. But a part of her was still scared for Presten and Ava; what if they got caught? "I'm going to trust you on this one," she said to Oz after a long pause. "I don't know what's gonna happen, but I feel like we all need to get it together. I'm proud of us, I really am, but this is only just the beginning."

The other three nodded solemnly, and then Oz reached his hand out to Isabel, motioning for her to get up. "Come on," he said. "Let's go down there… we don't have much time."

Isabel took his hand and squeezed it. "Wait," she breathed. "I'm, I'm scared."

"Don't be," Oz said, blinking at her. "I'm going to be right there with you... we're going to do this together." He pulled her hand just a little bit more until she couldn't resist him. They exchanged brief glances before Oz pulled the trapdoor open and climbed down. He nodded towards Gavin's cell, and as Isabel slowly started tiptoeing her way across the dungeon, he crouched down in the corner, trying not to draw any attention to himself. The cells were so silent that even Oz was afraid. It had occurred to him that a hostage's silence was not an indication of desperation, but of confidence. The vampire council already had their eyes out; maybe these hostages were just waiting for the right time to be rescued. Oz held his breath while Isabel made her way for Gavin's cell. Deep down, he prayed she could do this on her own.

"Hello, Isabel," Gavin said, lifting his head off the floor. He had been lying, half-asleep, on his stomach, and had raised himself on his elbows when a pair of feet that he immediately recognized as Isabel's, came into his line of vision. His gaze travelled up and down her body like a hungry wolf eyeing his prey. "What brought you here?" he asked, standing, then raising himself up on the balls of his feet before sinking to his knees again. He had a smile plastered to his face, that smile Isabel despised so much.

She squatted down in front of him. "I'm here," she started, "to ask you a few questions."

"And what might those be?" Gavin asked, his pearly teeth showing through his smile. Isabel opened her mouth to speak but no words came out. *It's happening,* she thought to herself. "Come on, Isabel, cat got your tongue?" he asked. Isabel could feel the heat boiling up inside her.

"What's the council's next move? When are they coming for us, for you?" she asked, leaning in close to him. Her face was only inches from his, and she could feel his hot breath against her skin; it made her sick.

Gavin chuckled. "Ah, Isabel, you're still naive... I thought you would've learned by now, but you're still your old gullible self, how amazing!"

"You tell me, now!" Isabel hissed, reaching out and grabbing Gavin by the collar. "What's the council's next move?!" Gavin's face drooped to a scowl. Their eyes locked on like magnets. Isabel figured she'd have to do a little bit more if she wanted him to talk. She found herself focusing on an empty space in the air between them, her hands slowly retreating from his collar and latching onto his neck. Gavin didn't wince. Eyes narrowed and he got a vertical wrinkle between his eyebrows. His lips pursed slightly.

"Home, home," he breathed. Isabel stared brazenly into his eyes.

"Home?" she said.

"Home, home," he hissed. "Home is where the heart is."

Isabel's hands shook. She knew she had him right where she wanted him. She couldn't lose her focus; she had to hold on. At the far end of the dungeon Oz lay with his eyes clenched shut. Little did Isabel know that he was right there with her. "What home?" Isabel asked, her grip around Gavin's neck tightening. "Gavin, what home?"

"Get off me!" he snarled. Isabel's arms fell limp to her side. Suddenly the whole dungeon fell silent. For a moment, she knew she had him, but then it all dwindled away for no apparent reason. Isabel turned around, her eyes scanning the place. Oz was still tucked away somewhere; she was glad no one could see him. "Oh, Isabel, did you really think it was that simple?" Gavin asked, raising an eyebrow at her. His lips curved to a menacing smile, and when Isabel tried to reel him in again, he snapped his fingers repeatedly, ordering her to stop. "We don't have to do this, you don't have to do this," he said, shaking his head frantically. "You're getting to me, you're getting to me."

"Home is where the heart is?" Isabel asked, popping her head in through the gap between the iron bars of his cell. "Tell me, *what is your secret?*"

"Isabel, stop, you don't want to do this… you know you don't, you still care about me and we both know it," he said, his eyes boring into hers. His voice softened and his grip on the iron bars loosened; for a second, Isabel thought she would give into his orders. Her mind conjured up images of the two of them together; Gavin's arms were around her, he was cradling her to sleep. She thought she would melt into his arms, but then she snapped out of it. Like a slap across the face, Isabel felt a gush of cold air hit her, but it wasn't coming from outside. She knew it was Oz. He was the one controlling her.

"I won't pity you," she snarled. "That's enough."

Gavin shot her a glare before he retreated back into his cell. He crawled up into a fetal position and started cradling himself to sleep.

Isabel rose to her feet and climbed out of the cell, and when the coast was clear, Oz followed her. "Well, what now?" Isabel asked, her eyebrows furrowed. "I don't know what to make of this."

"Neither do I," Oz said, slamming the trapdoor shut. "You did a good job, though, I'm proud of you."

"Not good enough, apparently," she said, rolling her eyes. "Or else we would've had more information by now."

"Hey, just cut yourself some slack, okay? Even the two of us combined couldn't control him... but we almost had him, maybe next time..."

"There won't be a next time, don't you see?" Isabel asked, a look of frustration on her face. "The council are going to break in eventually... they're probably plotting right now."

"Which is why Presten and Ava have a job to do... they're on their way right now," Oz said, brushing a hand through Isabel's hair. "I don't want you to worry, Isabel, just be patient. Everything will fall into place." But Isabel wasn't listening. In her mind's eyes, she could see Gavin's face shining in the dimness of the cells, mouthing the words "home is where the heart is" to her. She thought about what that could mean. She thought about whether he was just trying to fuck with her. Gavin repulsed her and all she wanted right now was to get rid of him. "Isabel, I think you should get some rest." Oz's voice seeped into her consciousness.

"Yeah, you're right," she said, sighing. "I think I just need to lie down for a while."

"Do you want me to come with you?" he asked, his lips coming to a smile.

"I think— I think I just need to be alone."

Isabel ran for the stairs. She felt like she was going to hurl. She swung the door to her room open and collapsed into bed, her mind racing with a million thoughts at once. At that point, she was filled with doubt. She heard a knock at her door; she knew it would be Oz. But she decided she just wanted to be alone. She rolled over away from the door and the first thing she saw was the pile of books from last night. Immediately, she grabbed them off the floor and started skimming through them. *The Earth and the Supernatural,* one of them read, but the rest were untitled. "Well, what do we have here?" she asked herself as she flipped the book open. Deep down, she was scared to even look at it. *This literary work taps into the role of the supernatural in shaping the natural world we know today...* Isabel clutched the book in her hands for a moment before she flipped it open again. Shapeshifters, vampires, the vampire council and the succubi; it was all in this book. *The origin of vampires, angels and shapeshifters,* one of the chapter titles read. "Looks like I'll be up all night reading this," Isabel thought. Oz continued to knock on her door and she continued to ignore him.

CHAPTER 6

Oz sat by the fireplace, not moving. His eyes were fixated on the rising flames, and when he heard a knock at the mansion door, he shot up, startled, thinking it must be Presten and Ava. "Welcome back," he said, his lips coming to a smile the second he saw them standing in the doorway. Behind him stood four or five strangers, who Oz immediately recognized as fellow angels and succubi. "Hello," he said graciously. "Come on in."

"See, I told you we wouldn't disappoint you," Ava said playfully. "No one knew it was us and we managed to rally up some allies, too."

"Hi," one of them said, peering at Presten through her bangs. He shook her hand and smiled at her, and it wasn't long before she realized she needed to introduce herself. "I'm Nadia, a succubus from a small town here in France."

"Hello, Nadia," Presten said. But he was too distracted. The rest of them stared at him with wide eyes, like little kids meeting their teacher on the first day of school. "It's nice to meet you all," he said finally. "Are you all succubi?" They nodded in robotic motion. Presten didn't know if this was a sign of discipline, respect, or just weak character. "Where's Isabel?" he asked, looking around.

"Isabel has been in her room for quite some time now," Oz said, his eyes dropping to the floor. "I don't know what's with her. She seems... distracted." The truth was, he couldn't stop thinking about her. He just wanted to crawl into bed with her, pull her close. But she was too "in her head" to even talk to him right now.

"Did anything happen?" Ava asked eagerly. "Did she talk to Gavin?"

"Home is where the heart is," Oz said, avoiding eye contact. "Does that saying ring any bells for you?"

Ava shook her head. "No," she said. There was a pause. "The vampires are still working on renovating the house. They're still assigning everyone their rooms, still taking care of their injured. I would say we still have time."

"That's... optimistic," Oz said, seemingly distracted. "Let's not rely on that thought. I think it would be best if we plan ahead."

"You're right," Ava said, folding both her arms across her chest. "Do you think we should go check on Isabel?" she asked.

"I tried, but she won't answer the door," he said. "But anyway, right now, we need to assign everyone their rooms. Ava, where would you like to stay?"

"I think it's about time I stayed in the tower," she said teasingly. The others stared back blankly. "Right, not a time for jokes?"

"Most certainly not."

"Alright, I think we should spread out; Presten and Isabel already have rooms next to the dungeon… you and me, we can move a bit higher up," she said.

"Sounds about right," Oz said, folding both of his arms across his chest and shifting his weight to one leg. "Oh, hey, look who decided to crawl out of their cave." Isabel smiled at him as she thumped her way down the hall. Her feet were clammy against the hardwood floorboards, but she couldn't be bothered to put any shoes on.

"Hello," she said, a smile plastered to her face. Her eyes immediately went to the five strangers standing next to Ava and she nodded at them graciously. "I see Ava has brought along some allies, welcome," she said.

"Where have you been?" Presten asked, walking over to her.

"I've been reading," Isabel said. "Oz, those books we found... I skimmed through them a little bit."

"Gavin's memoirs?" he asked, his eyes wide.

"No, I've left those till the end," she said, flashing him a smirk. "I went through some history books, here, check this out." She threw him the leather-bound book she had been reading for the past couple of hours. "This is... this is pretty interesting stuff. Did you know that Presten and my names are written in there?" she asked, a glimmer in her eyes.

"Of course they are! They don't call them prophecies for nothing," Oz said, flipping through the book without actually reading it. Isabel wondered why he was so disinterested. "Does it say anything about the final battle?" he asked.

Isabel felt her stomach churn at the mentioning of a final battle. "I don't know, I haven't come across anything about that just yet," she said, shaking her head. Deep down, she didn't really want to know. "Oz, I really think we should go back and look for that key."

"I think we should... but first, let's go down and see how the hostages are," he said, nodding towards the trapdoor. It looked so ominous, as if something would spring out of it at any second.

"We should feed them," Isabel said to Ava and Presten.

"It's your turn," Ava said slyly. "Just be careful... Gavin's an aggressive one."

"You're telling me," Isabel said, turning to look at Oz. But he was already gone. A few minutes later he came back with no less than four trays of food, stacked on top of each other. Isabel slid down the trapdoor and walked to Gavin's cell. She just wanted to get this over with. After their last confrontation, Isabel was weary of how he'd react to her presence. *Stop being so scared of him, what could he possibly do?* She needed to stop being ridiculous. Isabel had Gavin right where she wanted him; she knew she had the upper hand. As she walked quietly to his cell she realized he was asleep, so she just set the tray down on the floor next to him and stared at his black mass of a body for a while before turning to leave. "Wait, what?" she whispered to herself, turning to look at him again. In the darkness, she caught a glimpse of a tiny glint on Gavin's chest. She moved in closer, not sure if what she was seeing was real or just a figment of her imagination. She moved in closer and realized it was a key. *Holy shit.*

"Isabel, Isabel," Oz whispered from the other side of the cells. Isabel jumped. She couldn't let Gavin hear him. She crouched down and focused all her powers towards Oz; maybe, just maybe, she could get through to him.

Oz, Oz, listen to me, can you hear me? I'm inside your head.

The silence was too dense to bear. Somehow, Isabel was trying to penetrate this silence without being heard. *I can hear you,* Oz came through. For a moment Isabel couldn't believe this actually worked. Had she been capable of telepathy all along?

Alright, I'm going to need you to hide... I think I found what we were looking for. She clenched her eyes and waited for an answer, but when she never got one, she figured Oz already got the message. The air was so still that even the sound of Oz's breathing went unheard. She shouldered her way through the iron bars, her eyes still fixated on the small glittery spot on Gavin's chest. The floor creaked beneath her and she wondered if Gavin would wake up. She wondered if any of the vampires would wake up. They all looked so weak. By the looks of it, some of them wouldn't make it through the night. But Isabel needed them to hang in there; she needed to use them as bait for the council. Gavin wasn't moving. His chest was rising and falling to the beat of his breath and when Isabel got close enough, she made sure that this was the key she was looking for. If Gavin kept it secure around his neck, then it must be valuable. She reached out and grabbed it, slowly pulling it off his neck. The rope brushed up against his skin and his head jerked to the left, as if he was being tickled. Isabel let go of the key. For a second, she thought she would run, but when she realized he was still asleep, she knew now was her chance. In one swift move, she snatched the key and took off, but before she could make a run for it, Gavin's eyes shot open.

"Oh my God," Isabel said, feeling his fingers tighten around her wrist.

"What do you think you're doing?" he hissed, getting up. "Do you think I'm stupid, Isabel? Do you think I'm some kind of an idiot?"

Isabel wanted to run. Her eyes were darting back and forth frantically, and she let out a gasp. Suddenly she saw a pair of feet landing into the cellar. *Presten.*

"Who the fuck are you?" Gavin asked as Presten's face swam into view. Maybe Oz was right; maybe the council really didn't know what Presten looked like. "Isabel, you've got some explaining to do," Gavin said, his grip on her wrist tightening. Isabel winced.

"Hey, you stay away from her!" Presten snarled. Gavin didn't flinch.

"You think that just because you've got me locked up in here that I'm going to do whatever you want me to? Well, you're wrong!" Gavin said, letting go of Isabel's arm. She let out a squeal. "Izzy, honey, what's wrong, are you hurt?" he asked, tilting his head to the side. Isabel looked at him and then looked away. "I didn't mean to hurt you," he said again. "You know I wouldn't do that… I just want you to mind your own business, that's all."

"You don't get to tell me what to do," she hissed.

"And what about this guy over here?" he asked, ignoring her. "Who is he and why have you brought him here?" There was silence. "My, Izzy, you're still so gullible... always trusting the people you shouldn't trust."

"You don't get to talk about trust," she snapped. She realized he was only trying to mess with her head. Isabel recognized that now, and she was doing all that she could to stop it. She turned to Presten for help and he nodded at her, trying to channel all his energy towards her. Suddenly Oz appeared from the far end of the cell and it was three against one. Gavin's eyes started drooping, like he was being hypnotized.

"I, I," he stuttered, and then, without warning, his head drooped like a deflated balloon. Gavin was spent. There was no way he could resist all three of them exercising their powers over him. Isabel breathed out a sigh of relief.

"Well that was definitely... intense," she whispered, grabbing hold of Gavin's key. "Got it," she said, flashing Presten a smirk. They climbed out of the basement and Isabel quickly made her way for the stairs. "Who's coming with me?" she asked.

Without much hesitation, Presten followed her, the two of them hurrying up the stairs like little kids going on an adventure. Oz sighed and turned around. Was this jealousy he was feeling? Either way, he decided to mind his own business. Isabel was free to do whatever she wanted, no matter what he felt.

CHAPTER 7

"That must've been scary, what you did in there," Presten said, looking at Isabel out of the corner of his eye.

"It was," she said, shaking her head frantically. "And when his eyes shot open... that shit freaked me out."

Presten chuckled. "I probably would've peed myself," he said. "I hate to say this, but Gavin's a scary motherfucker."

"You're telling me," Isabel said, rolling her eyes. "I can't believe I used to sleep with that guy." There was silence. Isabel didn't know if what she said was inappropriate, but deep down, she didn't care. She knew she had bigger things to worry about than what Presten thought about her.

"I can't believe you used to sleep with him, either," he said, grinning. "You did a pretty good job, though, I'm proud of you."

"I don't deserve that, you guys did most of the work," she said, looking at him through her eyelashes.

"I don't think you give yourself nearly enough credit," Presten said. "And I'm not just saying that... you're way stronger than you think."

Isabel didn't know what to say. She wanted to believe him, she really did, but a part of her felt like he was lying. Isabel just wanted to step out of Oz's shadow, to explore things on her own. But she knew that wasn't possible: it was too risky. "I really appreciate you saying that," she said after a long pause. "Right now, we just need to find Gavin's room so we can try this thing." Presten nodded. "I just need to remember where it was... oh, right there," she said, pointing to that familiar swinging door at the far end of the hall. She pushed it open and stepped inside, immediately heading for

Gavin's closet. "Let's hope it works." The key rustled in its lock before the little door at the back of the closet creaked open. Isabel couldn't believe her eyes. She pushed past some cobwebs, which hung from the ceiling like drapes, her knees bending involuntarily as the walls closed in on her bit by bit. "Hey, are you good back there?" she asked, struggling to turn her neck around.

"I'm okay," Presten said. "I'm right behind you." They were crammed in such a tight space that Isabel eventually found herself crawling on all fours. But it was not long before the rabbit hole of a passageway opened up again and Isabel found it possible to stretch herself out again. "There a light at the end of this tunnel?" Presten asked, peering over her shoulder.

"I think so," she said pleasantly. "Just follow that glow." Isabel stopped at the end of the hall. "Check this out," she said, jumping out and landing on lower ground. She spun around, trying to take in what she was seeing. The ceiling arched over them like a dome; Isabel felt like she was stuck in a snow globe. She looked around and all she saw were books covering the entire length of the walls. "Presten," she breathed. "Where the fuck are we?"

"I think we just unlocked Gavin's secret library."

There was silence. The place was so quiet, like a place of worship. "That explains a lot," Isabel said after a long pause. "You wanna check it out?"

"I wouldn't know where to begin," he said, his eyes darting from one bookshelf to another. "How old do you think this place is?"

"I have no idea," she said. Isabel was still in shock. How could someone even hide a place like this? It made no sense to her. Her head was buzzing with questions, questions about Gavin and what he possibly could be doing with all these books. They lined every shelf, every inch of this library; Isabel didn't know *what* to think. She got up on a stool placed usefully underneath one of the shelves and started skimming through the leather-bound books.

All along they ran from black, to brown, to beige, to black again. Isabel grabbed one of them and started skimming through it. *The Art of Mind Control.* "I am definitely keeping this," she said, tucking it under her arm and hopping off the stool. "Hey, check this out." She tossed it to Presten and then went on looking.

"Are you sure we should be going through Gavin's shit?" he asked, folding both arms across his chest. If anything, he looked weary. He didn't know what it was about this place that freaked him out. Isabel looked at him like he was a crazy person.

"What do you mean?" she asked, raising an eyebrow at him. "This place is a goldmine... look around you! We can't possibly leave here without looking through his things." She moved the stool and climbed up again, running her fingers along the line of books. She took them out, one by one, examining them carefully. "There are a lot of interesting titles over here... you might want to check them out."

But Presten was reluctant. He moved in closer to Isabel, but his feet didn't carry him far. She just stared at him, her eyes reeling him in closer. "Just hand me over those books," he said, holding out his hands.

"Here," she said. "Catch." Presten grabbed the books and started to flip through them.

"This is— this is pretty dangerous," he said, not taking his eyes off the page. "He has spells in here, mind control spells."

"Which is exactly why we're going to need those books," she said with her back to him. Presten eyed her as she swayed back and forth between shelves; her curvaceous body was absolutely mesmerizing.

"You have a really nice figure, you know that?" he asked, shifting his weight to one leg. Isabel froze. For some reason, she hadn't expected him to say that.

"Oh, I'm flattered that you think that," she said coldly. But in reality, she could feel the fire boiling up inside of her. Her mind was conjuring up images of Presten fucking her in that library; that big, empty library. Her body quivered at the thought.

"That's all you're going to say?" Presten asked, putting the books down and walking over to her. His eyes were on her, she could feel them, but she kept trying to convince herself that she didn't want that, that she didn't want him. A part of her felt like she belonged to Oz, that nothing and nobody would ever compare to him. But she shook her head at the thought; since when did succubi get into monogamous relationships?

"I really don't know what to say," she said after a long pause. *That's it? That's all you can come up with?* "I mean, I do find you very attractive, Presten, it's just that—"

"It's just what?" he asked, wrapping his arms around her waist and pressing her body to his.

Isabel let out a sigh. At that moment, she knew she wanted him, and she knew he wanted her, too. The hunger was tugging at her insides; she had never wanted anything so bad. But Oz lingered at the back of her mind. What was it about him that made her so reluctant to be with anyone else? She recognized that her desires were completely independent from her feelings for Oz, but she just couldn't shake off the feeling that she was doing something wrong. Something didn't feel right. But she knew she was going to go ahead and do it anyway.

"It's nothing," she said finally, pressing his head down to her pelvic area.

She caught a glimmer of a smile on his lips as his face disappeared, and she felt his strong hands grasp her from behind. The fabric of her robe slithered across her thighs as he nestled his nose in between them, pushing them apart, his hot breath against her pussy igniting the desire inside her even more. She kept her eyes locked on him; her fingers entangled in his hair, and she almost automatically draped one long leg over his shoulder.

It was all the invitation Presten needed. Her grip on his hair tightened and she threw her head back at the first touch of his tongue against her. She could feel how wet she was, how much she wanted him, and it was no secret to him. His tongue flickered slightly before his hands brought her hips closer to him and he buried his face in between her thighs.

Isabel couldn't hold back the satisfied moan that erupted from within her. And why would she? They were alone in the library, with only the books to keep them company, and the thought of Oz locked too far back in her head to care. All she wanted now was more of what she was feeling, more of Presten's tongue against her pussy, more of his hands squeezing her ass cheeks as he did things to her she had never felt before.

Soon she was rocking against him, both her hands now clutching his hair as she grinded, pulling him even closer to her with her leg. He responded with vigor, his tongue finding its way inside her, circling her clit, sending wave after wave of orgasm rocking through her body. She closed her eyes, screaming in pleasure, lost in this feeling of satisfaction.

Her eyes flew open when she felt her body being lifted off the ground, Presten pushing her higher up against the wall and throwing her other leg over his shoulder. Bolts of electricity shot up and down her legs as his tongue moved and for an instant she thought that she couldn't take any more.

Presten turned around and let her slide down his body, Isabel's feet finding the ground and her knees buckling. Presten grabbed her by the hair as she stumbled down in front of him and with one hand quickly undid his pants. Isabel's eyes widened at the size of him.

"You like what you see?" Presten smirked.

Isabel looked up at him and before he could say anything else, grabbed his cock and squeezed, pumping him. Presten groaned and threw his head back and Isabel quickly wrapped her lips around his cock. She felt her lips stretch around it, only a third of it finding its way into her mouth before she felt she couldn't take any more. She felt Presten's hands tighten on her hair and he immediately began to rock against her, sliding in and out of her mouth slowly at first, and then picking up speed.

Isabel matched his rhythm, determined to keep up with him. She felt his throbbing inside her mouth and knew he would explode within minutes if this continued. She braced herself, wrapping her hands around his thighs, anticipating the flood that would explode from him.

"I want you," Presten growled, pulling out of her mouth.

She felt his grip hard on her arm as he brought her roughly to her feet. Isabel smiled to herself. Somehow his aggressiveness was turning her on and as he led her back to the bookshelf and pushed her against it, she could feel her wetness dripping down the inside of her thighs, waiting for him. She opened her legs, feeling his cock pressed against her as he positioned himself.

She looked back at him, her eyes catching his as she bit her lip. His hands squeezed her ass cheeks and she squirmed. Without taking his eyes off her, Presten pushed and slid inside her, grabbing her by the waist as he buried his cock as deep as it would go.

Isabel's screams echoed off the walls of the library as Presten fucked her. His hips made slapping sounds against her ass as he moved, his pace quick, his cock stretching her and touching places inside her she never knew could be reached. He was like a jackhammer, grabbing her by the hair and pulling her head back as he slammed against her. Isabel had to grab onto the shelves just to keep her balance, toppling books over as she pushed back against him, matching his rhythm, their moans and groan of pleasure intertwining in an animalistic desire.

It seemed to last forever and Isabel didn't want it to stop. His hands suddenly tightened around her hips and she could feel his cock expand inside her. She knew what was coming even before he pushed in one final time, pulling her against him, burying himself to the hilt and exploding inside her.

She fell back against him, panting and exhausted, worn from his assault on her body. She let his arms wrap around her, his cock still inside her. She felt limp in his embrace, and she knew that if he let her go, she would crumble to the floor. She didn't have to worry about it, though, as Presten guided them both to the ground, softly, their bodies lying side by side on the cold surface and their muted panting a reprieve from the screams and grunts that had filled the room just moments before.

Isabel wanted to turn to him, to say something, but felt her body give out and her eyes close slowly. Exhaustion enveloped her and within seconds she had drifted away.

CHAPTER 8

Isabel opened her eyes. Her arm was stretched out to her side and for a second her fingers felt numb. She was lying on the floor of Gavin's library, her body feeling like a slab of dry clay against the cold marble. She tried to roll over but her whole body was aching; Presten must've done a pretty good job. She marveled at the events of last night, but she still couldn't stop thinking about Oz. It was true she got what she wanted, but she couldn't help but compare. Oz was gentle; Presten liked it rough. Images from the night before were zapping through her mind: images of Presten, images of herself. She couldn't take her mind off it, but she was conflicted. If she were to tell Oz, would he get jealous? Would he be happy for her? Would he be indifferent?

Did she want him to be jealous?

All those questions were racing through her mind, but she knew she was being ridiculous. Even in her previous life, she was never a monogamous person. What changed? She rolled over to look at Presten, her eyes travelling up and down his naked body. He was spread out over the cold ground, and so was she, and they basked in the moderate chill of the night. Isabel tried to get up, but her back hurt like hell. "Holy shit," she whispered, getting up on the balls of her feet. She sat up and looked around. There were books splayed out all around them and she wondered how many of those would actually come in handy sometime. Her eyes went straight to the one about mind control and when she realized Presten had tossed it aside last night, purely for the sake of making his advances on Isabel, she rolled her eyes, reaching for it again and making a mental note not to forget it.

"Good morning," Presten said, rolling over to face her. He clenched his eyes in pain. "Holy fuck, I think I hurt myself."

"Me, too," Isabel said, smiling. "But it was worth it."

"I'm glad," he beamed. "I don't know why I thought you'd be reluctant at first... it was probably all in my head."

But it wasn't. "I'm guessing it was," she said.

"Well, I can go for another round, anytime," he whispered, his eyes boring into hers. Isabel was starting to feel hungry again.

"We really need to control ourselves if we want to make it out of here alive," she said, shaking her head. "I think we should go tell the rest about this place... they'll be more than thrilled."

Presten's face drooped to a scowl. "Do you promise me, though, that this place will always stay our little safe haven... for whenever we need to get away from everything and everyone?" he asked, his head cocked to the side. Isabel couldn't resist his eyes; they glimmered with his desire for her. The truth was, she was flattered, and she couldn't help but feel attracted to him.

"I promise," she said finally. "Listen, I had fun last night, I don't want you to doubt that for one second. It's just that I've been a bit… preoccupied lately, with all what's been going on."

"I know, I understand," Presten nodded. "And I want you to know that I've been just as pressured as you have lately… but we'll get through this, together."

"I know we will," Isabel said, reaching her hand out to him. "But for now, let's just get out of here." They made their way back; it felt weird having to crawl through that little cave again— it was making Isabel claustrophobic— but when they finally jumped out of the closet she felt a tide of relief wash over her. As soon as they both stepped out of Gavin's master bedroom, they ran into Oz, who was waiting for them outside.

"Where have you been?" he asked, his head cocked to the side. "We looked everywhere for you."

"Good news," Isabel said, flashing Oz a smirk. "We've uncovered something, something big."

"And what is that?" he asked, his eyes darting between them. There was something about the way he was gawking at them that made Presten uncomfortable. If he wasn't mistaken, Oz was displaying some signs of jealousy. "Come on, you two, say something!"

"It's Gavin's secret book library," Isabel blurted out. "He has hundreds, if not thousands of books in there and this is one of them," she said, handed the book over to Oz. He narrowed his eyes at the title and then began skimming through it.

"This is a dangerous book," he mumbled, rather to himself. "I think we can make use of this… good job keeping it with you," he said, raising his eyebrows at Isabel. "We'll go back and take a look at this place later… I have a feeling we will need to revisit it. But for now, I want to let you in on our plan."

"Your plan?" Isabel asked, her eyebrows furrowed. It wasn't long before Ava and the five strangers showed up at the doorway.

"We're going to visit the council," one of them said. "We'll show up at the other mansion and demand that they hear us out in exchange for the hostages."

Isabel thought about that for a second. "That sounds like a good plan... and now that there are more of us, we're going to sound more convincing. They're going to have to listen to us because they know we have the upper hand."

"We do have the upper hand, but do you know why?" Oz asked, looking at Isabel through the corner of his eye. "It's not because we're a larger number, but because we've got Gavin."

Isabel let that sink in for a second. She knew Oz was right. She knew Gavin was one of the most influential vampires in the council. "That makes total sense," she breathed. "Now that they know that Gavin's with us, they're going to have to hear us out," she said.

"Absolutely... or else we kill Gavin," one of the angels said. Isabel locked eyes with Presten. He had been gawking at her all throughout the meeting, and the truth was, she was beginning to crave his attention all over again. Just the thought of him and Oz taking her at once made her feel all warm on the inside, but she knew she couldn't think about that now.

"I think this is the perfect plan," she said after a long pause. "But I do think we need to recruit more succubi before we head over there."

"I'll handle it," Ava said. "They didn't recognize me at the other mansion... they have no idea who I am. I'm going to sneak in there, maybe scope out some new members to join our clan."

"This is a dangerous game you're playing," Oz said, shaking his head.

"Got any better ideas?" Ava asked, raising an eyebrow at him. "I don't see you doing anything."

"I'm just saying... you need to be very careful. Those people might not know you, but sooner or later, they'll realize that some people went missing, and they're going to pin it on us," Oz said.

"He's right," Isabel said. "Be careful, Ava, and I do think you should take Presten with you like last time. You guys can protect each other." Presten shot Isabel a worried look. Somehow, it made her feel guilty. Was she throwing him into the monster's den?

She thought about it for a little while longer. "I have an idea," she said. "Why don't we all go?"

"Remember how the last time you suggested that we all shot you down, because, as I'd like to remind you, the vampire council already knows you?" Oz asked, agitated this time. "You're risking our plans, Isabel, I don't know why you're being so stubborn about this."

"I'm not stubborn," she said, narrowing her eyes at Oz. "I just have a plan."

"And what would that plan be?" he asked. Isabel wondered why he was being so critical towards her. She wondered if it had anything to do with Presten.

"You know how we've all come to master mind control?" she asked, searching Oz's face for a reaction, and when she didn't get one, she moved on to the rest of them. "Some of us haven't exactly mastered it... but you know what I mean." They nodded. "Alright, well, I was thinking we should all go to the mansion together, but I don't think we should go inside." There was a pause. "How about we all gather somewhere out in the forest... and try to lure the succubi, make them come to us?"

"And how will we do that?" Ava asked, staring at Isabel with heavy lidded eyes.

"Mind control," she said. "If all of us go, we've got a better chance at getting through to them. That way, we can lure the succubi out of the mansion, and then all of us, as a collective group, can use our powers to bend the vampires."

Oz thought about that for a second. "And then?"

"And then we all head out to the vampire council to make our case."

"You do know where the council is, right?" Oz asked, raising an eyebrow at her. Isabel shook her head.

"I'm guessing it's somewhere around here?" she asked.

"It's in Nice. We're going to have to take a train there," he said, matter-of-factly. At that point, Isabel was just annoyed by him. The truth was, Oz was probably the most sensible person in the room, but there was something about the way he was dealing with Isabel that made her furious. She hated when someone talked down to her and at that point, Oz was making her feel like an idiot.

"Listen, we were going to pay the council a visit, anyway," she said after a long pause. "So we might as well just do it now, all of us."

"It's a risk, you being there," he said, his lips barely moving.

"It's a risk I'm willing to take."

The silence poured into the room from all directions. Like a cloud, it descended on them and just lingered there; Isabel was suffocating. "Alright," Oz said finally. "Do what you wish. I just don't want you to get hurt in the process."

"I won't," she said. "Now, what do the rest of you think about heading over to the mansion right now?"

"I think it's a brilliant idea," Presten said, his deep-set eyes boring into Isabel's. "We just need to stick together and clear our minds from all the negative energy; if any one of us is distracted during the time of summoning, our entire plan will go to shit."

"You're right," Isabel said, nodding. "I think we've all gotten the hang of this whole telepathy thing... it's controlling the vampires that's going to be tough."

"You know what the best thing is?" Presten asked, his lips curving to a sly smile. "We've got an entire book dedicated to mind control on our hands. Don't forget to use that, Isabel."

"Oh I won't," she said. "I've read quite a big chunk of it so far... believe me, it's going to come in handy."

"Alright, should we get going?" Oz asked, already making his way for the door.

"And the prisoners? Who's going to stay with them?" Ava asked.

"Presten, you can stay," Oz said with a smile. "Seeing as though you're probably the most powerful incubus in this room, I think you should keep an eye on the hostages."

"Alright," Presten said, his eyes darting from Oz, to Isabel, and then to Oz again. "I'll take care of it.

"Okay, let's go," Isabel said, turning to leave. She eyed Oz as he swung the door open and stepped outside. "Boy, do you look pissed off," she said, walking over and standing next to him. She just didn't understand why he was acting the way he was. Something was off, but she knew that now wasn't the time to confront him about it. Ava joined them and the three of them marched across the yard.

"Oh, hey," Ava said, her eyes fixated somewhere over Isabel's shoulder. She looked over and saw all five succubi— the "newbies", as she liked to think of them- huddled at the far end of the field. "I don't know why we keep forgetting about them," Ava said, skipping across the yard.

"I didn't forget about them," Isabel said. "I keep an eye on them all the time... I knew we would find them out here."

"They're always in a group," Oz said, looking at Isabel with glassy eyes. "I wonder if we should be worried."

Isabel shook her head. "No, I've been watching them very closely lately... they seem alright," she said.

""Alright" doesn't necessarily mean dedicated," Oz said. Isabel rolled her eyes. She couldn't believe how negative he was being. She wanted to scream her lungs out to him, to tell him that she couldn't take it anymore. It was all so frustrating, given the fact that she needed to feed. And it's not like she needed to feed on just about anybody, she needed to feed on Oz. She didn't get why he was pushing her away, why he was shooting her down. She thought he would be more supportive of her by now, but it didn't look to her like he was going to get over this anytime soon. Whatever "this" was.

"Well, I guess we're going to have to find out," she said, waving to the group of people standing at the far end of the field. They dispersed for a moment before they came together again, marching towards Isabel and the others.

"I really hope you prove me wrong," Oz said, crossing both arms across his chest.
"Oh, I will."

***

"Alright, I think we're getting close," Isabel said, catching a glimpse of the old mansion. They had been hiking for around an hour. When the tip of the tower came into view, Isabel crouched down amongst the weeds. "Let's stop here," she said. The rest of them crouched down next to her and eyed the mansion apprehensively.

"Do you think it'll work if we try and tap into them from all the way over here?" Ava asked.

"It has to," Isabel said. "I don't think we can get any closer, it's too risky."

"There are a lot of us. I think this might work," one of the succubi said, her eyes fixated on the mansion. She got down and hugged her knees to her chest, rocking back and forth repeatedly. Isabel clenched her eyes and tried to focus. She looked around once to make sure everyone else was doing the same and then she went back again, trying to immerse herself in her own little world. No one had taught her how to do this; it was all a matter of instinct. She took a deep breath. The wind caressed her face and she could feel every muscle in her body turn flaccid. It was like she was doing yoga. *Alright, now, tell them to come out. Come out, come out, come out.*

"Come out, come out, come out," Oz said out loud.

"Come out, come out, come out," all seven of them said in unison. "Come out, come out, come out." The silence lingered in the air. Isabel tried to focus all her energy on that one thing, on luring the succubi out of the mansion. It was like her soul was leaving her body— or at least it felt that way— and she was watching herself from afar. She felt like she was floating around freely, that she was communicating with people and things she never thought she would be able to communicate with. *Come out, come out, come out. Come out from the mansion, join us.*

"Join us, join us," Oz breathed. The rest followed. Isabel opened her eyes and stared out into the distance. She could see the trees swaying back and forth in the wind, but no people. She wondered if this was actually working. The air was so still, despite the wind. She had never felt so peaceful, yet so worried. A series of paradoxes, a chain reaction of impending events that were yet to come. Isabel felt connected, not only to the people in the mansion, but also to the circle of people around her.

They were all crouched down on the ground, taking up different positions, positions that were quite peculiar in their nature. Oz stooped down next to Isabel and she could feel the heat radiating from his body. She basked in it, wishing she could let him know how much she loved him, but then decided to stay focused, clenching her eyes again and ducking her head down low. Suddenly, she heard rustling sounds. Her eyes shot open and she started scanning the place, trying to discern the source of the noise.

"Did you hear that?" Oz asked, turning to look at her. Isabel nodded.

"It's coming from over there," she said, looking somewhere over her shoulder. Suddenly a bunch of figures appeared from amongst the trees. They staggered towards Oz, Isabel and the rest of the gang, and when they spotted what seemed to be the source of the frequencies, they nodded at them, as if to acknowledge their presence. Isabel noticed that one incubus lead the pack.

"Hello," he said, smiling at her. "We heard you from over there."

"Welcome," Isabel smiled, motioning for him to sit down.

"We can't," he said, seemingly distracted. "We need to get out of here as soon as possible, it's not safe here."

"How did you get past security?" Oz asked, rising to his feet.

"We fed off your energy and tapped into their consciousness," he said, his hands balled up into fists. He wouldn't stop looking around; Isabel thought the vampires would strike at any second. "For the first time, we evaded them, something we thought we would never be able to do. I'm Jared, by the way." He reached his hand out to Isabel.

"Isabel," she said. "Have you sedated the guards?"

Jared nodded. "Yes, we have. But not for long... we better get out of here before they wake up again," he said. The rest rose to their feet, and in a matter of moments, they were back on the hiking trail again. "So, Isabel, what brought you to us?" he asked, glancing at her.

"I know you," one of them said. "You're Isabel, the chosen one."

Jared paused. "Wait, you're Isabel?" he asked, his eyes wide as a set of plates. "I don't know why I never made the connection, this is awesome!"

Isabel didn't really know what to say. She wasn't used to people recognizing her. "Thanks," she said after a long pause. "I'm sorry, I've just never been put in a situation like this before."

"What, no one has ever recognized you before?" he asked, tilting his head to the side. "That's strange. You see, I'm an old succubus. I'm quite old, actually and I've been imprisoned for quite a long time now. I hear things, things about impending battles and about the chosen ones. I know about you and Presten," he said.

"Presten is at the other mansion," Oz said. "You'll get to meet him in a little while."

Jared smiled. "I'd be honored to," he said. Isabel started making her way downhill again, motioning for the rest to follow her. "Where are we headed now?" Jared asked, a cheesy smile plastered to his face.

"To the rebels' mansion."

CHAPTER 9

It wasn't long before the pack arrived outside the mansion again. Isabel had gotten used to hikes; somehow her transformation had given her the unbreakable stamina of an athlete, the kind that's not even comparable to normal human strength. She signaled for Presten to step outside, so he did, and when he was confronted with seventeen people standing out in the field, his lips curved to a smile. "I see you've done a good job," he said, marching to them. Jared stared at him in awe.

"You're Presten," he said, pushing past his mates and reaching his hand out to him. "I'm Jared, I've heard a lot about you at the old mansion."

"Oh, wow, I did not expect that," Presten said, taking Jared's hand and shaking it. "It's a pleasure to meet you, Jared."

"Pleasure to meet you, too," he said. Presten could feel the eyes of the crowd on him. He peered over his shoulder and the rest of newcomers were staring at him like he was some kind of god. He knew he was the chosen one, but never in a million years would he have thought people would actually recognize him. "So, should we head out to the train station?" he asked, turning to Isabel.

"Yes," she said, averting her gaze to Oz, who just nodded at her.

"It's a long way to the train station," he said. "We'll need to take the bus. But remember, none of us are allowed to talk about internal affairs in public, especially when there are a lot of people around."

"Roger that," Isabel said. The pack made their way downhill again, Isabel and Presten walking side by side. The four succubi had decided to return to the rebel mansion to keep an eye on the hostages while the rest were away. Isabel put all her trust in them, after all, it was Ava who recruited them, and she trusted her judgement over anything. Isabel and Presten were lost in conversation, Isabel mostly forgetting that Oz was even there. There were times when she would feel his eyes on her, but she didn't care. He was emitting so much negative energy that even Isabel couldn't handle it. She bumped into Presten as they walked, their bodies colliding intermittently as they made their way downhill. The air was crisp and for the first time in a long time, Isabel felt free, and no one could take that away from her. She wasn't trapped inside a musty mansion anymore, and neither was she confined to a green patch of a yard. And the truth was, it felt great. "You know, I can't believe we're doing this," she said, the steady thump of her footsteps setting the beat for her movements.

"I can't believe we're doing this, either," Presten said, his eyes on the ground beneath him. "We need to be careful, though; once we get there, we need to have come up with a plan. We can't just barge into the council."

"I know," Isabel said. "We need to settle down somewhere first." The pack made it to the bus station and when they got on the bus, Isabel took the seat next to Presten, the two of them not speaking a single word to each other on the way to the train station. Isabel just stared out the window, her eyes following the road. The landscape shifted from rural to urban as the bus made its way downtown. "This is really weird," Isabel whispered, her lips barely moving. In a way, she felt like she was relearning everything all over again. It was almost as if she had forgotten how to deal with people, how to smile at them as they passed her by and how to properly thank them when they held the door open for her. All those little things, she needed to learn all over again. She had been trapped in this tiny community for so long, that everything she once knew had become so foreign to her, so unnatural.

"What's weird?" Presten asked, looking over her shoulder at the view outside. "The view's beautiful."

"Exactly," Isabel jumped. "Aren't you stunned by it? Don't you miss it? Don't you miss being outside?"

"I do," he smiled. "I actually haven't stopped freaking out ever since we left the mansion. I feel like an alien."

"Me, too," Isabel said, not taking her eyes off the road. "Everything is so... dynamic, but in a different way. Cars are hurrying by; people are going about their lives. But they have no idea we exist. They mock people like us, because they only see us in storybooks."

"You're right, but that's where we're meant to live. Otherwise, the vampire's prophecies will be fulfilled," Presten said. Just the mention of them made Isabel's skin crawl.

"Alright, well, we don't want to talk about this too much... we don't want anyone to hear us," Isabel said, resting her head on Presten's shoulder. She closed her eyes and dozed off for what felt like a couple of minutes but was probably longer. When she felt Presten's hand come over her shoulder, she flinched awake, staring at the people around her as they grabbed their things and hopped off the bus.

The pack stood on the platform for a while before Oz realized they were too early. "Alright, well, we have time to sit down for some tea, who's in?"

"I am," Isabel said, nodding to a few chairs spread out over the pavement. "Let's go sit there."

There were so many of them now; a part of her wondered if they would be able to devise a concrete plan with that many people involved. She wasn't used to working with a big group and she wasn't used to devising plans like this. Suddenly it dawned on her that she was responsible for this whole thing, well, she and Presten. "Alright," she said, slumping down on one of the many foldout chairs spread out in front of the coffee shop. "Now, first thing's first: how about we all get to know each other?" The succubi exchanged brief glances before they pulled out some chairs and sat down in a circle. Isabel eyed them expectantly, waiting for them to introduce themselves.

"I'm Solange," one of them said. Isabel tried to identify the source of the smooth, sultry sound, and when she realized the voice belonged to the woman sitting next to her, she smiled.

"Hello, Solange. I'm Isabel," she said.

"I know you, Isabel," the dark-skinned woman said. "We all do. You're a legend and we can't wait to work with you."

"Solange, where do you come from? I want to know more about you," Isabel said, leaning forward in her seat. She brought her hands together and turned to look at her. Instantly, the woman's eyes dropped to the floor.

"I come from a humble background," she said. "My brother and I, we're both from Nigeria." She pointed to one of the incubi sitting across from her. He nodded at Isabel to acknowledge her, and then continued to fumble with the pepper shaker.

"Hello," he said. "My name is Abeo. It's nice to finally meet you, Isabel."

"It's great to meet you, too, Abeo," she said, reaching her hand out to him. "So, how long have you been living here?" she asked, her eyes darting back and forth between the two siblings.

"Our parents brought us out here when I was five," Abeo said, his pearly teeth showing through his smile. "We were practically raised here."

"And what about you, Solange? How old were you when you came to France?" Isabel asked.

"I was five," she said. "Abeo and I are twins."

Isabel's lips curved to a smile. There was something about them that felt very warm, very friendly. But she knew she had to be careful, nonetheless. "That's interesting," she said. "And, if you don't mind me asking… when did the two of you transform? How did you cope with your transformation?" she asked.

"Well, it's kind of awkward to talk about that time you had sex with two women on the same night in front of your sister," Abeo chuckled.

Isabel laughed. "You're probably right," she said, looking somewhere over Abeo's shoulder. She could see him out of the corner of her eye; he was smiling, a smile so radiant that Isabel couldn't help but smile, too. "But how did you cope? Was it hard for you?" she asked again.

"It was extremely hard," Solange said, knitting her brows. "Abeo and I... we both suffered, but then we realized we were better off this way."

"You were better off away from your family?" Isabel asked with her head tilted.

"Yes," Solange nodded. "Our father... he was very abusive. So when Abeo and I were abducted by the succubi, we couldn't have been more grateful."

Isabel wished she knew what to say. Most of the time she tended to avoid thinking about her family and friends. She didn't want to face that. There was a chance that she would never see them again; they were probably convinced she was dead. She thought about the heartache she must have caused them by disappearing so suddenly, without a trace. They knew nothing about her, and they probably never will. Isabel shook her head; she didn't want to think about this right now, because if it sank in for one second, she knew she would probably have a nervous breakdown. "I'm glad to hear that," Isabel said after a long pause. "You see I've always imagined transformations to be struggle stories, something mostly negative… but you, guys, you've changed the rules completely."

"And what about you, Isabel, what was transformation like for you?" Solange asked, her head cocked to the side.

"It was pretty hard," she said. "I had to leave my family, I couldn't cope with the fact that I didn't even recognize myself in the mirror most of the time. And when I learned I was the chosen one, well, it freaked me out even more."

"Yeah, I was going to ask… how did you react to that, realizing you were the chosen one?" Abeo asked.

"I didn't take it very well," Isabel admitted. "I was in denial… I didn't know what was being asked of me. Basically, I freaked the fuck out."

Abeo and Solange chuckled. The conversation trailed off, and soon enough, all thirteen of them had to get up to catch the train. Isabel felt her lungs inflate with the cool air. She knew they had a long journey ahead of them.

***

"Are you sure you know where it is?" Isabel asked, turning to Oz.

"Pretty sure," he said, letting the cold fuel his walk. He hurried along the sidewalk, his eyes fixated on a red brick building with a glowing sign that read "motel" on its side. The gang would be spending the night there while they came up with a plot to infiltrate the council. They walked in through the revolving doors, Isabel wrapping her arms around herself to keep warm.

"Nice is way colder than I thought it would be," she said, turning to Presten.

"I can keep you warm if you want me to," he said, flashing her a smirk. Oz rolled his eyes and looked away. Isabel noticed. She went up to him and just stood there, searching his face for a reaction.

"Can I talk to you?" she asked, shifting her weight to one leg. Oz wasn't being himself and she thought that, if they were going to work together, it was about time they patched things up.

"Yeah, what's up?" Oz asked, his eyes fixated on a faraway point.

"You wanna sit over there?" she asked, nodding towards the seating area.

"How about we just go up to our rooms? It's late," he said, nodding towards the elevators, instead. Isabel shrugged, making her way for the automatic doors. She pressed the button to the elevator indicating the up direction, which, ironically, was made to glow red. Oz put one foot in front of the other, slowly following Isabel, and when they both stepped inside that elevator, she could feel nothing but the hunger gnawing at her. She missed Oz more than anything, but she told herself she wasn't going to give in. He was giving her the cold shoulder and she didn't really know why. Somewhere down the line between getting there and booking their rooms, Isabel had made the decision to talk to him. The elevator doors parted and after what felt like an eternity of trying to pull herself together, Isabel stopped Oz on his way to his room.

"Wait," she said finally. "I need to talk to you."

CHAPTER 10

"What's wrong?" Oz asked, folding both arms across his chest. He eyed Isabel intently, as if waiting for her to blow up in his face. "Well?" he said again, tilting his head to the side.

"You've been acting pretty weird lately," Isabel blurted out. She didn't know how Oz would react, but she decided she was going to take the chance, anyway. "I don't know what's going on inside your head... I don't know anything."

"Why do you say that?" Oz asked, making his way down the hall. Isabel stopped him again.

"You know why," she said, her eyes fixated on his. "You've been so cold to me lately, I don't know what to make of it."

"Isabel," Oz said, grabbing her by the shoulders and looking her in the eyes. "There is nothing wrong. Everything's changing, everything's moving so fast. It's stressful and I'm scared for you."

"I don't want you to be scared for me," she said, grabbing his hand and squeezing it. "I'll be okay and so will you. We're strong like that."

"I know, it's going to be okay," he said, twisting a lock of her hair around one of his fingers. "I don't want you worrying about me, either."

Isabel smiled. If anything, she was relieved. But then it dawned on her that there was something else she wanted to talk to him about, something important. Or at least, she thought it would matter to him. "Oz," she said again. "I kind of wanted to talk to you about something else."

"Something else?" he asked, raising his eyebrows at her.

"Yeah," she said. "Can we maybe sit down?"

"You're scaring me." Oz opened his hand and there was a key. Isabel didn't even know when he had booked the rooms. He hurried down the hallway, his eyes darting from one door to the other until he stopped in front of one of them. "This one is mine," he said. The key rustled in its lock for a while until Oz practically kicked the door open. "French motels, huh?" he said, turning around and stepping inside. Isabel followed.

"Fancy room," she said, looking around. She saw something, like a bug, scurry across the floor the minute they flicked the lights on. "Oh, God," she said, her hand flying to her mouth. She went over to the bed and just stood there, contemplating whether or not she should sit down.

"I wouldn't sit on that if I were you," Oz said, his lips curving to a wry smile.

"Yeah, just sleep on it, instead," Isabel said, rolling her eyes. There was a pause. Oz let out a chuckle. He went around the room, pretending to arrange the knick knacks on the shelves.

"So, what did you want to talk to me about again?" he asked.

"Oz, listen," Isabel said, placing a hand over his shoulder. "When I began my transformation, I didn't really understand the idea of hunger. I couldn't comprehend it— I still don't sometimes— but right now..." She paused, clearing her throat. "I guess I've come to understand my own needs and how to quench them."

Oz turned to look at her. He was still fumbling with some wine glass he found near the TV set. "Go on," he said, staring at her through heavy-lidded eyes.

"I had sex with Presten," Isabel blurted out. A part of her felt like she just confessed to cheating on him. The air was so still, that she could hear the sound of Oz's breathing. And her breathing. She was nervous as hell.

"Alright," Oz said after what felt like an eternity of scrubbing down the wine glass. "And why did you feel like you needed to tell me that?" he asked.

"I— I don't know," Isabel said, turning away. Suddenly she felt like an idiot. Oz was just looking at her with glassy eyes, not moving. "I guess I just thought I owed it to you," she continued.

"Isabel, you know I love you, right?" he asked, walking towards her. He moved slowly across the carpeted floor; Isabel wasn't sure if he was going to kiss her or yell at her. "Right?"

"And I love you, too," she breathed. "Which is why I felt like I needed to tell you this."

"Our love for each other is independent of who we sleep with," Oz said. "I knew you were sleeping with Presten... it wouldn't be normal if you didn't."

"I just really needed to feed at the time, and you were giving me the cold shoulder and I—"

"Isabel, you don't need to justify yourself... you have needs, and so do I. Sometimes we're going to turn to each other for those needs, and sometimes, we're going to have to resort to other people to get what we want."

Isabel nodded. For some reason, she still felt uneasy. All her life she kept jumping from one person to the other, but right now, the idea of monogamy appealed to her more than ever. It was ironic, she thought, given that her entire being depended on promiscuity. "You're right," she said, despite herself. "I don't know what I was thinking, I guess I just didn't want to hurt your feelings."

"Is that all this was?" Oz asked, folding both arms across his chest. He stared at her playfully, his eyes looking as though they were about to pop out of their sockets. He bit his bottom lip and looked away again, inspecting the dusty utensils randomly spread out over the table. "This is one weird-ass motel room," he said.

"It's nothing, just forget about it," Isabel said, brushing her fingers through her hair. It had gotten so long over the past month that she felt like she could almost trip on it. "I think we should all stay up tonight and plan what we're going to say at the council," she muttered. "How about we call the rest of them in here?"

"Sure," Oz said, sprinting for the door and swinging it open. "Hello, ladies and gentlemen, would you ever so kindly step in here so we can arrange what we're going to say tomorrow?" he called down the hall, motioning for them to step inside. Isabel peered over Oz's shoulder and she could see Abeo and Solange pacing the hallway, trying to find their rooms.

"Hello," Abeo said, popping his head in through the inched open door. The rest of the succubi slowly followed and they poured into the room, one after the other. Jared sat on the bed; Solange pulled a chair and slumped down on it. It creaked under her, but she couldn't care less. Suddenly Isabel felt overwhelmed by what was happening, so she retreated into the bathroom for a while before stepping back out again, trying to take in the fact that they only had a few hours to prepare. They would need to stay up all night, plotting how to present their case. This wasn't going to be easy.

"Alright, ladies and gentlemen," Oz said again, putting his hands together. Isabel thought he surely must possess the skills of a public orator. He stood with such poise, such confidence that a part of her felt like he had already prepared his speech. "When the sun comes up, we're going to make our way for the council to present our case, and by the end of tonight, we will have come up with a plan for this." The rest of them nodded, like disciples listening to their master. "Now, Isabel, what do you think is going to strengthen our case?"

"The fact that we've got Gavin locked up in our dungeon," she said, staring back at him. "Along with the rest of the vampires."

"This is a rather dangerous statement," he said, not taking his eyes off her. "We cannot claim to be holding the "rest of the vampires" captive because then we would be fabricating the truth. We're only holding some of them captive, but not all."

Jared smiled. "He's right, we need to be very precise in what we're going to say."

"So, we've got Gavin... what else do we have to strengthen our case?" Oz asked again, scanning the room with his eyes. Isabel felt like she was back in college again, and Oz was that sonofabitch professor always looking for the right answer but never getting it.

"We've taken control over the rebel's mansion," Ava said, shifting her weight to one leg. She had been standing by the door this entire time; Isabel hadn't even noticed that she was there.

"The rebel's mansion is a useless thing to being up in our case," Oz said coldly. "The vampires have already taken over the old mansion, the original mansion... they've wholly reshaped and constructed it. As far as headquarters go, the vampires already have the upper hand." There was silence. Oz was pacing back and forth, eyeing them as they pretended to be deep in thought. "Come on, you guys," he said again. "Think small, think about what's next to you. Think!"

"I, I don't know," Isabel said, her voice boiling down to a hoarse whisper. She thought back to scenario time when her college professor wasn't even directly addressing her and she felt the need to get up and leave the lecturing room because she was so overwhelmed. But she wasn't going to leave this time. This time, she was going to see things through.

"You, of all people, should know," Oz said, eyeing her coldly. "It's *Isabel*, you guys! Isabel is the chosen one! She's one of the strongest most powerful succubi to ever walk this Earth! She's our most valuable weapon."

Isabel could feel a weight being dropped to her chest. It's not like she didn't know it from the very beginning: this whole thing, start to finish, rested on her, and her only. Everyone else was at the periphery, or at least that's what it seemed like. Ultimately, when Oz had done his part as the orator, when Jared has done his part as the loyal follower, when Ava has done her part as the gutsy rebel, it was only Isabel who remained.

"And what about Presten?" Abeo asked. "Isn't he the chosen one, too?"

"Ah, I'm glad you asked," Oz said, his lips curving to a wry smile. "Do you know why I never mentioned him, even though he's the chosen one?"

"Because no one knows him," a voice said from the far end of the room. Isabel turned around to see who it was. To her surprise, it was a girl she had never spoken to before; she was one of the people they had summoned outside the old mansion, but she hadn't really gotten the chance to get to know her.

"This woman is a goldmine," Oz said, his pearly teeth showing through his smile as he looked at the woman who had spoken. "Tell me, what's your name?"

"Abigail," the woman said, hugging her knees to her chest.

"It's so nice to meet you, Abigail. Do you mind telling us a little about yourself?"

"I'm a shapeshifter," she said, her hands clasped around her ankles. "That's pretty much it."

Isabel opened her mouth to speak but no words came out. She and Oz exchanged brief glances before he smiled again, trying to conceal his confusion. Isabel was weary of shapeshifters, especially after what happened with Mikael. This woman was dangerous and she had to be recognized as such. "Interesting," Oz said after a long pause. "I'd love to get to know you after our meeting... if that's okay with you, of course."

Abigail just nodded and looked away. It wasn't like she was uninterested, but there was something weird about her, something peculiar. Isabel thought maybe she was just introverted, but then again, she knew nothing about her or where she came from. It was a bit worrying.

"Now, back to what we were saying… the council doesn't know Presten. Or, of course they 'know' him, they just wouldn't *recognize* him if they saw him," Oz said, searching their faces for a reaction. "And so, that makes him our secret weapon. What do you think, Presten?"

"I think you're absolutely right," he said, peering at Isabel. She was still stuck in her own head.

"So basically, I'm the front, Presten's our secret weapon, the hostages are the bait," she said finally.

"Exactly."

"Well, I think we've got most things sorted out," Ava said, rising to her feet. "I have a good feeling about this."

"Will you sit back down?" Oz asked, agitated. "We still have a lot to cover, right now we're just trying to figure out where we are."

"Oh, I'm sorry, I didn't know you were my college lecturer," Ava said, folding both arms across her chest. Of all the girls that Oz knew, Ava was probably the sassiest.

"I'm sorry," he said after a pause. "I just don't want us to screw this up, because if we do, we might never get another chance."

"We're not going to screw up," Ava said, slumping back down on the floor. She sat cross-legged, gawking at Oz as he tried to gather his thoughts. "We're a strong group, I think we'll be okay."

"Alright, well, the night is still young, ladies and gentlemen! We have a lot of time on our hands… and a lot more planning."

CHAPTER 11

Isabel was dead tired. It was approaching four AM; she had been stuck in the same position for hours now. She rose to her feet, cursing under her breath, as her legs seemed to have fallen asleep. When she peered out of the window, all she saw was the blue dark seeping into the room. "I think we should call it a day," she said finally.

"I think so, too," Ava said, rising to her feet as well. "I'm gonna go out for a walk right now, anyone wanna join me?"

"I do," Abeo said, getting up on his elbows and bouncing to his feet. Solange followed, and so did Abigail. One by one, the rest of them began pouring out of the room, flashing Oz a coy smile as they did so.

"Well, I guess that just leaves the three of us," Presten said, cocking his head towards Isabel. She smiled at him and averted her gaze to Oz, who had finally settled in one place. At one point during the night Isabel began to wonder if he would dig a hole in the ground just pacing back and forth. Suddenly she felt an overwhelming urge come over her. She could see Presten out of the corner of her eye; he was gawking at her, following her every move. The bed looked tempting despite the spotted sheets and she could see herself crawling under the covers with not one, but both of them. Silence settled in the air; Isabel knew something was going to happen. She said to herself that she wouldn't even try to stop it.

"Well, what do you feel like doing?" Oz asked, his eyes fixated on Isabel. He didn't even look at Presten; it was like he wasn't even there.

"What do *you* feel like doing?" she asked, her eyes darting from Oz, to Presten, and then to Oz again. The two men couldn't even stand being in the same room together, let alone the same bed, with the same girl. Oz was so protective over Isabel, but then again, so was Presten. They had both grown so fond of her, that it was difficult, almost impossible, for her to imagine them allowing her fantasy to come true.

"You tell us what you'd like us to do, and we'll do it," Presten said boldly. He eyed Isabel with such lust, such passion, that she felt the need to be fucked by him, right then and there. But not only him... Oz was just standing there, gawking at them, biting his bottom lip and then clenching his jaw. He couldn't stand the idea of another man being with her, but the thought of fucking her with Presten around was so compelling. He wanted to blow her mind, to make her wish she never even considered another man in the first place. He could see it in her eyes, how much she wanted to be fucked by him. And he could see it in Presten's eyes, too. He wasn't all that competitive. In fact, he didn't love Isabel half as much as Oz did. Oz just wanted him to be a bystander, to show him that nothing and nobody could make Isabel feel the way she did when she was with him.

"I'm hungry," Isabel said, her lips barely moving. The words slipped out of her mouth like dark confessions and when she raised her eyes to

Oz, he was already smiling. He had been waiting to hear her say these words.

"And what do you want us to do about that?" Oz asked, stepping in closer to her. His hands were stuffed inside the pockets of his jacket, and when he came close enough, Isabel went ahead and kissed him. She felt his lips caress hers softly at first, and as her hunger grew, her hand wrapped around the back of his head and Oz's hands grasped her waist as their kiss intensified.

Presten watched the couple with a small smile on his face, but deep down, he knew there was no way he could just sit back and watch. The scene in front of him was mesmerizing and when Oz's hands slid Isabel's robe off her body, her naked curves on full display, Presten felt his cock instantly grow hard in his pants. He got up, slowly, calmly, straining to maintain his control as he walked up behind Isabel and rested a hand on the small of her back.

Isabel broke the kiss and looked back at Presten. A part of her longed for him, while the rest of her body itched for Oz. She remembered the last time she had been between two men, when Gavin had shared her with the angel, but something told her that this would be different. She could feel it with every goose bump that broke out across her skin.

Presten pushed up against her, his hardness nestled against her cheeks as Oz brought her face back to him and kissed her again. Her hands quickly stripped him of his shirt and as she was about to remove his pants, she felt herself being turned around forcefully to face Presten.

She gazed into his eyes and the smile on his face reflected exactly what he was thinking. He knew how hungry she was and exactly how far she was willing to go to quench that feeling. With a strong hand on her shoulder, he pushed her down onto her knees in front of him. He slid his pants down, revealing himself to her and she wrapped a hand around his thigh as she let her tongue slide up and down his shaft. She heard a sharp intake of breath from above her and she smiled seductively before taking him into her mouth. Her lips wrapped around him, sliding him in as far as she could take him.

There was a flutter of clothes behind her and she slipped Presten's cock out of her mouth to turn and look at the chiseled nakedness of Oz. She felt herself get instantly wet at the thought of running her hands across his skin, the feel of his muscles at the tips of her fingers. She wrapped a hand around his cock, bringing him closer, and swallowed him into her mouth. Isabel looked up at the angel and she could see the challenging smile he shot at Presten.

She alternated between the two, hungrily attacking them, a feeling of unbridled sexual desire racing through her. She made her mind up quickly as she watched the reactions on their faces, the mix of smile and desire, the tension that was building up. She was going to have them both, right here, right now.

Isabel stood up, quickly jumping to her feet as she pushed Oz back and onto the couch. She wasted no time straddling him and with a quick motion guided his cock to her pussy and slid him in. He entered her easily, effortlessly, penetrating deep inside her as she moaned in pleasure. She looked back at Presten and gestured to him and when he was close enough, pulled him onto the couch beside Oz as she began to ride the cock inside her.

Isabel bent down, taking Presten's cock into her mouth as her hips moved against Oz. Her pace quickened, the fever and lust inside of her growing at the feeling of both men inside her and she felt a tingle race up and down her spine. She hadn't expected how much pleasure this would give her and despite her conflicting feelings for Oz and her hunger to be satisfied by both men, she found herself reveling in the rush of emotions coursing through her.

Presten suddenly stood up, his cock sliding out of Isabel's mouth, and he moved behind her.

She looked over her shoulder, knowing fully what he intended to do as her hips bounced up and down on Oz. She met his eyes and as he positioned himself directly behind her, she pushed a hand against his chest and slowed her pace.

"Slowly," she said, breathing heavily, her chest rising and falling. She felt Oz's lips wrap around one of her nipples and suck hard, and she closed her eyes against the needed distraction. She waited, losing herself in the attention Oz was giving her breasts, and inhaled sharply as she felt Presten push against her from behind.

Slowly, carefully, he slid inside, and she clenched her teeth against the pain of being stretched in places she had never been stretched before. Presten's hands squeezed her cheeks as he continued to enter her. Fire shot up from her asshole and through her body and she wrapped her arms tight around Oz's neck.

Then Presten stopped. She waited for the pain to subside and Presten was patient enough to give her the few seconds she needed to get accustomed to his cock inside her. She opened her eyes and gazed into Oz's and he gave her a reassuring smile.

"You're okay," he said, brushing the hair from her face.

Isabel nodded, and Presten began to pull out slowly, and then push back in. He took it slow, and after a few strokes, the pain had subsided and all Isabel could feel was the pleasure that came with his movements. She began to move her hips against him and gasped at the dual feeling of both Oz and Presten inside her. Presten picked up the pace, reacting to her movements, knowing that she no longer needed the gentle treatment.

Isabel pushed up against Oz's shoulder, staring down at him, their eyes locked as she moaned in pleasure. A mix of emotions raced through her then. For some reason, she was almost glad she couldn't see Presten. She was loving every inch of them inside her, the feeling she was getting as both man slammed against her, faster and harder. Yet, she could only see Oz, and it was almost as if this fulfillment was an intimate feeling between the two of them alone.

Presten began to slam harder against her and Isabel knew it was more a way of reinforcing his presence than sexual desire. She let him have his way with her and soon she was screaming in orgasm, both cocks sliding in and out of her and sending bolts of electricity shooting through her.

She looked down at Oz, his eyes rolling in their sockets, and knew he was close. She picked up the pace, and Presten picked up his, and with a few more grinds, Oz grabbed her by the waist and exploded inside her. She felt Presten bulge, as if growing in size, and soon he too was coming hard, thrusting deep as he emptied himself. Isabel felt another wave of orgasms course through her, and she collapsed on top of Oz just as Presten pulled out of her.

"What do you say we move this somewhere a little more comfortable?" Presten asked.

Isabel looked at Oz, his chest beaded with sweat, his breaths coming in deep inhales and exhales.

"Still hungry?" he asked her.

Isabel smiled and licked her lips. "Always."

***

"Today's the big day," Isabel said, climbing out of bed, slipping into her robe and preparing to step out into the world again. Presten had already left a few hours ago and she was alone with Oz, who had been cuddled up beside her. He got up and looked at her, a triumphant smile on his face.

"I have a feeling we'll be okay," he said. "We've already spent a whole night planning... I know what I'm going to say, you know what you're going to say. Our thoughts are in order. What could possibly go wrong, right?"

"You know what happened the last time a man said that?" she asked with a smirk on her face.

"He died?" Oz asked, putting his shoes back on. Isabel smiled and nodded at him. She got up, dusted herself off and took his hand, leading the way out of the room. They made out a little in the hallway, until Abeo appeared around the corner.

"Oh, I'm sorry to interrupt," he said, his lips curving to a smile.

"No, no," Oz said, shaking his head frantically. "We've got to go now, all of us. We need to start making our way to the council." It took a couple of minutes to assemble everyone out in the courtyard, and once Isabel had made sure everyone was present, she led the way to the bus station again. They got on the bus and immediately retreated into their own little bubble of silence. They knew better than to speak of their lives in public. Isabel was lost in her own little world, her eyes growing more accustomed to the surrounding landscape. She told herself that, as soon as they get that visit to the council over with, she would reward herself with a day on the beach.

"Let's get off here," she said, getting up. "Alright, you guys, we've still got a long hike ahead of us, so before we start up the hill, I suggest we have a coffee here," she pointed to a small coffee shop nested under the trees at the bottom of the hill.

"I'm dying for some coffee," Abeo said, practically sprinting to the shop.

"I'm gonna go stand in line," Isabel said, making a beeline for the cashier. She got on her tiptoes and peered at the people standing in queue. "That's a long ass line," she said to herself. Suddenly she felt like something was tugging at her robe, so she turned around, and, realizing it was only a little girl, she smiled and ignored it. *Wait, what the fuck?* A pair of bloody eyes stared back at her; Isabel didn't know whether to run or ask the mother if her child was okay. She almost resembled a porcelain doll in the way her curly hair fell down her back.

Her eyes were glazed over, her lips were slightly parted and her skin was the palest Isabel had ever seen. Something told her to get away, to ditch the breakfast while she still could. Suddenly her eyes darted to the mother; there was nothing comforting about watching her, either. Isabel felt a strange sense of recognition towards them, like she had seen them somewhere before, in another dimension, perhaps. But there was something unsettling about the way they stared at everyone, how they seemed to be gawking at the people in line like predators stalking their prey.

"Isabel, you're taking too long!" she heard a voice say. She recognized it as Abeo's, who was probably just joking with her.

"I'm coming!" she said after a long pause. She poked out of the line like a splinter and walked back to them, a worried look on her face. "Guys," she started.

"Alright, I think that's all of us," Oz said, not paying any attention to Isabel. It looked to her like no one could hear her cries for help. It was like she had just come in contact with the devil, like she was forced to be in his presence for what felt to her like an eternity. Nothing had ever made her more uncomfortable. She opened her mouth to speak but no words came out. As they exited the coffee shop and started walking and she found herself peering behind herself every couple of seconds, trying to make sure that no one was following them.

"Hey, are you okay?" Presten asked, worried. His eyebrows were knitted together, and he looked at Isabel like her water had just broke. "Isabel, what's wrong?"

"Nothing," she said after a long while of staring out into the distance.

"Isabel, you seem distracted," Oz said, glancing at her briefly before he led the pack to a large patch of shade at the very bottom of the hill. His eyes darted from one person to the other, as if counting all the kids at a field trip. "On our way up, please be careful," he said, his hands clasped behind his back. "We're here to make our presence known, but that doesn't mean we should cause a racket on our way up."

The rest nodded at him like soldiers ready to go to war. A cold war, that is. They started up the hill, their boots sinking into piles of crunchy leaves as they walked. Isabel clutched her stomach, trying to stop herself from hurling. "You don't look okay," Presten said, staring at her. "What did you see over there?"

"I saw this lady standing in line... she had her daughter with her. Presten, I'm pretty sure they were—" she paused for a second, as if caught in a trance. The truth was, she had a hard time trying to remember exactly *what* they were. The pictures that were popping up in her head were nothing but ashen faces resembling egg heads, and they were staring at her. She could've sworn the mother had a red blotch at the corner of her mouth, but then she re-visualized the cherry lemonade she had in her hand.

"They were what?" Presten asked, concerned. Isabel could already feel the incline of the hill taking its toll on her calf muscles. She felt drained, like something had sucked the life out of her.

"I don't know, it's not important," she breathed, her eyes fixated on the ground underneath her. It was muddier than last time; Isabel concluded it had rained heavily overnight. Her feet sank into the mud like quicksand and she could feel the strain on her ankles as she wrestled with the ground for her shoe.

"You look like you just saw a ghost," Presten said, peering at Isabel through the corner of his eyes. "You didn't even get your coffee."

"I'm just paranoid," she said, looking behind her. Oz lingered at the back of the pack, which was now sandwiched from both sides by their protectors. The council was still quite a way up; Isabel almost imagined it to be nested amongst the clouds. She hated to admit it, but she was growing tired. It felt like her legs would give way and she would fall face first into the mud. "Superhuman strength, my ass," she murmured, rather to herself. She could still feel Presten's eyes on her, but she didn't mind. On the contrary, a part of her wondered what she did to deserve him in the first place. He was so patient with her, despite her love for Oz and her mood swings that could rattle oceans. He loved her despite herself and she couldn't help but feel grateful for it.

"Anyone tired back there?" Presten asked, turning to look at them. They ducked down and shook their heads, but Presten could tell they were panting like dogs. "We're almost there," he lied. Oz was giving him orders telepathically; telling him where to go, where to turn and which routes to avoid. He was like a compass, the directing force guiding them all throughout. Finally, Isabel caught a glimpse of something, something other than trees and rocks and gravel. She caught a signal from Oz telling her that was it: the vampire's council.

"Alright," she said. "From this point onwards, I'm going to ask you guys to be careful, to watch your step and, most importantly, to keep an eye on what's around you." The pack trekked carefully through the woods. What was once a hiking trail eventually levelled out into even ground and Isabel found herself able to breathe again. She focused on staying confident, on putting on a brave face. This wasn't a break in. This wasn't an invasion. This was court.

The gang reached the gates and didn't hesitate once before going in. The guards looked at them through heavy-lidded eyes; Isabel knew right then and there they were expecting them. They stood in one line with their hands brought together and their eyes darting sideways, as if contemplating whether or not to open up the gates of hell to those asking for it. One of them flashed Isabel a wry grin; he knew her, he knew she was the chosen one. He was staring at her so hard, Isabel didn't know if he would welcome her in or throw her out. But he didn't do either. He looked at the one beside him, but his body didn't move. He blinked at him once, and instantly, as if triggered by some telepathic force, he swung the doors open, and they parted with a loud creak. Isabel didn't hesitate. She stepped inside, watching as the shadows danced on the walls. Oz went up next to her. He could feel the guard's' eyes on them, but he wouldn't dare do anything stupid. Presten stood to Isabel's right, his eyes bouncing between the seemingly endless set of stairs and the crystal chandeliers hanging from the ceiling like nooses.

Suddenly he sensed some sort of movement. A black mass was coming down the stairs, followed by another black mass, followed by another. They reached the bottom of the stairs and just stood there, their ashen faces not moving. Isabel didn't recognize any of them, except one woman she was sure she had seen at the mansion before. She visualized her standing in the hallway with Gavin, the two of them looking as though they would burn the place down. She stared at her with such contempt, such intolerance that Isabel thought she would grab at her throat at any second. The silence leaked into the air and it wasn't long before Isabel saw something that made her gasp. Standing at the very end of the line was the little girl she had seen at the coffee shop; she had a smile plastered to her face, much like the one Isabel had seen that morning. There was no way she could have mistaken that girl for somebody else. Her mother wasn't there but she was, and for some strange reason, Isabel didn't feel that intimidated by her. It wasn't because she was young, but because there was something about her: something warm that Isabel couldn't really see in the light of day. Only in this darkness, the darkness of the mansion, could Isabel feel the warmth shining through that girl, and the truth was she had a good feeling about her. She looked over at the rest and they were gawking at her like hawks. Now, *they* were intimidating.

"Good evening," Oz said solemnly. "I suppose you know why we're here."

"Oh, do we, now?" one of the vampires, a seemingly ageing woman with sparkling silver hair, said. "Consider us ignorant. Tell me, young man, why *are* you here?"

"We're here because we want to reach some kind of agreement; in the past, we have tried to do that, but unfortunately, when all else failed, we had to resort to extreme measures," he said.

"Extreme measures? And what would those be?" the woman asked, peering at her mates through the corner of her eye. She had a smile plastered to her face; Isabel knew she had something up her sleeve. "Speak, for I want to know!"

"Gavin's with us," Isabel hissed. The house fell silent again. The vampires were exchanging weird looks, looks that even Isabel couldn't understand. It was like they were speaking in some sort of secret language governed by brief glances of sheer suspicion.

"Oh, is he, now?" the woman asked, rather sarcastically. She tilted her head and stared at Oz, her grey eyes boring into his. He opened his mouth but no words came out and when Isabel turned to look at him, he knew he had to say something. He was their orator, the person they were depending on the most. How could he just let them down like that?

"Yes, he is," he said again. It was like he was trying to speak but his words were barely finding their way out of his mouth. They rolled off his tongue like alphabet soup, and Oz found himself almost blabbering. "He, along with some other hostages from your pack, are with us at the rebel mansion. They're being watched over, monitored by our guards, and in order to let them out, some conditions need to be met."

"And what would those be?" the silver-haired woman asked, folding both arms across her chest. Her hands were veiny: just the sight of them was freaking Isabel out.

"The council needs to drop all intention of starting a war," Oz said, rather confidently this time. "They need to make peace with the angels and they need to stop recruiting people for their own wicked deeds."

"What else?"

"They need to evacuate the old mansion... as that was never their home to begin with... and lastly, they need to acknowledge the power of the succubi and incubi as the leading powers of the supernatural world."

"Wow, that's a lot you got there," she said, raising an eyebrow at Oz. She then pursed her lips, turning to the vampires standing next to her. There must've been at least seven of them and when Oz was done presenting his case, they all just glared at him, as if offended he had even opened his mouth at all. Suddenly the woman started laughing. "Tell me, Oz, why are you here?"

"I think I've already provided a sufficient answer," he said, his lips barely moving.

"No, seriously, tell me why you're *really* here," she said again.

"Listen, we're not here to play around," Isabel snapped, stepping out from the line. The woman looked amused, almost pleased, to have heard her said that. She eyed her up and down condescendingly; nothing bothered Isabel more than when people underestimated her. "We're here to negotiate, and if you're not willing to do that, then I guess we're going to have to make a choice for you."

"And what choice is that?"

"We're going to have to kill Gavin and the rest of the hostages."

The silence fell again. Judging by the look on the woman's face, Isabel could tell she had made a horrible mistake. "Guards, lock them up."

"What, no," Oz said, his eyes darting back and forth frantically. "No!"

Suddenly, Isabel felt herself being hauled off the ground. The room was spinning and she could hear nothing but the sound of the guards' heels clicking against the hardwood floor. She tried to look down but couldn't; she could barely even move her neck. She could hear Oz's screams in the distance. And Abeo's. And Solange's. Isabel felt like her body was shooting through the air, like she had no control over it. Suddenly she felt like she was being carried down a set of stairs. *Oh, no, not again!* That old musty dungeon. She couldn't bear the thought of going back there. "Let me go, let me go!" she yelled. A rattling sound could be heard and Isabel concluded they were unlocking the gates to the cells. That sound haunted her; she couldn't believe she was going back there again and that Oz was too. Nothing made sense to her anymore. She felt like, no matter what she did, she would still end up defeated, and nothing frustrated her more.

"You thought you could get away with this?" the woman snarled, leaning in close to Isabel. Her breath was sour; Isabel couldn't help but squirm away. She hugged her knees to her chest and watched as the ashen faced woman disappeared behind the cells.

CHAPTER 12

"Oz, Oz," Isabel whispered. She had been stuck in the same position for a couple of hours now; it was getting cold and she had no extra clothes, nothing to keep her from shivering convulsively. The cells were darker than last time; she thought it was because the winter was setting in. "Oz," she said again, and this time, she felt a movement in the cell next to her.

"Hey," he said, his knuckles the only thing visible behind the wrought iron bars. "I'm sorry, I've been trying to lay low, don't want to cause any more problems."

"Yeah," Isabel breathed. "How are you feeling?"

"I've been better," he said, his lips curving to a wry smile. His teeth had a yellowish tint to them; Isabel couldn't care less. She leaned in and kissed him, but he pulled away, his eyes dropping to the floor. "I'm sorry," he breathed. "I just can't focus on anything right now. I won't be able to give you my full attention, I'm sorry."

"Don't be," she said, the silver of her eyes glowing in the moonlight. It seeped in through the barred windows, illuminating Oz's face. Suddenly she felt a hand come over her own, and she let out a gasp, pulling her hand away.

"Isabel, it's Presten," a voice said. Isabel reached out and, realizing the iron bars didn't hinder her, touched Presten's face.

"Presten, is that really you?" she asked. "It sounds like you."

"It is me," he said, grabbing her hand and kissing it. Isabel didn't know whether to feel awkward or flattered. The place was pitch dark; it was almost impossible to make out the faces of the people in there.

"Are we in the same cell?" Isabel asked, feeling around for his hand again.

"Yeah," he whispered. "I just didn't realize it until, you know, I heard smooching sounds."

Isabel's chuckle sounded more like a sigh. She was careful not to make a noise, but in the silence of the cells she was secretly suffering, Presten's presence was but a roadblock to her, a reminder of how hungry she felt. Suddenly she heard a sound that made her jump. "What was that?" she asked. Her eyes were darting back and forth, trying to discern the source of the noise. Her gaze landed on the ashen face of a little girl staring back at her through the bars. Strands of her hair were glowing in the light and she smiled at Isabel as if trying to reassure her. A little more light seeped into the room, illuminating the girl's face. Once again, Isabel recognized her as the girl from the coffee shop.

"I know you," she said in a small voice. "I've seen you in my dreams."

"You know me?" Isabel asked, blinking at her. "What do you know about me?"

"I know that you're the chosen one," she said, her pearly teeth showing through her smile. "And I know he's the chosen one, too." She patted Presten on the back, making him jump. "There, there," she said again. "You don't have to be afraid."

"How do you know me?" Presten asked, squirming away.

"Like I said, I've seen you in my dreams." She patted Presten on the back again, but this time, he didn't flinch. She flashed Isabel an even wider smile, but before Isabel could say anything, the girl's face fell away from the light, and she disappeared again.

"Isabel! Isabel, look," Presten said, nudging her with a piece of rolled paper.
"What is that?" she asked, taking it from him.

"She left this. It literally just fell off my back," he said. Isabel unrolled the paper and lifted it up in front of her. The blue haze of the night allowed her to read what was written; *I will be back by sunrise.*

"I will be back by sunrise?" Isabel asked, her eyebrows furrowed. "Who do you think this girl is, and is she on our side?"

"Guards!" a woman's voice echoed across the cells. "Bring them to me!" The gates swung open and Isabel found herself being handcuffed and forced to leave the cells. Presten was right behind her, but they didn't take anyone else.

"Isabel! Isabel!" she heard Abeo yell, his voice getting more and more distant as she went up the stairs. She squinted at what seemed to be the light at the end of the tunnel, but when she saw that same old woman standing at the top of the stairs, she rolled her eyes in disgust.

"You don't look so happy to see me," the woman snarled, her eyes darting from Isabel, to Presten, and then to Isabel again. "Now, let's just cut to the chase; is Gavin dead or alive?"

"He's alive, but not for long," Isabel said.

"So you're dead set on being stupid, on being reckless?" she asked, her nostrils flared. Isabel didn't say anything. "Alright, then. Guards, take them back! And listen here, Isabel, we're going to send out rescue missions all over Paris... and we're going to find Gavin and the others, whether you like it, or not!"

"Well, good luck finding them," Isabel said coldly.

"Oh, we're going to," she hissed. "And when we do, we're going to kill off all the rebels, including you!"

Presten snarled at her like a dog before the guards took him away. A million thoughts were racing through Isabel's head and when she finally settled into the depressing quietude of the cells, she felt powerful again. It was ironic, but she reminded herself that this was all cause and reaction; if they didn't intimidate the vampires, none of this would've happened in the first place. "It's almost dawn," she said, rather to herself. A little under an hour later, the sun's rays slashed through the windows and Isabel could breathe again. She waited for the girl to show up and when she noticed her shadow on the wall, Isabel rose to her feet attentively. Her hands were balled up; Isabel could tell she was holding something. The girl walked slowly towards Isabel and, making sure no one could see her, she handed Presten another note, and Isabel, a brown cloth bag.

"What is this?" she asked, but before she could even raise her eyes to the girl again, she was gone.

CHAPTER 13

"Are you sure you want to do this?" Isabel asked with her eyes fixated on Presten's.

"Do we really have another choice?" he said, reaching into the cloth and pulling out a bronze handled dagger. He stared at his own reflection in the blade before he cut his hand with it. The blood came gushing out of his palm. "Fuck," he said.

"Are you okay?" Isabel asked, her eyes wide as a set of plates. Presten grimaced, but nodded. She took the dagger and cut herself too, smearing her own blood all over the blade. "It's the only way," she said, rather to herself.

"Are you in a lot of pain?" Presten asked.

"Kind of, it's not too deep, though," she said. "Alright, there are only a few hours left… all we have to do is wait until lunch time."

"Did the note say two o'clock?" Presten asked, clenching his eyes. A sharp pain shot up his arm, but he ignored it.

"Yeah," Isabel said, putting the blood-smeared dagger back into its cloth. She held onto it like dear life and when her gaze met Oz's, her lips curved into a smile.

"Do you want me to go over the note with you?" he asked, his lips barely moving. Isabel could tell he had gotten weak.

"No, that's okay... I think we've got it covered," she said. "Listen, I don't want you to worry about me. The note carries clear instructions of what we're supposed to do, and I promise you, Oz, I promise you... we're going to make it back safe."

"My part here is done," he said with the contentedness of a great master. "Now it's all up to you to get us all out of this mess."

"No pressure," Presten laughed.

"So is it true that the rebels have infiltrated the council?" Oz asked, turning to Isabel.

"Yes, it says so in the note. They've been there for a long time, but they were dormant. It turns out they were waiting for Presten and I."

"They are a strong force," Oz said, his voice boiling down to a whisper. "And they tend to form rallies... they're probably more in number than you think."

"That's probably the most reassuring thing I've heard all day," she said, her lips curving to a smile. She exchanged brief glances with Oz, and then he got up on the balls of his feet.

"Listen to me, both of you," he said. "Be careful of the King Vampire... they don't write about him in books for no reason."

Isabel's face drooped to a scowl. She thought back to that day when she and Presten discovered

Gavin's secret book library. She thought back to that book she had been saving all this time. She had seen pictures of the King Vampire all over the pages; he was strong, intimidating. Isabel thought he resembled the devil. She couldn't help but feel afraid, but somewhere at the back of her mind lingered the little girl's face, and it was telling her how to act.

The hours rolled by and Isabel knew it was time to go. "It's almost one thirty," she said. "We should probably get going."

"Do you think they've set up the lunch table yet?" Presten asked.

"Of course not, which is why we need to get there early… we need to go into the kitchen first so we can, you know, seep it into their drinks."

"Do you have the map she gave you?" Presten asked.

"Yeah, it's in my pocket," Isabel replied. "We should take one last look at it." She spread it out in front of them; it was a hand drawn map. The little girl had slipped it into the prison cell the very first time Isabel had been down in the dungeon. Presten inspected the map and then he checked his watch, motioning for Isabel to follow him outside. "Did she leave the door open?" she asked.

"Yep," Presten said, pushing it open. They both crept outside, and as they were about the leave the dungeons, Abeo called them.

"I pray that you come back to us safe," he said, his voice trailing off.

"We'll be waiting for you," Solange said, beaming. Isabel looked around and they were all staring at them, smiling. Isabel could tell they were filled with hope, that they depended on them. She nodded towards the door; they didn't have a second to spare.

"Wait," she whispered suddenly, stopping dead in her tracks.

"What?" Presten asked?

She squeezed her eyes shut and clenched her teeth. Her body shuddered momentarily before she let out a sigh and opened her eyes again. Presten heard a loud thump.

"What was that?" he asked, rushing up the stairs. The guards were scattered over the floor like dead birds. Isabel felt a strange energy being channeled towards her. She turned around to look at Abeo; he was also crouched down on the floor with his eyes clenched. Isabel knew straight away he had helped her hypnotize the guards.

"Thank you," she said, her eyes moving over to Solange, who was also fixated in that same position. Isabel then turned back and followed Presten. "Did you really think there would be no vampires standing out there?" she asked, casually trotting up the stairs. Presten's lips curved to a smile. He had to admit, he was quite impressed.

"Well, we should probably get going if we want to make it there on time," he said, stepping over the guards' motionless bodies.

Presten and Isabel tiptoed across the halls. Isabel had the map memorized in her head and Presten followed her. The mansion was almost completely empty; according to the little girl with the ashen face, most of the vampires would be out on a mission to find the hostages. "We're almost there, it should be right around that corner," Isabel said, slowing down a bit.

"Are you okay?" Presten asked.

"I'm okay," she said after a pause. She clenched her jaw and carried on. The kitchen was completely empty, but Isabel knew the cooks would be there soon. She held onto the cloth, picturing herself ripping that poison open and slipping it into the drinks. But she didn't have to picture it anymore. There were wine glasses lined up on the kitchen counter like soldiers. Isabel looked left and right before she walked up to them and after making sure that no one was around, she ripped the bag open and put just a little bit of the poison in each glass, except one. This last one, she needed to spare. Isabel had a special gift for the King Vampire. She exchanged an alarmed glance with Presten as they heard footsteps. *Fuck.* When Isabel turned around, she was faced with one of the cooks. He was staring back at her with the bloodshot eyes of a vampire, but he didn't say anything. He just smiled at them and popped the cork open on one of the wine bottles, pouring some in each glass.

"Don't worry," he said. "I'm on your side."

Isabel breathed a sigh of relief. "Does he sit at the head of the table? You know, the King Vampire?" she asked.

"Yeah… only you can kill him, Isabel. No one else."

"I know that," she said, clutching the bag in her hand. Her mind kept going back to Gavin's book; *only she who bears the ivory dagger shall hold the power to terminate the King.* For the past couple of weeks, she couldn't take that verse out of her head. It lingered in her memory; it propelled her forward towards her goal. Outside, she could hear the sound of plates clicking. She knew it was time. It was approaching two o'clock; the cook took out the salad first, setting it down on the table before returning to the kitchen. He eyed both Isabel and Presten, motioning for them to lay low and be quiet. They held their breath while he went out again with a tray in his hands. Six glasses of wine, all contaminated with the venom. He set them down on the dining table, one after the other, and then retreated back into the kitchen. He peered out the door at the council members as each of them drank their wine; Isabel couldn't believe this was it. According to the little girl, they would be dead in a matter of minutes. The time dragged on. Isabel could feel her heart beating like a jackhammer. Suddenly she heard a loud crash, followed by coughing. She peered out the door, and soon enough, all six of the diners were coughing. One of them fell off his chair and his body began to shiver. He was going into a seizure. Finally, Isabel caught a glimpse of the King Vampire as he rose to his feet, his eyes wide as dinner plates. Her body shuddered at the mere sight of him. He was clad in black with peculiarly sharp white teeth that protruded over the lips, whose remarkable ruddiness showed astonishing vitality for a man of his years. He watched as the council members dropped, one after the other, and it was only then that he realized someone had poisoned them. Isabel looked over at the cook, who was shivering so convulsively that she thought he would have a heart attack. She knew it was time to act. She clenched her eyes shut for a moment, her fingers wrapped tightly around the cloth, and then she took the dagger out and charged for the King.

It all happened so fast. He was so caught up trying to figure out who had poisoned him that he didn't think twice about Isabel, or Presten. With her eyes fixated on his, she hurried along the length of the table, the blood-smeared blade in her hand. Without thinking, she jabbed the dagger into his chest, but she didn't stop there. With the force of a fighter, she stabbed him repeatedly; Presten couldn't believe what he was seeing. The blood splattered all over her face; it was like she was possessed by some kind of energy, and it kept her going. She pulled out the blade one last time, watching as the blood dripped from it. She was panting like a dog, eyeing King's body as it lay motionless on the floor. "It's done, it's over," she said, standing over him. Presten stumbled back a few steps and then he motioned for her to follow him outside. All seven council members were lying on the floor; only the King was lying in a puddle of his own blood. Isabel was left breathless, victorious. Her hands were balled up into fists; she knew what she had to do next. "We need to get to Oz, we need to head back to Paris as soon as possible."

"Do you think you can get to him telepathically?" Presten asked, his head cocked to the side.

"Yeah," Isabel said confidently. "But I'm going to need your help." They closed their eyes and focused their powers. Isabel hadn't felt this assured in a very long time. Her head was throbbing, but she soldiered on. She had found some kind of a happy place in her head, somewhere she could channel all her energy without many obstacles. And finally, her thoughts linked themselves to Oz's, and she could feel him answering back to her. *It's time to go back to Paris,* he said.

CHAPTER 14

Isabel wished she knew who the little girl was. But one thing was for sure: the vampires hadn't paid her much attention, or none at all. They were all so preoccupied with council related matters that it didn't even cross their minds a little girl might be a rebel in disguise.

"It feels good to be back again," Presten said, staring out the bus window and onto the streets of Paris. Straight after King's death, the rest of them had managed to break out of the dungeon. As soon as the bus pulled over, Isabel hopped off, gathering her allies around her.

"We've come a long way, all of us," she said. "Now, all we need to do is show a little bit of courage, a little bit of fearlessness. The vampires are probably on their way to the old mansion right now to free Gavin, and when they do get there, we need to be there to stop them." Oz smiled at Isabel. If anything, he was proud of her, what she had accomplished. She had grown so fierce, so heroic that even Oz felt like he couldn't keep up with her. The pack started up the hill for one last time, one last battle. Isabel knew they were going to win this.

When they got to the top of the hill, the first thing they saw was that the gates had been busted open. The vampires had gotten there before them! Isabel rushed inside, her eyes scanning the place carefully. Suddenly, she heard a crashing sound. Were they breaking the hostages out of the dungeon? Isabel turned around, only to find that the enemy was slipping from doorways and corners. The pack had stalked in, unseen, converging from all directions.

Isabel pulled out her dagger. She charged at one of them, running her blade into his chest. He collapsed momentarily and then got up again; that was when Isabel knew she had to get her hands on a wooden stake. Presten approached her with a chair leg, which was already smeared in blood from a previous killing, and she ran it into one of the intruders. Both Solange and Abeo fought like warriors, and although they were severely outnumbered, nothing could beat them now. Gavin was still trapped in the dungeon and despite the vampires' untiring attempts to break into the cells they were left defeated. A familiar stink of death rose in the air; Isabel basked in it, she knew they deserved it. She found herself anticipating her attackers' every move, and she killed them, one by one. They fell down to her feet, some begging her to spare their lives; for the first time ever, Isabel believed she was the chosen one.

"Where's Gavin?" Presten asked. "Is he still down there?"

"We need to go check." Isabel climbed down into the basement, and all she saw was Oz. He was just standing there, his eyes fixated on Gavin's. His hands were balled up into fists; Isabel could see them shaking. She approached him and handed him the chair leg. She knew exactly what he wanted to do. He wanted to see Gavin suffer, he wanted to be the one to end him. Slowly, he walked closer to him; Gavin had a smile plastered to his face, that smile Oz despised so much.

"You want to get rid of me?" he asked, raising an eyebrow at Oz. "Well, you can go ahead and do it! Take my life! The King is dead, so why should I live?"

Oz didn't say anything. With his hair disheveled and his eyes wide as ever, he drove the chair leg into Gavin's chest. He fell back with a horrible thud, his clothes torn halfway off him. His eyes were open and fixated on the ceiling. His face froze in a terrible grin. Oz kicked him in the abdomen, walked away and never looked back.

"It's done," he said. "It's over."

THE END

Newsletter

This exclusive **VIP Mailing List** from Persia Publishing focuses on delivering high quality content to your inbox that will bring more passion, excitement, and entertainment to your life. Weekly insights, specials offers and free giveaways that you will love!

You are just one click away from getting exclusive access to the **VIP Mailing List**!

Click the "**Get Access Now**" link below to join today!

GET ACCESS NOW

http://www.persiapublishing.com/subscribe-to-romance-lucy/

LIKE US AT

https://www.facebook.com/LucyLyonsRomance/

CAN YOU HELP?

PLEASE leave a quick review for this book if it gives you any value. It provides valuable feedback that allows me to continuously improve my books and motivates me to keep writing.

Thank You!

Made in the USA
San Bernardino, CA
11 December 2018